TIL

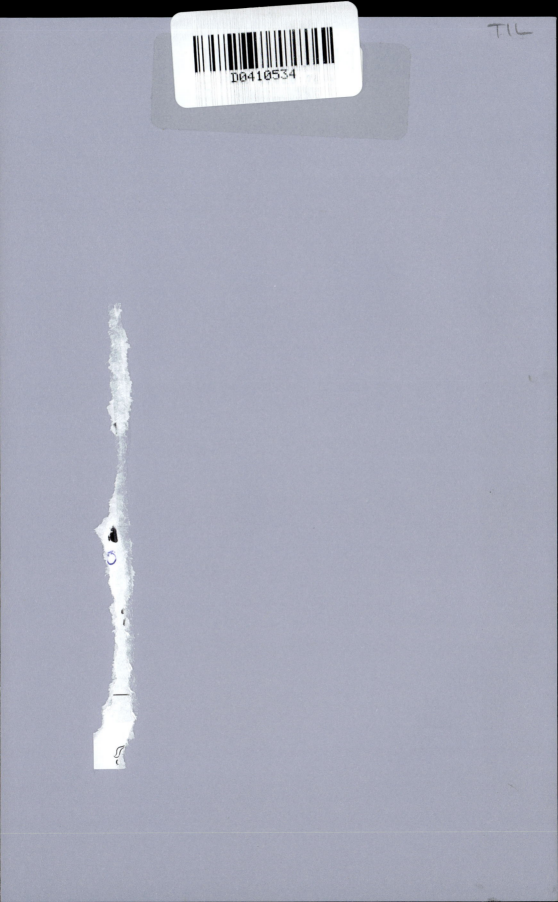

New Lives for Old

ROGER KERSHAW AND JANET SACKS

New Lives for Old

the national archives

First published in 2008 by
The National Archives, Kew, Richmond Surrey, TW9 4DU, UK
www.nationalarchives.gov.uk

The National Archives brings together the Public Record Office,
Historical Manuscripts Commission, Office of Public Sector
Information and Her Majesty's Stationery Office.

A catalogue card for this book is available from the British Library

ISBN 978 1 905615 17 9

Jacket design by Goldust Design
Page design and typesetting by Ken Wilson | point 918
Printed in Great Britain by Biddles Ltd, King's Lynn

Jacket images
FRONT: Boys from Dr Barnardo's Homes enjoy their first ship's
rations on board the *Largo Bay*, February 1923. The party was
sailing to Australia.
BACK: A shipboard photograph of children bound for the
Fairbridge Farm School at Pinjarra, Western Australia, 1931.

Contents

INTRODUCTION 7

1 Two women pioneers · *19*

2 Journey to a new life · *51*

3 Barnardo, the biggest player · *90*

4 The Catholic emigration movement · *119*

5 Farm schools and Kingsley Fairbridge · *142*

6 Second World War child evacuees · *170*

7 The final phase · *192*

AFTERWORD · *230*

Notes on the text · 234

Tracing records of child migrants · 240

Useful addresses · 246

Selected websites · 249

Bibliography · 250

Index · 252

Acknowledgements · 256

Introduction

VICTORIAN BRITAIN did not smile upon the poor—and the big cities were full of them. Those who swelled the slums in the mid-19th century had flocked to industrialized cities from the country, seeking jobs in factories and at the docks. Many were Irish refugees from the Potato Famine of 1845–9, especially in the ports of Liverpool and Glasgow, and all of them struggled to eke out a marginal existence. Food was scarce, epidemics of cholera, smallpox and other diseases were rife and the housing shortage grew more and more acute. Many dwellings were demolished in the 1860s to make way for the railways, and new ones were not within the reach of the poor. By the 1880s, problems of accommodation were chronic, as more and more people crowded into the tenements and slum landlords made huge profits. Crime and lawlessness—unsurprisingly—flourished. In this hostile environment children grew up with little food and no education, sometimes abandoned by their parents and often exploited for their work.

Into the chaos stepped several philanthropists, most of them imbued with an evangelical mission to spread the word of God and rescue the poor from sin. They set to work with energy and dedication, setting up shelters for the destitute and schools and homes for their young. But the stream of those in need was never-ending and, as unemployment rose in the late 1860s, charities and Poor Law Unions began to send people to Canada, releasing space in the workhouse to accommodate others.

Maria Rye was the first of the philanthropists to send a large party of children, in her case girls, to Canada. They were destined to become domestic servants, and the project proved successful. The fact that most of the girls were under 11 was in their favour: the Canadians felt that children were more able to adapt to a new life at a young age. Once the door was opened, others were quick to follow suit. During the 1870s—ironically a more prosperous period in Britain—Annie Macpherson, Father Nugent, Thomas Bowman Stephenson, William Quarrier and John Throgmorton Middlemore were all involved in sending pauper children to Canada. In the 1880s, when unemployment rose again and the housing shortage became even more severe, Dr Barnardo, James Fegan and, later, the Catholic Emigration Association also started to emigrate children. Joy Parr notes that the number of children sent to Canada by the philanthropists rose from 540 in 1880 to 2,104 in 1888.[1]

From the point of view of workhouse authorities and child-rescuers, emigrating children had practical advantages. It gave children from the city slums a new chance, rescuing them from moral as well as physical decay. Life in Canada was healthier, and in general the Canadians were regarded as more pious. It was also very much cheaper to send the children to work in Canada than to bring them up at the British rate-payers' expense, followed by a possible future of destitution or crime. There were also disadvantages, of course, largely relating to how the children themselves experienced life overseas—not a primary concern of most of those involved in emigrating them.

The abrupt transition to Canada was for almost all children stressful and challenging. They had to adapt to conditions very different from those they were familiar with, such as living on a remote farm in rural Ontario rather than the streets of London. The climate could be harsh, particularly the extreme cold in winter; even young migrants were expected to work very hard all day, sometimes in the evening as well, often with no one to care much how they fared. Far from adult help, some of the children experienced terrible cruelty. They also endured the stigma of being a 'Home Child' (as child migrants were called in Canada), something many of them never admitted, even to their spouses, because of the shame (wholly undeserved) associated with the name. Worst of all was their loneliness. The children had been used to the friendship of others in the same situation as themselves, but now they found themselves alone among strangers, with no one to confide in. Many had brothers and sisters from whom they were separated, as well as relatives back home, yet maintaining contact was problematic. Despite this, most children proved to be survivors, growing up to hold down jobs, marry and establish families, and make new lives for themselves in Canada. Others, of course, did not. Some returned to Britain when they could; and a few could not cope with the hardship, abuse and friendlessness and took their own lives.

The children sent to Canada were not all orphans. On the contrary, most had a parent, but they lived in circumstances where they had to fend for themselves and were thought likely to come under bad influences. The philanthropists sought to remove them from inauspicious conditions to new environments in which they had the chance to make different lives for themselves. In Canada, they were placed in the open spaces and clean air of the countryside, away from the city and its temptations—certain to strengthen them and make them healthy in body and spirit. In many cases emigration took place with the parent's consent, but this was not always the case; sometimes it was done through 'philanthropic abduction', a practice which Barnardo admitted, believing it necessary for the children's physical and moral wellbeing. And yet, although the children were so far away, a large number of them kept in touch with their families—even those who were discouraged from doing so.

In the early 20th century, a new force reared its head—one that the British government could support wholeheartedly: imperialism. The child-rescuers began to change their tune, with Barnardo describing his children sent overseas as 'Bricks for Empire-Building'. An imperial vision of Dominions prospering under young settlers of good British stock complemented the moral benefits of child migration. Despite reservations, such as those from socialist workhouse guardians in northern counties (who objected to young children being sent abroad to earn their living) and from trade unions in Canada (who resisted British workers competing for low wages with their own home-grown ones), the number of children emigrated to Canada continued to rise until the First World War. After the war, however, the situation changed. Lives lost in Europe meant falling birth rates, and over-population was no longer an issue. The Bondfield Report and the Canadian Immigration Branch put an end to the arrival of unaccompanied children under

14 in the mid-1920s, and in the 1930s economic depression meant there was much less work available for older teenagers.

However, Australia offered an alternative destination just as Canada began to recede. Kingsley Fairbridge, a fervent supporter of Britain's empire, described a vision in which the orphanages of Britain were shifted to 'Greater Britain' (the Empire) 'where farmers and farmers' wives are wanted, and where no man with strong arms and a willing heart would ever want for his daily bread.'[2] He captured the Edwardian imagination, and in 1909 was offered land by the premier of Western Australia; four years later the first 13 boys were sent to his farm school at Pinjarra.

Fairbridge broke new ground, but it was after the First World War that child migration to Australia really took off. Casualties in the war had been high and emigration—especially of those of solid Anglo-Saxon origin—was encouraged. Physical stamina was important, and children were prepared for the outback by sleeping outside in tents and learning to swim. They also underwent a range of medical tests. Eric L., who arrived in Australia at the age of 11, noted the eugenic aspect of the selection process. 'It was better if you had mumps and measles and didn't have flat feet or anaemia. They didn't take anyone wearing glasses or who was colour blind to Australia.'[3]

Helped by government grants, both Fairbridge and Barnardo sent more children to Australia, but other organizations were also getting involved. In 1924 the Big Brother organization was formed by philanthropist and businessman Richard Linton in Sydney, seeking to help young British men settle in Australia. And in 1938, even as another conflict loomed, the first Catholic child migrants from Britain arrived at orphanages run by the Christian Brothers. Supported by the Prince of Wales (later Edward VIII), other members of the royal family, politicians and charities across the Empire, the momentum of migration was driven by the enthusiasm of the age.

Whether in Australia or Canada, life as a child migrant was often hard. Institutions could be bleak, strict and lacking in affection—so much depended on the character of those looking after the children, and this was largely a matter of luck. Children left the orphanages and farm schools around the age of 15 or 16—many were younger—and were sent out into the world with very little support. Boys worked long hours as farm hands in unfamiliar terrain, grappling with searing heat or bitter cold; girls' options were even more limited, as they were sent into domestic service and only the exceptional ones could develop any form of career. Systems of aftercare were often very limited or ineffective, and the children's loneliness and isolation also left them vulnerable to abuse.

Such problems existed despite the authorities' attempts to regulate child migration from the 1920s onwards. As the practice became more closely linked to an imperial vision, the Empire Settlement Acts of 1922, 1937, 1952 and 1957 sought to control how children were selected and to ensure some degree of consultation with parents and the children themselves. This was often a token process, however, relying on parents' lack of options and children's lack of understanding about what was involved. There are stories of very young children being asked to select their destination by shape—did they prefer Canada or Australia?—with older children desperately trying to steer the responses to prevent the family being split up over the globe. Even children excited by the prospect of travel had no real concept of what life would be like in either country. In *After Barnardo*, Howard and Leonard quote Mary A., aged 11, who when asked in 1939 why she wanted to go to Australia said, 'I wanted to see kangaroos hopping down the street!'[4]. At the same age, Eric L.'s view was a little more realistic, if incomplete: 'We got the impression that Australia was a vast, sun-drenched country where we would ride ponies.'[5] Life-changing choices could also be overridden without notice. Ernie R., for example, decided at 14 that Canada offered better prospects of escape if necessary, but found himself instead in 1937 en route to Australia:

> I thought I was going to Canada and thought it strange we left from Tilbury because ships bound for the New World left from Liverpool. We asked Mr Stables at Australia House before we left and Mr Bertram who was in charge of our party where we were going but they were coy about answering. When we went ashore at Gibraltar and sailed down the Suez Canal we worked it out for ourselves![6]

Working things out for themselves became a characteristic of many child migrants' lives. Isolated from family and friends, they had to make their own way in life with little support—a particular problem for those leaving institutional regimes at a young and impressionable age. Eric B. sums up their predicament:

I think the worst thing about being in an orphanage is that you have no one really to turn to. Every decision you have to make on your own and it is a fifty-fifty chance you will make the wrong decision when you are young. Between the time you leave the home and get married, loneliness is a major problem… It would be so easy to slip the wrong way when you have nobody to guide you, and get into drugs, drinking heavily or turning to crime.'[7]

As Eric notes, the fact that so many child migrants across the world 'made it', despite these inauspicious circumstances, is a tribute to their courage, self-belief and strength of character, and to those who helped to instil such qualities when they were in their care.

From a modern perspective, the separation of children from family and past lives seems one of the cruellest aspects of emigration policy. Nineteenth-century evangelicals believed that severing children from destitute or depraved backgrounds was the key to their moral welfare, but even in the mid-20th century young migrants were often surprised to discover their true family circumstances—or, conversely, the misrepresentations of these by officialdom. Violet B., who sailed to Australia on the SS *Berrima* in 1928, discovered her records on the voyage; they referred to her as an only child and an orphan. Violet, in care since before her second birthday, subsequently learned that she had a brother who had been sent to Canada aged eight, as well as another sister and brother. She also had a living father who had been imprisoned for attempting suicide following her mother's death.[8]

Laurie Humphreys, who was sent to the Christian Brothers' Bindoon Farm School in 1947, also had some family surprises to contend with. 'I was mystified when one of the Christian Brothers told me that my younger brother, Terry, was to arrive in Australia on the next boat in December. To this I hastily replied, "Can't be. I haven't got a brother" as that is what I had always believed.'[9] For those who discovered relatives only in adulthood, meetings were not always easy, but at least today's greater awareness of child migration issues can provide support and assistance to those seeking to make or renew family contact.

Migration of children in the 20th century came to an end in the 1960s, the result of changing social attitudes and an increasing preference for fostering in family units rather than large institutions. As the British Empire drew to a close and countries became independent, there was also political resistance to taking children from overseas;

both inside and outside Britain, it was felt that underprivileged or orphaned children should be cared for in their country of origin. Child migration to Australia effectively ended in 1967 and even New Zealand, which had remained enthusiastic into the 1950s, received its last party of children from the Overseas League in 1952.

Three centuries of child migration

Although well rooted in living memory, child migration schemes had existed in various guises since the 17th century. In 1619, the Virginia Company took 100 street children from the City of London to Virginia in order to supply labour to the plantation owners. Some were as young as 10, deemed, like their 19th-century counterparts, a nuisance to the authorities and a burden to the taxpayers; moreover, they were suspected of spreading the plague! This set a precedent, and in 1622 the Council for New England also asked for poor children to be sent to them. And so the emigration of children to the colonies began.

Children were also transported to the colonies as criminals, since those over the age of seven were considered adults and were punished as such. As the penalty for most crimes was hanging, transportation must have been a welcome alternative. After 1615, it became increasingly common for convicted individuals to be offered a pardon on condition of transportation. America was their destination, for a period of 14 years for those entitled to conditional pardons. Transportation for seven years was also introduced as a sentence in its own right for non-capital offences.

Thousands of children were transported to the American and West Indian colonies between 1615 and 1776 (before the American Revolution), and to Australia between 1787 and 1868. When the First Fleet sailed to Australia in 1787 it carried children such as 13-year-old Elizabeth Hayward—a clogmaker tried at the Old Bailey for stealing a linen dress and silk bonnet—among the 717 convicts on board. As poverty and destitution soared after the Napoleonic Wars (c.1793–1815), concerns over crime increased. A purpose-built penal station for boys was opened on Van Diemen's Land (Tasmania) in 1834; known as Point Puer, it sought to rehabilitate 'little depraved felons' through a harshly disciplinarian regime, along with a very basic education and the chance to learn a trade. Point Puer closed in 1849, after 2,000 boys had passed through its doors. Transportation was not formally abolished until 1868, although it had effectively stopped a decade earlier.

Back in Britain, Poor Law administration had become so scandalous that a Royal Commission was appointed to look into it; their report was made in 1834. The first real attempt to tackle the problem of child destitution on a national scale, this led to the establishment of a responsible body with a duty to all pauper children in England and Wales. The Poor Law Act of 1834 sought to regulate workhouse regimes, appointing Poor Law Commissioners and Boards of Guardians to oversee the running of institutions and monitor conditions for those 'behind doors'. In 1847, the Poor Law Board took over the Commissioners' responsibilities, and they were assumed in turn by the Local Government Board in 1871 and the Ministry of Health in 1919. Gradually workhouses were replaced by Children's Homes from which the children went out to school, and towards 1900 boarding out was again expanded. In the second half of the 19th century more and more private voluntary organizations were founded, including Dr Barnardo's Homes, the Church of England Waifs and Strays (later the Children's) Society, Quarriers and the National Children's Home. These were the organizations that became prominent in arranging migration of children overseas.

Crime and punishment

Child poverty had been associated with crime since well before transportation, and it preoccupied reformers of the late 18th and early 19th centuries. The Philanthropic Society was founded in 1788 by Robert Young to reform boys convicted of petty crimes, and the Society opened a refuge in Southwark in 1792. Half a century later, in 1849, it bought a farm of 133 acres, later expanded to 350 acres, in Redhill, Surrey (plate 10). It was the first organization to try such an approach, its attitude illustrated by a description in an annual report:

> ... the boy has been left untaught and uncared for — has been the subject of much ill-treatment and neglect — and ... the gentler influences of a mother's care and the comforts of an honest and happy home have been unknown to him.[10]

The boys at the farm were either very young and sentenced to transportation or attending voluntarily after spending time in prison —on a form of rehabilitation programme in which they could learn farming skills. Charles Dickens visited the farm in 1852 and praised it for having few rules, for putting trust in the boys and teaching them to think for themselves. After the Reformatory School Act was passed in 1854 the school began to receive boys directly from the courts, and numbers grew considerably. At the end of their training on the farm, many boys were helped to emigrate to parts of the British Empire.

The Quaker Peter Bedford, a silk merchant in Spitalfields, was another philanthropist concerned with poverty and crime among young people. He founded the Society for Lessening the Causes of Juvenile Delinquency in London, which produced a detailed report on children and crime in 1816. It cited copious case histories and suggested the establishment of reformatories, but the government was slow to take the initiative. Bedford then set up his own refuge where boys were given training in tailoring, shoemaking and other skills, so that they were equipped with the basis of a trade when they left. Many of the boys were helped to emigrate to South Africa through a government scheme since, in 1819, the British government had set aside £50,000 for emigrating people to the Cape Colony in order to counter the Afrikaans influence and to help fight against the indigenous people. In South Africa they worked mainly as farm labourers, as later child migrants were to do in Canada and Australia.

South Africa was also the destination of many of the boys from the Children's Friend Society. This was founded in London in 1830, as the Society for the Suppression of Juvenile Vagrancy, by retired naval captain Edward Pelham Brenton. Brenton's aim was to prepare destitute children for emigration with training to enable them to support themselves. He opened two homes: the Brenton Juvenile Asylum in Hackney for boys and the Royal Victoria Asylum in Chiswick for girls. The children who went there were those who had lived on the streets, begging and stealing. Some were unmanageable children with whom the parishes could not cope, and others had got into bad company; but Brenton's attitude to all was very enlightened for the time. He emphasized that they should be kindly treated and that punishment should be used sparingly. Flogging was forbidden and, although there was 'strict discipline, prompt obedience and perfect regularity', the only punishment was six to seven hours of solitary confinement for theft. In the Homes, the children were taught to look after themselves, to grind corn, to bake bread and to cook.

In 1832, the first party of Brenton's children were sent to the Cape of Good Hope; by 1835, a committee had been set up there to super-vise the boys and girls and make sure they were treated properly in their placements. Despite this, a complaint at the end of the 1830s from an apprentice who had been sent out to South Africa sparked off rumours of bad treatment, to the extent that Brenton asked the gov-ernment to investigate the situation and clear his name. Sir George Napier, Governor of the Cape, sent four magistrates to report on 434 apprentices (over half those in the colony), asking them about their treatment, their education, their church attendance, whether they had been taught a trade and the conditions in which they lived. Their report concluded that the concerns were largely groundless. Nonetheless, many of the children felt lonely in the isolated farmsteads dotted around the vast open country, where even opportunities for attending church were limited. And since most of the farmers were Dutch-speaking, the children placed with them were beginning to lose their English, coun-teracting the British government's reason for sending them there in the first place. Sarah Piper's story sums up the situation in which many of the children found themselves:

> I am about 15 years old; my parents are living in England: I cannot read or write; my general health is good but I am much troubled with sores on my neck; never go to church but hear the family prayers at home. I can't speak English now. I am employed nursing or housework; sleep in the same apartment with my mistress; have no complaints to make.[11]

One of the magistrates, H. Piers, observed that the children were gen-erally treated well, were healthy and well clothed, but that their educa-tion and religious instruction were neglected, if only because of the isolation of the farms.

> The result must inevitably be, when out of their indentures, that having learned nothing that can procure a comfortable or respectable living, they must continue in the same degraded, hopeless position of farm labourer ... without a chance that I can perceive of their ever rising higher.[12]

Children who had been apprenticed to tradesmen, such as masons, generally had a better future than those who were settled on remote rural outposts. They lived in towns where they could go to school and attend church, and had a good chance of being masters in their own right once they had finished their apprenticeships.

Napier, however, was angry that the inquiry had taken place at all as it cast aspersions on the settlers' conduct. Although the report was generally in their favour, he believed that it 'had created the strongest disinclination on the part of the Local Commissioners to receive or take charge of any more of the Society's children'.[13] In fact, Brenton's Society was already reaching further afield—it had sent children to the Swan River Colony in Australia as well as the Cape in 1832, and in August 1833 its first party of children was despatched to Toronto, Canada. However, the majority of the apprentices were South Africa-bound, and when the Cape would no longer accept them the Society closed. A year later, the disappointed Brenton died.

Another attempt to combat the criminal and depraved influences surrounding destitute city children was the ragged schools movement. Unofficial teachers tried to inculcate the four 'R's—reading, 'riting, 'rithmetic and religion—from schoolrooms in stables, lofts and railway arches which pauper children were encouraged to attend. By 1844, there were about 20 ragged schools in London and the Ragged School Union was founded to centralize their organization and promote the cause. Lord Shaftesbury, a celebrated champion of child emigration, was appointed chairman, and 150 boys and girls were sent from the ragged schools to Australia in 1848. Shaftesbury tried to persuade the government to fund an official migration of children to the colonies, without success; despite this, small groups of children from the schools continued to be sent out, funded by donations. To promote the concept, the *Ragged School Union Magazine* of 1849 published a series of engravings depicting the changing fortunes of a young migrant—beginning as a pauper among London squalor, he discovers a happier, somewhat idealized existence as a shepherd in Australia. The magazine also bore witness to the real experiences of the young migrants by publishing their letters. One boy wrote:

> I have to get the breakfast and supper ready for the shepherds, and that is all I have to do; then I go out native cat hunting and make rugs of their skins. I am going to have a dog for the purpose of hunting kangaroos.[14]

And another boy described his day:

I go out of a morning at sunrise, and all I have to do is to see that my flock don't part. I lay down and read all day, then at sunset I come home... Coming from England to Australia is like coming from a dirty town to the garden of paradise.[15]

This early phase of emigration to Australia ceased with the Gold Rush in 1853, when conditions in that country were judged unsuitable for children. In a reversal of later developments, the young migrants were sent to Canada instead. However, in 1870 the passing of the Education Act, requiring all children between 5 and 13 to attend school, saw the beginning of the end of the Ragged School Union. New school boards took over some of their existing schoolrooms and embarked on a major programme of school-building and teacher-training. By the mid-1870s many ragged schools had closed and the movement changed direction, moving out of schooling and into other areas.

The decline of ragged schools also saw the winding down of their child migration activity, but the opportunities it offered were not to be neglected for long. The initiative was seized by evangelicals, philan-thropists, reformers and those with an eye to business, and new organ-izations to rescue and dispatch children were set up. It was a practice that captured the imagination of officials and individuals, and seemed to offer possible solutions to each age's different needs. Thousands more lives were destined to be changed in the next hundred years — some for the better, others to end in loneliness and disillusion. By 1869 the first of a new wave of children — frightened, excited, vulnerable — was on its way across the Atlantic. And with these small girls sailed the undisputed first lady of the second phase, Maria Rye.

Chapter 1

Two women pioneers

Occasionally during the first days of our distribution work, there would be a hue and cry from the children, 'A farmer's coming!' 'Oh, let him have me, Mrs Birt!' 'No, let him have me. I want to be a farmer and earn my own living.'

LILLIAN BIRT, *The Children's Home-Finder*, 1913

THE LATER PART of Victoria's reign brought new awareness of the poverty and destitution blighting Britain's cities, and of the philanthropists and reformers battling with them. Many of those working in the slums, ragged schools and missions, including several involved with emigration, were inspired by the evangelical movement, and they used its literature and resources to publicize and raise money for their reforms. Children became a natural focus of such campaigns, as sympathy for their often wretched circumstances blended with moral concern for the degenerate lives they would probably grow up to lead. Emigration was presented as a solution to both issues, enabling children to flourish in a more wholesome environment under sound religious influence. Enthusiasm for the project fuelled more organized, larger-scale migration, developed in the first instance by two remarkable, very different Victorians, Annie Macpherson and Maria Rye.

Although the women's names are often linked, and they shared the same fierce dedication to the child migration cause, Rye and Macpherson never worked together and their relationship was remote. This was partly due to differences of background—Rye came from a privileged, professional family, able to enlist the help of establishment figures such as Lord Shaftesbury and the Archbishop of Canterbury, while Macpherson was a devout, 'twice-born' evangelical, skilled in using the Christian press to promote her activities but with a much lower social profile. She drew upon a network of close family and friends in her emigration work, while Rye preferred to remain in charge of all as a dominant, prestigious figurehead, liaising with a few favoured organizations and remaining close to the Anglican church. Both possessed a natural ability to lead, motivate and defy obstacles, and, despite the controversy their work could and did inspire, both continued to display the courage of their convictions—an unshakeable assurance that they were doing the best thing for those in their care.

The redoubtable Miss Rye

Maria Susan Rye was born into a London legal family in 1829 (plate 2). Well educated herself, she became frustrated by the limitations that Victorian society placed on women, offering them few opportunities outside the home. She joined the Langham Place Group (active 1857–66), a small number of determined, middle-class women who campaigned on a variety of fronts to improve their situation, and for a short time she served as secretary of the committee to reform the law on married women's property.

Dissatisfied by her parochial work at St Luke's, Chelsea (where the rector was the father of author Charles Kingsley), Maria began to think about helping middle-class women, such as herself, find work. She became a member of the Society for Promoting the Employment of Women, founded in 1859, and one of her initiatives was setting up an office copying legal documents in Lincoln's Inn Fields, helped, no doubt, by her family's connections with the law. She went on to found the Victoria Printing Press and a telegraph school for girl clerks, and also wrote articles for *The Englishwoman's Domestic Magazine* under the initials MSR.

At the Society for Promoting the Employment of Women, Maria found herself deluged with applicants for a limited number of posts. Emigration was considered a solution to problems caused by the population explosion, and Maria decided that sending women abroad to work would help them out of a difficult situation. The Female Middle Class Emigration Society was therefore founded in May 1862, with the fund-raising assistance of Barbara Bodichon (a founder of the Langham Place Group) and with Lord Shaftesbury as its first president. The Society aimed to provide interest-free loans to enable educated women to emigrate, and it established contacts at both departure and arrival points. With the energetic Miss Rye behind it, progress was swift, and the first party, in Rye's charge, sailed for New Zealand in the autumn of 1862. The long journey and the responsibility of a hundred women in her care did not daunt Rye; it reinforced her sense of purpose, and being on the high seas with only herself in charge may well have given her a sense of freedom. She wrote of the 'pleasurable' 90-day voyage in the *John Duncan*, and seemed proud that the women went 'as quietly as they would have done in London'.[1] However, it became clear that employers wanted domestic servants rather than middle-class governesses, so the enterprising Rye turned her attention to emigrating working-class women.

Her first trip to Canada was in June 1868, in the SS *Hibernian*, when she accompanied a party of 119 women, 21 men and 5 children to Quebec, for which she received $500 from the Canadian government. She found work for the women in Quebec City, in Montreal and Toronto. The immigration agent stated that '… all the girls left by her in Montreal, about 40 in number, turned out well; and had she left the whole of them there, they could have been easily disposed of and thus have saved the expense of their Western journey.'[2] Buoyed by success, Maria Rye organized another trip to Canada that year. She also travelled to New York where she met the Reverend W.C. Van Meter, founder of the Howard Mission and Home for Little Wanderers, opened on 10 June 1861. Van Meter had been engaged for several years in rescuing 'children of the street' and placing them in carefully selected homes, chiefly in the country. In these new homes, they were to be treated as part of the family and receive a school education, attend Sunday school and church, and be given some kind of training. Most importantly, Van Meter retained the power to remove the children if they were not properly treated.

This visit inspired Maria Rye. It occurred to her that she could do something similar with the street children of London and other cities, only instead of the English countryside she could take them overseas and board them in Canada. She was confident that the Canadians would welcome them with open arms: there were plenty of families who wanted help on their farms and the children would benefit from clean, country air. With renewed energy, Miss Rye set about implementing her plan.

Ever the publicist, she wrote a fund-raising letter to *The Times*, published on 29 March 1869. In it she described Van Meter's work, explaining how it had inspired her 'to take the "gutter children" of London, Manchester, Birmingham, Bristol and Liverpool and emigrate them to Canada'. She justified such an intervention by pointing out the perils of their present plight. 'What treatment will they receive from the cold, the starvation, the temptation they receive in our gutters...? Can anything I introduce them to in Canada ... be worse that that to which they are doomed if we leave them where they are now?'

The children's response, could they have made it, would have been that at least it was familiar to them, and they had people around them whom they knew, even valued family ties. The cartoonist and temperance campaigner George Cruikshank replied by publishing a pamphlet denouncing her plan. Entitled Our 'Gutter Children', it featured a stark cartoon depicting street children being carted away like rubbish, their pitiful cries overridden by voices of authority and a Maria Rye-like figure which proclaimed, 'I'll drive off to pitch the little dears aboard of a ship and take them thousands of miles away from their native land so that they may never see any of their relatives again.' Cruikshank's belief was that emigration was not the solution to child destitution and that money should rather be put into reforms at home. This was not a popular view, however, and there were many who rallied in support of Maria Rye's scheme. Only a few months later she was ready to begin.

'Our Western Home'

Before emigrating any children, Rye needed to find a place to serve as a distributing house in Canada. For this she chose the old court-house and gaol at Niagara-on-the-Lake (a district described by the Toronto Standard as 'the fruit garden of Canada')[3], situated on two acres of land. The property was bought with money donated to the project, yet it subsequently emerged that the building had been purchased in her name and was thus Rye's personal possession. Despite the concern this aroused in certain quarters, Rye did in later years hand over the property, together with the rest of her work, to the Church of England's Waifs and Strays Society, never attempting to retain it for her own use. The house was christened 'Our Western Home' (plate 1) and her conversion transformed the building, the court becoming a dormitory for a hundred girls and one of the cells a larder. Many years later it still impressed visitors; in 1877 the correspondent of the Toronto *Standard* noted the 'cleanliness, space and airiness' of the home, distinguished by its 'deep verandahs and jalousies'.[4]

Sourcing the children to fill the new structure was not so straightforward. Rye had also established a distributing Home in Peckham, south London, but although she had launched an appeal for 'gutter children' on the premise that their circumstances could hardly be worse, most of those she emigrated to Canada were girls from the workhouse. Street children in reality were undisciplined, lacked education and were not ready material to take over to Canada as domestic servants. Maria Rye had no inclination to train girls for the work; in any case, workhouse girls had the benefit of some schooling and were used to living in a house under a certain amount of discipline. Most advantageous of all—and a point her detractors were swift to perceive—the Board of Guardians would pay their fares.

Maria Rye took her first party of girls to Canada in October 1869. Their departure was reported in the *Illustrated London News* of 6 November: 'By the Allan Company's steamer *Hibernia* [sic] which left the Mersey for Quebec yesterday week, Miss Rye took with her a hundred young girls she has selected—seventy of them, from five to eleven years of age, being from the Liverpool industrial schools.' They landed in Quebec City, from there travelling by train to Toronto and crossing Lake Ontario by steamer. The party was met on the far side by local farmers who carted the luggage to 'Our Western Home'. Rye, always one to make an entrance, arrived some time after the children with a local reporter in tow. In the *Niagara Mail*, 17 November, he wrote a glowing description of the scene: 'The confidence and trust of those children in Miss Rye is unbounded. They regard her with the strongest affection, which they show in a thousand artless ways—fondling around her, kissing her hands and the like...' The party was also enthusiastically welcomed by the *Daily Telegraph* of St John, New Brunswick, which observed, in an article published on 14 November, that 'the children are all smart and intelligent looking, and can all read, write, and sing... We trust that Miss Rye will be induced to bring another troop of these fine children to homes which are always awaiting them in this province... Mr Shives expects that those who have applied will call for the girls now in his charge before Saturday next.'[5]

Back in England, Miss Rye reported to the Board of Guardians at Kirkdale Industrial School, Liverpool, on how she had placed the children in Canada. Those Canadians who wanted a child had to fill in an application form, and if this was satisfactorily done a child was put in their care — in Rye's words, 'regularly and legally' placed. She had two forms, an Indenture for Adoption and an Indenture of Service, in which the signatories were bound to act in a particular way towards the child, but neither had any legal standing and could not be enforced. Nor had Miss Rye put any system in place to observe whether the terms of these indentures were carried out, believing that this was the responsibility of the Canadian government. She had asked the mayor and a Justice of the Peace in Niagara to keep an eye on the children, although how they were to do this was never clearly explained. Nor was her argument that anything must be better than the lot of street children applicable to young migrants brought from workhouses. None of these matters seemed to concern the Liverpool Board of Guardians unduly, however, or else, conscious of financial pressures, they were highly motivated to emigrate as many children as possible. In all events, convinced by Rye's assurances, the Guardians agreed to fund more journeys to Canada for the young girls in their care.

In 1870, at a meeting of the National Association for the Promotion of Social Science, presided over by Lord Shaftesbury, Miss Rye gave a speech about the economic realities of keeping pauper children on relief. Noting that in London alone there were more than 10,000 children in the workhouse and another 46,000 on outdoor relief, she revealed that she could take girls to Canada for £10 a head, placing them with respectable families. In this way the children's lives would be greatly improved, and the cost of supporting them at home would be materially reduced.

This point was taken up by Dr Hayward in a lecture to the Liverpool Literary and Philosophical Society that same year. His paper, entitled 'Emigration of public orphans', stated that Miss Rye had already saved the Liverpool ratepayers £5,000, which would have been the cost of maintaining the children she had taken to Canada from eight years of age to 18. Not only that, he claimed, but the workhouse notoriously contributed to the ruin of girls; they should be emigrated at the age of eight to benefit both the colonies and England.[6]

The London Board of Guardians was pleased to be convinced, and it agreed that Maria Rye could take children from its workhouses to Canada. Under the Board's auspices, 461 children were sent away in 1871, by which time 36 Unions were entrusting their children to her. Although there were mainly girls in her party, boys were sometimes included, and New Brunswick, as well as Ontario, was their destination. Girls remained her preference, however, and in a letter to *The Christian* in 1870 Rye proposed dividing the sexes between Annie Macpherson's operation and her own: 'Miss Macpherson could place a thousand little boys, the younger the better, and I and my workers could place a thousand little girls wisely and safely in Canada for the next ten years.' Macpherson was not interested in the suggestion.

As Rye's work became higher profile, she sought to defend herself against detractors by publishing judiciously chosen letters (from supporters and some of the young migrants themselves) rather than filing reports. A selection quoted by Gillian Wagner reveals the children's deep-rooted anxieties, especially about lost siblings or friends, underlying the superficially positive accounts. A girl from Chichester workhouse in Sussex, for example, begs for news of her brother, 'I thank you for getting me such a good home … I have heard that my brother as got a home, but I have not seen him or heard of him … I know I don't feel quite so happy as I should feel if I knew where he was and hear from him.' Another girl, Selina N., travelled in Rye's original Kirkdale party; she also requests information about her friends and sister. 'Would you please tell me where my sister is … would you tell me were Jane Tatlock is, and how she his [sic], for I like to know … I would like to see my sister, if I could get to see her.'[7]

Energy and dedication characterized Rye, and she was relentless in pursuing her goal. Even her arch-critic, Andrew Doyle, was amazed by her vigour, recognizing that she had placed 190 children in three parties in 1873 alone. She had made the draining Atlantic crossing three times and had journeyed more than 6,000 miles visiting children, as well as exploring the slums of cities at home. Yet a backlash to her operation was starting to grow. Doubts about her work had surfaced as far back as 1868, when William Dixon, a Canadian emigration agent based in Britain, had condemned her organization. He called Rye 'a passenger agent of the sharpest description', explaining his rationale:

> She appeals to the public through the press for contributions to aid her
> in assisting poor girls to emigrate… She then applies to the registry

offices for girls and asks them how much money they can raise towards the price of a passage ... she also applies to the unions of factory towns and ... the guardians pay all the expenses. If the girls have two pounds and Miss Rye's subscriptions come in freely she supplements what is required, retaining what she considers reasonable ... it is a profitable business...[8]

More public concerns were expressed in 1874 through a letter to the Islington Board of Guardians. It was written by a Mr Allendale Grainger, who was married to a girl who had once worked for—and been dismissed by—Maria Rye. The letter queries whether the children were benefiting from emigration and if Miss Rye was making undue profit from the ratepayers, who seemed to be overpaying for her services. He pointed out that the girls were friendless in a strange country where they needed protection, and that the work they were doing was hard. He ended by saying that the Local Government Board should send out a person with knowledge of Canada and its farmers to look into the project.

Miss Rye countered this argument with a list of prominent people who supported her work in Canada. She also pointed out that England had no right to criticize any other country, 'for as a nation we are guilty of wife-desertion and beating, of child-selling and child neglect to an extent to which there is no parallel in any other civilized nation under the sun'. She offered to submit accounts to rebut the charge of profiteering and emphasized that she did not object to anyone inspecting her work. Her defence ended on a typically high note, sweeping away all criticism: 'And I thank God this day, and say it without fear of contradiction, that my work is a glorious success and has in many ways exceeded my most sanguine expectations.'[9]

The Board of Guardians backed her—perhaps it was in their interest to do so. Nonetheless, the Local Government Board did take note of one suggestion made by Mr Grainger. In 1874, it commissioned Andrew Doyle, one of its senior inspectors, to report back on the schemes for emigration of workhouse children to Canada.

The Homes of Annie Macpherson

Annie Macpherson was also to be involved in Doyle's investigation. A very different character from Rye, she was born in Campsie, Stirlingshire, in 1833, the eldest of seven children. Her father James, a teacher and a Quaker, was asked by Lady Lovelace to establish schools on her estate and his daughter accompanied him there, assisting him with correspondence. He died while she was still in her teens, and in 1852 the family moved to Eversden, Cambridgeshire, where her sister Rachel married Joseph Merry—their sons would later help Macpherson in her work. An uneventful life in Eversden, teaching Sunday school and Bible classes, was changed by a day trip to London in 1861, when she attended a Christian Revival meeting. Its effect was gradual; as she later said, 'I had not the slightest thought that this would open up a way by which my life could be spent in serving and helping little children in London.'[10]

On her return to Eversden she set up a Mission, including evening classes where Cambridge University students gave lectures. Her work here continued until 1865, when she and her mother moved to London and Macpherson became active in the evangelical movement and charitable work in the East End. She attended the sick, distributed food and held meetings for mothers, witnessing the reality of destitution at close hand. The impact of alcohol on impoverished lives disturbed her, especially when it was used as a panacea for children:

> While yet in their mothers' arms, gin is poured down their infant throats, and a little later as a natural consequence childish voices beg for coppers to be spent in drink. Alas! no uncommon sight is it to see little girls of ten years old reeling drunk along the streets.[11]

Worse was to come. A visit with a colleague, Clara Lowe, to a house in Bethnal Green brought her up narrow stairs to an attic where she was confronted with a 'group of palefaced little matchbox makers'. They spent all their waking hours bending pieces of wood, sanding them and covering them with paper—many of the children had raw, blistered fingers from the sandpaper. Some were only three years old, and all had lost their childhood years to earn three farthings for every 12 dozen boxes made. Macpherson brought their plight to public attention by writing a booklet called *The Little Matchbox Makers*. The readers of the evangelical journal *The Revival* (later called *The Christian*) were moved by her description—a tribute to Macpherson's talent for publicizing her work. Fellow evangelicals donated enough money to rent the old cholera hospital at 60 Commercial Street, Spitalfields, and Macpherson successfully converted the warehouse space into 'The Home of Industry'. Complete with dormitories, schoolrooms, workshops and kitchens, it was a place where children came to work and some to live. Macpherson commented, 'The children are no idlers themselves; tailoring, shoemaking, matchbox-making are all being pursued on different floors of the building.'[12] Yet assistance with day-to-day living always underlay her main intention—to bring the children to God and save their souls.

The project was successful, as were other fund-raising campaigns in *The Revival*. Three further Revival Homes were established, formally opening in May 1869, and Macpherson involved herself closely with the children they housed. Her skill at raising funds was, like that of Thomas Barnardo, crucial to her success, and she used it to the full, perceiving the value of 'before' and 'after' photographs to promote her achievements. In this and other ways she influenced the young Barnardo, still a medical student when her Homes were opened, not least in her enthusiasm for emigration to save her protégés from the criminal future looming before them. Moving children on was also a practical response to what was becoming an untenable situation—the numbers of destitute children were more than Macpherson and her assistants could manage. As she explained to her readers, faith helped them find a way: 'Our walls had limits and our failures in finding employment for many away from their old haunts became a great difficulty, and the God-opened way of emigration to Canada was pressed upon us.'[13]

Macpherson, like Rye, had been impressed by Van Meter's work in New York as he sought to board or foster out west children left orphaned by the American civil war. She opened a fund for public donations to assist families to go to Canada, and in April 1869 was able to send a party of 500 people to Montreal, from where the adults were dispatched to farms in Quebec and Ontario. Then in May 1870, she herself took 100 boys from London across the Atlantic on the *Peruvian*.

It was a bold step, as those on the first trip had no receiving house, having to rely on the emigration agent. It was clear that Macpherson's parties needed a Home in Canada to stay on arrival, providing a base for any child that arrived ill and for keeping an eye on the new arrivals in their foster homes—rather than depending on the goodwill of farmers or civic officials. One place where Macpherson was sent with the children was the town of Belleville in Ontario, and it was here that the Warden of Hastings County, A.F. Wood, gave her a letter from the county council encouraging her to select the town for her distribution house by offering to pay the rent. Macpherson could not refuse the generous offer, and Belleville duly became the site of her first receiving Home, known as Marchmont (plate 4). Ellen Agnes Bilborough, a stalwart friend who had accompanied Annie Macpherson on the journey from England, was put in charge, where she remained as honorary superintendent for the next 30 years. Macpherson supplied a lyrical description of the Home for readers of *The Christian*—'a home of love … a sweet foretaste to these unloved and uncared for children of their home in heaven', but it burnt down in 1872, with the loss of a six-year-old child. It was suggested that Macpherson's organization should buy a bigger property, and another Marchmont was purchased with funds raised for this purpose. In 1875 this was also devastated by fire, but rose from the ashes rebuilt in brick by local people.

For Macpherson, securing Marchmont as a base was a huge relief, but for the children she escorted the journey was still traumatic. A twelve-year-old boy quoted by Bean and Melville describes the rigours of the trip, involving as it did a five or six hour train journey to Belleville on top of the Atlantic voyage. He arrived fearful, homesick and exhausted: 'We were out in the [distribution] Home then and taken up to our rooms and put in bed. I was frightened … I cried and cried as I wanted to go back. I wanted to go to Canada, but when I got there I wanted to go back to Wales. I guess the other boys felt the same.'[14]

Both evangelical organizations and several workhouse Unions were by now requesting Macpherson's help in emigrating children to Canada. She was arranging several journeys a year to bring children to Canada, and with so many she needed to find more receiving Homes. In 1872 Macpherson established Blair Atholl, a 100-acre farm near Galt in Ontario, that provided a deliberately different sort of home. Galt had received mention in *The Christian* as the site of a flourishing religious revival, and Macpherson's visit to this town, of largely Scottish origin, resulted in their generous gift. Macpherson planned to use it 'to fit them [children] to be of value to the farmer', wanting children to work in the fields so that 'they might see the effects of new soil and climate in the growth of vegetables, shrubs, and farm produce'.[15] Annie's sister and her husband, Rachel and Joseph Merry, took over the farm in 1877. It was sold in 1882 and the Home moved to a house on several acres of land in Stratford, Ontario (plate 12). The third Home Macpherson acquired was at Knowlton, a small village in Quebec, in the Eastern Townships near Montreal. Two ladies from Knowlton, Emma Barber and Mrs Foster, had become interested in her work and raised funds in the area to purchase an old tavern, which became the Knowlton Home. Its comforts were basic, with paraffin lamps for light, wood stoves for heat and water pumped from a well, and the location was isolated and rather bleak. Despite the somewhat daunting conditions, Knowlton was opened in 1872, with Emma Barber in charge.

Macpherson differed from Rye in her attempts to keep an eye on the children once they had been found foster homes—a crucial difference between the two operations. The reports on the children seem to have been made by people in sympathy with them, although limited by the cultural attitude to children of the time. It is clear that what the agent expected was obedience above all, then honesty and piety—not qualities immediately associated with young teenagers today. The National Archives holds reports on children from the Bristol Incorporation of the Poor whom Miss Macpherson placed in Canada (plate 3); a series from Marchmont in October 1872 offers fascinating insight into the children's individual characters and lives (MH 32/20). Some were faring well, such as George S., aged eight, who was 'with kind people, has a good home, and goes regularly to school'. Others were more problematic, such as William G., aged 12, who had to be removed from his placement in the summer of 1872. The inspectors had 'found his master a lumber merchant and had a number of rough men in his employment, who had learned William to swear'. In March 1873, he wrote to the agent: 'Please would you write and tell Miss Macpherson that I have got a good place, and am getting on pretty well, and I can read and write pretty well.'

The reports show that inspections were generally made annually, and that most of the children seemed to be in good homes with people who did care about them. Those that were not were moved and, like William, appear grateful for it. Samuel L., for example, had been extracted in January from 'a bad home where his employer drank' despite the errant boss's kindness to the boy. By 20 September he had been reassigned to 'an excellent home' where he was doing well and attending winter school.

Education was deemed important, and children were taken away if not allowed by the farmers to attend school: Mary Ann B. (aged nine) was removed 'as she was not getting to school; quite a little drudge. Taken Aug 27th to get schooling, clothes, etc.' Mary Ann's story illustrated the different fortunes of divided siblings; her elder sister Hannah, aged 13, was 'getting on with her education' and 'greatly liked by her mistress' and the prospects for her younger sister Emily ('Adopted; has a good home and very much thought of') also looked relatively bright. The reports often reflect siblings' desire to keep in touch, and the responsibility shown by family members to one another, situated as they were so far from home. Frank H., aged 14, wrote to Marchmont to enquire about his ten-year-old brother William in February; by September he had managed to visit him with, according to the report, satisfactory results: '[he] found him well and happy, in a good place and getting to school all the time.' Some children asked for siblings to join them, such as James H. ('Is doing very well, and much liked; employer greatly interested in him') who wanted his sister to share in the opportunities he was making for himself. Others, such as James and Thomas B., were keen to maintain ties with their sister at Knowlton; as both boys seemed well placed, this was hopefully achieved. Family fortunes were often mixed, however, one of the saddest cases being a 10-year-old never adopted through no fault of his own. Charles T.'s 'paralysed face' had left him stranded at Marchmont while his two brothers and little sister, despite their attempts to stay in touch (all had visited earlier in 1872), were building new lives elsewhere.

Some reports show that youngsters who were once keen and willing could become troublesome when they hit puberty—something we would accept now, but which seemed strangely unexpected to those dealing with children in the 19th century. Mark Appleby was described as 'a keen little man, not very big for his age, but quick and trustworthy' at the age of 11, but 18 months later he is 13 and things have changed:

> He has become rather troublesome of late and disobedient to his mistress. If he persists in his obstinacy, I advised her to return him to the Home. He is not altogether to blame, as he is of rather boisterous temperament, and requires a man to manage him.

Rosina Dew, at nine, was a child that her foster family 'could not part with'. But aged 11, her report reads,

> Mrs — has had a good deal of trouble with R. She is high-tempered, fond of her own way and so untidy, but with firmness and love, she is being won over, and slowly improving. She is with kind Christian people who have the interest of the Children at heart.[16]

What is interesting about Rosina Dew's report is the obvious affection and commitment that her family had for her; she was confident enough about their support to show her bad qualities and her family responded with understanding. Many children who did not behave properly were in danger of being sent back to the Home, or of drifting like 16-year-old William H. who was 'rather idle and associating with bad company. At present working in the town of Belleville.' Nevertheless the reports, brief as they are, reveal a degree of sympathy and understanding towards the less 'satisfactory' children. James D., 'a poor delicate little fellow, in a good home but still very delicate', was relying on the support of the family's grandmother who thought he had potential to become a minister, and even the troublesome Edwin B., 'returned to the Marchmont Home several times, because of dishonesty and untruthfulness', had been given training and, eventually, another opportunity at a 'good home in the country'. Some of the reports include the children's own tributes to the success of the scheme; George H., aged 11, is described as 'a willing boy, and I think will make a useful man', while 15-year-old James W. expressed his appreciation in a letter dated March 1872: 'I have to thank you very much for the great kindness you have done me by bringing me to this country. I am a great deal happier than when in England.'[17]

In the early years Macpherson divided the children between the three receiving Homes, but by 1877 she felt that Blair Atholl in Galt was able to house them all. Her friend Ellen Bilborough took over Marchmont and it became a distribution house for many of the agencies in Scotland, including Quarrier's (p.62). Annie offered management of Knowlton to her younger sister, Louisa Birt, who had been involved in her charitable work since 1870. She had accompanied Annie to Liverpool as the first group of children were sent to Canada, and the sisters saw destitution there that was even worse than the East End of London. During the Irish Potato Famine (1845–9) thousands of Irish had come to Liverpool, enduring unsavoury and insanitary conditions in which diseases such as typhus and cholera ran rife—nearly five per cent of the population died during the epidemics of 1866. Concerned about the large numbers of orphaned and neglected children, a group of ship-owners in 1872 invited Macpherson to address a public meeting in Liverpool and discuss the establishment of a rescue Home. Conscious of her rapidly expanding workload, she sent her sister Louisa to speak instead.

The Liverpool Sheltering Homes

At the Law Association Rooms in November 1872, Louisa Birt explained the aims and methods of her sister's work. She must have been convincing, for it was decided that a Home be established in Liverpool, with fund-raising and management to be kept separate from the London organization. Premises on Byron Street were offered free of rent and running costs, and the Liverpool Sheltering Homes was formally opened on 1 May 1873. The first president, Stephen Williamson, was none other than the Member of Parliament for Liverpool, and a friend of the influential shipowner Alexander Balfour who had first approached Macpherson. Birt herself became the first superintendent and the committee included the wealthy merchant Samuel Smith, who later became a Liverpool MP and vocal supporter of child emigration, and Mrs Williamson—not only the president's wife but also daughter of the Reverend Thomas Guthrie, founder of Edinburgh's Industrial Ragged School. Backed by influence and practical experience of charitable work, Louisa Birt could learn fast.

The organization sought to provide a place of rescue for destitute children, where they would be trained for work and then sent to a new life in Canada. The training was described in a letter to Birt by one of the instructors:

> I instruct the boys you send me in the general anatomy and structure of the horse, cow, pig and sheep; how to cleanse, water and feed them, and at all times to be kind and gentle to all animals and make them their friends. I also teach them how to detect slight injuries to a horse's hoof, and how to apply simple measures for their relief. I also take them to a stable and make them harness and unharness horses and hitch them to a conveyance, with many practical hints how to handle

and drive them. They also attend a large dairy where they have to clean
the shippon, feed and water the cows, and help in the milking. By this
means, when lads go to farms in Canada, they are able at once to make
themselves useful in the daily routine.

Louisa emerges as a caring person, wholeheartedly committed to the
children. She was the mother of four herself, having married a merchant, Charles Birt, in 1858 — one daughter, Lillian, later took over her
mother's work. Louisa brought warmth and affection; she would sing
to the children, tell them stories and help to bath the little ones. The
children were given a little schooling; girls were taught domestic skills,
boys carpentry and work in the stables. All the children attended Bible
classes.

Not long after the Liverpool Sheltering Homes had been opened,
Louisa received a letter from an Englishman, Colonel James Wimburn
Laurie, who had been appointed as inspector of the militia in Nova
Scotia. He invited Louisa to bring a group of children to Halifax and
offered to take responsibility for each child, paying their costs once
they were in Nova Scotia until they were placed on a farm. He had even
managed to persuade the provincial government to help pay their passage from Liverpool. It was too good an offer to refuse and so, in
August 1873, Louisa took a party of 76 to Halifax: 26 girls, 44 boys
and 6 women. On arrival, Laurie entered each person's name in a
register saying who they were, where they were from and where they
were going. Occasional entries in another column were made later,
revealing that the child had been returned, but not giving a reason.

Laurie seemed particularly careful about conditions of placement,
perhaps more so than any other person or organization involved in
child immigration at that time. He was appointed legal guardian of
the children in Canada and was thorough in his investigation of the
families who applied for a child. He also required 'quarterly reports,
giving full particulars of the child's health, conduct, progress in and
out of school and this in every case certified by the local minister'.[18]
However, these reports were to be written by the farmer himself, which
did not necessarily make them accurate, and neither could the minister's certification be relied upon. Nonetheless, in three years — before
withdrawing from the scheme through ill-health — Laurie placed nearly
600 children on farms in Nova Scotia. Even by Canadian standards,
this was a cold and difficult place to live. It had been settled by poor

Scottish farmers who were eager for help on the farm but could not afford to pay a hired hand. Living on an isolated farm away from everything familiar must have been difficult for city children, and it is not hard to imagine the reasons for the 'returned' entries in Laurie's ledger. It is interesting to note there were so few.

The Doyle Report

The difficulty of transposing children from city slums to lonely farms is one of the concerns expressed in Andrew Doyle's report on child migration. Born and raised in Dublin, he was to prove a provocative figure to those emigrating children and to become the *bête noire* of Maria Rye. When chosen to report on the conditions of child migrants, Doyle was 65 years old and had been a Poor Law inspector for 25 years; for most of his working life he had been a civil servant, but he was also legally trained. His brief was to examine the way in which children were selected for Canada; how they were prepared for their new life; how the receiving Homes in Canada were run; how the farms and new homes were chosen for the children; and the aftercare of the children once they had been placed. He was to fulfil it meticulously.

In early July 1874, Doyle arrived in Montreal. His plan was to visit all the receiving Homes first and meet the people who ran them, including Annie Macpherson and Maria Rye. His first stop was Knowlton in the Eastern Townships, then he went on to Ontario to see the Macpherson Homes in Belleville and Galt, and 'Our Western Home' at Niagara-on-the-Lake, run by Maria Rye. He was interested in finding out about their systems of working, and when he had satisfied himself that he understood them he went out to visit 400 children on the farms (their names and placements were found on the registers in each Home). The work was hard, many of the places were remote and Doyle mostly travelled alone. He finally completed his research and returned home in October, to spend the winter collating his notes and writing his report. It was published on 8 February 1875 and caused a furore.

Essentially, Doyle's report was very critical of the idea of child emigration. He wrote that although Macpherson's organization was motivated by a missionary zeal, 'in reality it is an agency for the promotion of emigration involving schemes for providing cheap labour for Canadian farmers'.[19] Nor did he approve of the way in which emigration was handled by either woman, but especially not by Maria Rye. While he praised both for their dedication and their desire to help, their actual methods were forthrightly condemned. As someone who was involved with workhouses, Doyle was perhaps oversensitive to the fact that no distinction was made between the workhouse child and the 'street arab'. His argument was that the workhouse child had some education and was used to living with other people in a disciplined environment, whereas a child from the streets did not have these advantages; it would be difficult to rid them of their semi-criminal habits in a few months of 'moral and religious influence' provided by the Homes and 'place them out in service in a new country and under conditions that are certainly not favourable to their future success'.

Doyle found the receiving Homes lacking in some requirements; washing facilities, for instance, were inadequate, as were the arrangements for looking after the sick and isolating those with infectious diseases. They offered no training before placement and, worse, he found in Maria Rye's Home evidence of cruelty. In one instance, a girl was punished for 'violent temper' by being kept 'in solitary confinement for eleven days upon bread and water, without book or work to divert her thoughts'. Such treatment did not encourage the children to view the receiving Home as a place of refuge, which is how it was described by both Macpherson and Rye. Doyle's view was endorsed by a case 20 years later in which Miss Rye's treatment of two young girls, Bertha Alice and Mary St Claire H., was reported to the National Society for the Prevention of Cruelty of Children by their brother-in-law, who claimed that they had been 'used as little slaves'. A letter from Bertha to her sister which he sent to the Society is now held by the National Archives (HO 45/9991). It offers a tragic insight into the suffering of a young girl and is a strong indictment of Maria Rye:

> I will never be happy till I get back home. I must tell you I have been
> sick about all the time I have been out here. I am sick of living. That
> first place I was at I had to work so hard that I was nearly lain sick with
> consumption. My shoulders were as round as some old lady. I am so
> homesick. I do not know what to do with myself, dear Minnie, I long
> to see you all. I would have been dead if it had not been for the Exeter
> policeman stopping me. I was going to drown myself. I felt so unhappy

and homesick. I thought I would be better dead than alive... I ran away from the first place I was at, I went to Buffalo over to the States. It is a far better place than Canada ... old mother Rye took me away from that place in Buffalo and sent me to the place where I am now. I cannot tell you how I hate it. I have to work till twelve and one at night.[20]

Her sister Mary sent a heartbreaking reply:

Never mind we will get to see each other when we are 18 and then we can do what we might ... but Bertha you must not say anything about it ... they will not let me write to you ... they won't let me come and see you till I get big. I will tell you the truth, I have to milk 3 Cows night and morning and have to ... stable them and I have to do all the work and when they go away they leave me all the work to do ... I help in the harvest. I help them in the hay ... pluck wheat and oats and I move them all back then I drive the horses but Bertha, that is too hard for me and I am so tired.[21]

Doyle's understanding of the young shows very strongly in his condemnation of the system of selecting places for children. In this he may have been ahead of his time, since the Victorians generally viewed children as small, imperfect adults, not as emotionally vulnerable human beings trying to find their place in the world. His comments mix compassion with common sense:

When one thinks what must be the depressing effect upon a child of being sent back to the Home disappointed and discouraged by early failure, it is impossible not to feel strongly that those who assume the responsibility of finding homes for them should have patience—keeping the children, notwithstanding the additional expense, until they could learn something of their tempers, dispositions and fitness for service, and something too of the temper and disposition of the people to whom they send them, so that there might be a reasonable chance of employer and child getting on together.[22]

Applicants for children under the charge of Miss Macpherson had to send in a letter of recommendation from their minister; but as one farmer's wife who had received one of the children pointed out, although her minister described her as respectable, in no way could he determine whether she was good at bringing up a child. As for Miss Rye, Doyle acidly remarks that she 'trusts to the accident of being able to find persons in different districts who will relieve her from the responsibility not only of finding suitable homes, but of looking after the children when they are placed in them'.

In Britain the selection of homes was done by a committee of local citizens who could ensure that the homes were acceptable for the children placed there. However, Doyle notes that this system was not used in Canada, with the result that abuses could and did occur. He continues, 'Had all the homes been "selected" by persons who have an intimate knowledge of the locality, children would not have been placed in such homes as those in which I found some of the...' If, too, the documents which all applicants had to sign had been legally binding, they might have been taken more seriously by both the employer and the agency. Doyle wrote that 'The whole machinery of indentures ... appears to me to be worthless or delusive. To the employer it affords no security for the service of the child; to the child it affords no protection so long as there is no efficient agency to see to the fulfilment of conditions.' The word 'adoption' was loosely used, especially for older children; what was really meant was 'apprenticeship'. The children themselves were not fooled by this; one girl in her teens commented, ''Doption, sir, is when folks gets a girl to work without wages.'[23]

He was also unimpressed by the Canadian government's indifference to the children's legal situation. 'Whether children who are brought to Canada have been legally placed under the care of the persons who bring them is a point left wholly unnoticed by the authorities of the Dominion or of the Provinces.'[24] This lack of concern over legalities demonstrated by the authorities was reflected in the attitude to children's legal rights back home. In Britain the letter of the law dictated that a child could not be emigrated without the consent of a legal guardian, and yet children were sent abroad without it. Doyle observed, 'I met with several cases of children sent out as orphans who had one if not both parents living.'

The biggest criticisms in Doyle's report were aimed at the system of aftercare. While Annie Macpherson's organization made attempts to visit the children and make sure they were being well looked after, the number of children placed in Canada made this difficult to achieve. He added that 'the visits do not constitute the sort of inspection that is much use, having a good deal more the character of visits from friends and guests of the employers than that of an impartial inquiry into the conditions and treatment of the children.' This was borne out by some of the children, who said they were kept out of the way when an inspector came round. Maria Rye was utterly condemned, because she had 'no set plans, no rules, no sharply defined policy about overlooking the children in Canada'. Once she had found the children places, she asked a few friends in the area to keep an eye on them. But this was not a system to protect the girls she brought over. When Doyle arrived at some of the homes, he found the girls had left, and the farmers did not know where they had gone.

Doyle examined the financial aspect of sending children abroad and worked out that there was 100 per cent profit on each child sent out! He calculated this by adding the money paid by the Guardians for each child and the bonus paid by the Canadian government, and subtracting the fare and the cost of keeping the child in the Home. This left a profit of almost £5. In addition to this, Miss Macpherson had the nerve to ask her children to pay their passage back, quoting the cost as £6 or £7 when it was actually half.

Doyle did not find much to recommend in child emigration, except in the 'adoption' of the very young. Because children under five could not work, those who wished to take them in had to be genuine in their wish to look after a child. 'I visited several, from children adopted into the families of gentlefolks to those adopted by small, hardworking farmers, and I may say without exception, their condition was in all cases most satisfactory.' In conclusion, Doyle believed that child emigration could only work if there was a proper system put in place, one in which selected children were trained, where the homes in Canada were more rigorously chosen and where there was a clearly defined system of inspection that was carried out to the letter.

Doyle's report was important because it was the first time that the British government had looked in any depth into the emigration of pauper children. The fact that it was highly critical provoked a response from the Canadian government, who produced their own 'Report of the Proceedings of the Committee of the House of Commons on Immigration and Colonisation', after a hearing in March 1875. The document, held at the National Archives (MH 32/20), was a defence of the Canadian position and a rebuttal of Doyle's suggestion that Canada imitate the British institutions.

John Lowe, who was the minister responsible for immigration, gave his opinion:

I think the 'industrial establishments' which he proposes would
be really an extension into this country of the English workhouse system, and that it would not be found to be satisfactory. I think it would
be altogether unsuited to the ideas and condition of the people of this
country. I think if the children are properly placed, the sooner they are
so placed and absorbed into the population of Canada ... the better;
and that the less they would have of any workhouse mark, or any
'industrial establishment' mark, to distinguish them from the ordinary
children of this country, the better.[25]

It was true that there was a stigma attached to the pauper children who
had come out from Britain and, certainly, it was best to absorb them
into Canadian life, but this was not a straightforward process, and the
children had to be prepared for the new world they were entering.

Lowe went on to say that if Mr Doyle's report was accepted as it
stood, it would put an end to immigration of children from the workhouse and affect the amount of money raised to migrate street children.
At that point, two of the committee members expressed their support
of Macpherson and Rye and declared Doyle's report 'erroneous and
unjust'. They were two of many prominent citizens who supported the
women, believing their work to be 'of great value to the country'. As
the Lord Bishop of Toronto wrote to Miss Rye, 'From all I heard they
[the girls] were in great demand: and any check to your benevolent
enterprise through calumny or misapprehension would be a wide felt
disappointment.' From the Canadian point of view, this may have been
so, but, as usual, the feelings of the children were not recorded.

By 1875 Annie Macpherson had brought out 2,000 children to
Canada, and both she and Maria Rye appeared before the Committee.
They were questioned on every aspect of Doyle's report, and on their
own experience and practices, from selection to placement and
beyond. Macpherson's system is described in the Canadian government's report:

The schoolmaster in the Home [in Spitalfields] selected (after they had
remained a month) such of the children as were healthy enough in constitution and sufficiently educated. Those who passed the test were sent
to the Homes in the country for training. If the children were ragged
when they were taken in charge they were comfortably clothed and
otherwise provided for...
A doctor was in the institution every day to see to their health, even

before they were judged ready to be formally received... While they were in the Home they underwent a thorough system of education and discipline.

In their passage to this country [Canada] the children were in charge of her (Miss Macpherson) or her co-workers... They had never tried to make any special bargain with the shippers... She (Miss Macpherson) and her assistants did not trust to the services of the ship-servants for attendance upon and care of the children, but turned in and helped at the work themselves.[26]

The Report goes on to explain how the places in Canada were selected and what aftercare was provided:

They were, as far as possible, given out to persons whose requirements would be suited by the children, and who would be expected to use them well.

They always required a recommendation from a minister or other responsible person as to the respectability of those applying for children...

Since the children first came out in 1870, one of the schoolmasters had been travelling continually in Canada, making inquiries into the welfare of those who had been sent out... A horse was kept at Belleville for the use of the travelling agent and no limit was imposed ... upon the expense of his visits.

Macpherson also explained that her accounts were audited annually and produced a recent balance sheet to show that, far from making a profit, the expenses left each Home with very little; for instance the Galt Home expenses for 1874 were $4,002 and the Home was left with only $78. In support of her work, Senator Flint gave examples of the success of individuals, including a boy who had been with his son: 'He had no means, nothing but the clothes he had on; and had but little education when he came to him. He had since educated himself, not at schools, but had pursued his studies in the office and his boarding house. He had successfully passed his examination at Toronto and in two years, if his health were spared, he would be an Attorney-at-Law.'[27] Flint said that he had put several of the boys into different trades, but farmers offered them more money and they left, even though they were doing well. He was astonished that Doyle 'could so present the dark side of the subject to the people' and was sure that no system of government inspectors could better 'the one employed by Miss

Macpherson'. Despite this support, Macpherson told the Committee that she 'did not intend to bring out any more pauper children from the workhouse'. Her decision served to vindicate Doyle, at least in terms of his criticism of Annie Macpherson.

Maria Rye was another story. She was incensed by Mr Doyle's 'unjust, ungenerous and most inaccurate report' and spent some time repudiating his claims about the girl allegedly punished by having bread and water for 11 days—in reality, it was only for two or three. The Committee did not question whether this was cruel or not, nor did they examine the necessity of sending this girl to nine places in four years, apparently sharing Rye's superficial and expedient assessment. Rye freely admitted her lack of accounts, but stated this was because she was spending time on more important things: the number of children being brought out each year necessitated a huge amount of correspondence. As for supervision, it was not necessary because the homes they found belonged to good people. In a letter to *The Times* on 6 April 1875 she added: 'Why do I say inspection is not needed over the Canadian homes of these poor children? Well, first because of the tremendous espionage already exercised over the children by persons of all ranks, ages, and conditions all over Canada—an espionage so severe that it positively hinders and checks the work.'

Doyle had suggested that Rye could be cruel, and one member of the Committee asked how the children reacted to being returned to the Home. She replied by saying that she had invited Doyle to a party at 'Our Western Home', but he had not attended—and was thus in no position to judge. However, she added that naughty children would not look forward to coming back to the Home as they knew they would be punished. Her responses indicate that she was not fond of children, and that she could on occasion be harsh and uncaring. Rye was prone to dismiss children with problems as being of their own making, revealing very little insight or inclination to understand.

The Committee concluded, probably as it had intended to do, that Doyle's report was 'full of misapprehension and mistake'. The work of emigration was carried out by people who were religiously motivated and the Canadian homes belonged to good people in decent neighbourhoods where, if anything did go wrong, the children would be helped. However, they did recommend a Canadian inspection which was carried out later that year. Unsurprisingly, their findings claimed that child migration was good for both Canada and the children.

The Canadian press then began their attacks on Doyle—one way of addressing the slurs made on good Canadian people. The *Ottawa Free Press*, quoted by Bagnall in *The Little Immigrants*, accused Doyle of coming to Canada with the 'intention of reaping to himself pecuniary profit out of an agitation which he had initiated in the old country against the benevolent work of Miss Rye...' As part of their chauvinistic approach to the subject, the press made out that semi-delinquent British children should be grateful for being rescued by the good Canadian citizen. *The Globe* was of the opinion that:

> Any drearier or more forlorn prospect than what lies before a pauper
> child or guttersnipe in England is not easily imagined... Anyone who
> knows the character of the great majority of Canadian homes ...
> would feel insulted by any lengthened or grave discussion of the ques-
> tion, whether or not it be for the advantage of such to leave England.

In another article, on 2 October 1875, it offered some reassuring statistics, claiming that not more than 'twenty or thirty' out of 1700, girls 'turned out what could be said badly, while a very great number, indeed, are in circumstances of the greatest comfort and happiness.' The final nail in the coffin was the *Globe*'s explanation of why Doyle was so critical of Macpherson and Rye's work: it must be because he was a Roman Catholic. The ladies were pious Protestants and he envied what they were able to do for their own kind. The newspaper commented that 'in order to avoid the very appearance of proselytism, [the ladies] have always taken out the children of Protestants only, leaving the emigration of Roman Catholic children exclusively to the benevolently inclined of their own Church.'[28] In this way, Doyle's motivation was made clear and his hostile attitude explained.

In Britain the Doyle Report had been taken more seriously, and in March 1875 the Local Government Board had decided to suspend emigration of any further children from workhouses. For Macpherson, many of whose children came from other sources, the decision did not bring her work to an end. Nor did it dim her enthusiasm for what she could achieve. On the contrary; inspired by the development of railways opening up the great country of Canada, she wrote in *The Christian* of new opportunities for emigrants on the prairies of the northwest.

New lives on the land

Macpherson made no public response to Doyle apart from her appearances before the Canadian Commission, and the work undertaken by her and her sister went from strength to strength. In 1876 Louisa Birt accepted her sister's offer to manage Knowlton Home—a brave decision, as location and facilities made this a difficult property to manage —and appointed a Canadian woman, Elizabeth Meiklejohn, as superintendent there. Meiklejohn proved a good choice, and she stayed until her retirement in 1904.

The first party of 70 children that Louisa brought to Knowlton sailed from Liverpool on 19 April 1877 on the *Sardinian*, stopping a day later at Londonderry before heading to Quebec City. Louisa described her first experience of Knowlton with a characteristic passion:

> We arrived at the Distributing Home on the 1st of May. At Knowlton
> we received a most cheering and hearty reception, and every one who
> visited the Home seemed delighted with the children. We had over a
> hundred applications for them… On bringing in about half a dozen
> and letting the farmer speak to them, it was very funny to see these
> dear children stretch themselves up to their greatest height; and …
> the scene would become very trying with beseeching voices saying,
> 'Take me sir, I'll be such a good boy.'
>
>   I have seen both men and women weep, and reply, 'My dears, my
> heart is big enough to take you all, but my house ain't.'
>
>   … It is sorrowful work unbinding, as it were, the little twinings
> their sweet, obedient ways have already bound around us. Many were
> writing letters to friends in England, but many had not a love-link to
> earth. One little fellow said, 'I ain't got nobody to write to but you.'[29]

While it is clear from this description that Louisa was genuinely pleased with the success of the scheme, the loneliness and vulnerability of the children show through. The isolation of many of the farms, and consequent complete dependence of the children on the families with whom they were placed, is vividly revealed in the children's own words, such as the 14-year-old girl cited by Bean and Melville:

> I would sit down and cry … and think that I am going to run away
> from here, and then I would sit down and think *where* am I going to
> run away to? I've got nowhere to go… With no money, you can't do
> anything. And you haven't any friends and no way of making them
> because they would never let you out. They were always there with
> you… They did not allow you to go out on your own…[30]

Anxiety—even fear—was an integral part of these children's lives, with little opportunity to influence events or to determine their futures. Many, not surprisingly, seem to have been too exhausted by the daily drudgery to make long-term plans, and they endured wretched conditions and hard work for years on end. A girl of 11 brings to life the grim reality of her daily grind on a remote farm:

> I worked there for nine years and was too frightened to say anything to anyone. No inspectors came round. The wife had a baby every year and a half and I had dirty nappies to cope with plus the housework and I cleaned out the stables and in the summer I fetched hay and grain and also milked the cows… I worked *all* the time.'[31]

Child after child describes the near-despair of loneliness that surrounded the relentless routine of interminable chores. Expectations were probably often set too high—on both sides; the children's eagerness for a caring home echoes in their voices, and they probably gave no thought to the reality of living—and working—in a stranger's house. One can only hope that the children were able to find at least something of what they desperately wanted, despite the isolation and unfamiliarity of their surroundings, and that some of those who seemed to be settling in well in the reports from Marchmont did indeed establish secure futures for themselves.

The response of Maria Rye

The outcome of Doyle's report was very different for Maria Rye. The suspension of workhouse children's emigration brought her supply of children to an end, and she sent no more children to Canada for two years. In May 1877 a letter she had written to the president of the Local Government Board was made public. It was in defence of herself and an attack on Doyle; as she said, somewhat smugly, there was no need to comment on the great injustice done to her since 'the great glory of all true work that in the keeping of His commands there is the reward and a thousand Mr Doyles could not touch me on that point'. She reiterated her belief that supervision of the children, once they had been placed, was unnecessary beyond some correspondence, since the 'custodians of the children' were 'substantial, orderly, comfortable and well established'. Having stated this, she could not then explain how a number of young workhouse girls had had illegitimate babies, or why 28 children under the age of 15 had absconded and no one knew where they were. Those facts alone should have convinced her of the importance of an organized system of inspection, but on this, as on other things, she appears unseeing, obdurate and self-righteous—preferring to attack the records of reformatory and industrial schools in Britain than to accept defects in her own arrangements. Her less than sympathetic qualities came to the fore again when, despite owning to not keeping good accounts, she asked the Board to give her £12 instead of £8 so that she could build another Home for girls!

By the time Maria Rye's letter was published, Doyle was retired and living in Wales. His detailed reply, sent to the Rt Hon. Sclater Booth, President of the Social Government Board and dated 14 May 1877, is held in the National Archives (MH 32/20). In the letter Doyle reiterated his belief that 'no pauper children ought to be sent to Canada under Miss Rye's present system', explaining, 'There is a total absence of efficient supervision and consequently children are exposed to suffering and wrong for which they get neither relief nor redress'. Impatient of her tirade, he pointed out that Rye brought out far larger parties than she could hope to manage, and that nevertheless 'Regulations that are essential in other countries, and for other agents, she thinks may be dispensed with in Canada and on behalf of Miss Rye alone'.

The humanity underlying Doyle's response emerges in the examples chosen to reveal Rye's attitude to those in her charge. For instance, she stated '"The workhouse child" exhibits the most frightful and disheartening obstinacy and deceit.' He writes that she describes A.R. as 'a thoroughly bad and incorrigible girl quite beyond our management or anybody else's'. And he continues: 'E.H. "This girl," says Miss Rye, "ought never to be emigrated as … she had repeatedly been brought before the Guardians as an 'incorrigible'." But Miss Rye herself selected her.' He points out that everything that Miss Rye knows about the children comes from the employers themselves and gives examples of the results of her lack of supervision.

Elizabeth S. was sent at the age of 12 to Mr W. M. in Greenwich, New Brunswick. She was severely beaten by Mrs M. and when she complained to her brothers, her letter was intercepted by Mrs M. and she was forbidden to write to them without permission. When she was 16, she was seduced by the son, fell pregnant and was sent back to

Liverpool with just a few dollars to find her way back to the work-house that was responsible for her up to the age of 18. The girl had to manage on her own.

Ellen E. was luckier as she could turn to a neighbour for help when she became very ill and left her home. The neighbour took pity on her, got her a new position and sent her to the doctor; she was fulfilling the role that Maria Rye's organization should have assumed. The neighbour wrote to the home, saying that Ellen wanted news of her father and uncle and aunt, but Rye knew nothing about the girl. She obviously had no interest in the individual child, especially those posing a problem, but believed her role to be purely a conduit, sending the girls to a 'better' life in Canada. If the girls did not benefit from their new opportunities, there was something amiss in their character.[32]

Doyle objected to her lack of care in selection, for the children were 'collected without regard to special fitness and [some] are unsuited for such a mode of life'. One example of her casual attitude in finding positions for her girls creates a particularly poignant picture in the imagination; it was one to which Doyle angrily objected, and rightly so, as it has overtones of the slave trade. About 50 children had been taken to Chatham, Ontario, where 'they were ranged round the Public Hall, on view ... while persons seeking them came in one by one and selected the child which he or she might happen to fancy'.

This lack of sensitivity to the children was demonstrated by Maria Rye over and over again. When Doyle complained of the filthy condition of some of the children sent into service, Rye agreed with him, but said it was because they came from the workhouse. She accepted criticisms of the workhouse institution without question, publishing a letter from an anonymous person who pointed out to her that their dogs had 'more fresh good meat than any poorhouse child ever had'. Strangely for someone involved in charitable work, she had a detachment that was hard to understand; she did not seem to think that it was her responsibility to do anything about these criticisms or to explore their truth. However, it does in part explain why she did not concern herself with the children once they were out of her hands. 'Out of sight, out of mind' might have been invented for Miss Rye.

Finally, Doyle no doubt earned Maria Rye's eternal enmity by his praise of Annie Macpherson. The first report had criticized both, but Doyle believed that Macpherson had taken his comments on board:

'Miss Macpherson has I believe recognised the importance of most of the suggestions that I made and through her good sense and good feeling has adopted them in practice.' He particularly approved of Macpherson's alleged agreement that 'the strictest personal supervision was absolutely indispensable', and praised both Macpherson and Billborough, the one 'deservedly respected', the other 'guided by good feeling, intelligence and admirable judgement.'[33] In fact, the difference between the two women was probably not as large as he would lead us to believe, but it provided him with a good weapon to use against Maria Rye: they had become sworn enemies.

Despite these revelations and the questions surrounding her financial dealings, Maria Rye began two years later to resume her work, taking girls out to Canada two or three times a year. She was quick to seize the propaganda initiative, and the *Illustrated London News* of 25 August 1877—aware that emigration was a hot topic—published a letter from a lady who had accompanied Miss Rye on the *Sardinian* in May 1877 when 'seventy-three young persons, of whom ten were boys, seven girls in their teens, and the rest quite little children' were emigrated. The anonymous lady was full of praise for Maria Rye and her methods: 'Miss Rye is exceedingly particular in placing out these children, suiting the tender and timid ones to kindly and indulgent mistresses, and the wild, lawless ones to stricter managers... The results of her work are certainly wonderful.'[34]

The Toronto correspondent of the *Standard* (reported in the *Illustrated London News*, 29 September 1877) describes 'Our Western Home' with approval for interested readers, although he notes—with some understatement—that 'No-one in their senses ever expected that these waifs and outcasts were to be placed on beds of roses; that their days were to be passed in happy romping among the peach trees of their "Western Home"; that they were to be free from toil, and subject to none of the rough usage that falls to the lot of the children of the poor all the world over.' While acknowledging some of her failures, the writer nonetheless comes to Rye's defence, saying that it was too much to expect Maria Rye single-handedly to run a scheme to emigrate children and 'keep up also a careful systematic supervision over them for many years', ignoring the fact that other child rescuers had managed it. Apparently any disappointments were the children's own fault: no one could expect that 'with her workhouse clothes, the workhouse girl would "shed" all her moral delinquencies, not only those acquired by herself, but those inherited from, perhaps, generations of ignorant or vicious parents'. Bearing the sub-standard material in mind, the Toronto correspondent continues to commend Rye's work and the 'energy and enthusiastic devotion' that she had displayed. His final endorsement is firm if less than rapturous: 'the experimentation of importation has been on the whole, very satisfactory. This is the verdict of the Canadian public.'[35]

Certainly the policies sounded all right in principle. Rye tried to arrange that girls under nine were often 'adopted'—in the sense of being offered a home rather than a workplace. Those in families were to be sent to school until they were 14; at 15 a girl was to receive $3 wages a month, increasing to $4 at age 17. Girls remained Rye's preference throughout, and although her parties did include both, the boys were usually placed by Ellen Bilborough and her husband the Reverend Wallace, who had taken over Macpherson's Marchmont Home in Belleville.

In 1894, towards the end of Rye's career, the *Buffalo Express* wrote an article about her. There was now a schoolhouse attached to 'Our Western Home' which the girls attended in the morning. In the afternoon they did sewing and housework, or worked in the garden, 'to use their hands'. All were productive enterprises, the garden delivering vegetables, fruit and chickens for the Home, while the girls were described as 'ideal maidservants', complete with 'rosy cheeks, clear eyes, and short cropped hair'.[36] The reporter was amused by the cockney accents of the children and commented that most of them were from London; there were no Irish or Scottish girls. He went on to describe the building as showing signs of wear, and Maria Rye did not miss the opportunity of pointing out that the roof was in need of repair and she was 'wondering if there is not someone ready to give the money for this purpose'. When the reporter asked about her work, Rye's answer was typically robust: 'There are eight homes for the rescue of such children in Canada. In the last 25 years these homes have distributed 30,000 children through the Dominion. Of that number not 25 have been sent to prison. That's a pretty good record, isn't it!'

Yet even the indefatigable Maria Rye was, like the roof, showing signs of wear. She retired through ill health in November 1896, going to live with her sister in Hemel Hempstead, Hertfordshire, and handing her work (including 'Our Western Home') over to the Church of England Waifs and Strays Society—an organization with which she had long been associated and held in high regard. Sharp criticism of her past work continued, with the Canadian Inspector of Juvenile Immigration Agencies, John Joseph Kelso, launching a fierce attack on her record in a report of 1897. He was particularly concerned with the standard of aftercare, which he deemed 'far from adequate'; Macpherson and Birt, while not wholeheartedly approved, received a more neutral assessment: 'with increased care in selection and closer supervision in their new homes, it is likely that good result will follow the work of this agency.'[37]

For both women, however, time was running out; Rye died in 1903 and Macpherson only a year later, to be followed by Louisa Birt in 1915. That year also saw the closure of Knowlton and 'Our Western Home', as the First World War began to impact, yet their legacy was impressive—Knowlton alone had processed over 4,800 children (1,000 aged under nine) and Maria Rye's organization, with 'Our Western Home' at its heart, emigrated over 5,000 girls. As an era came to an end in Canada, Lillian Birt in Britain took over the Liverpool Sheltering Homes, ensconced in new premises in Myrtle Street since November 1889. Lillian also paid a poignant tribute to her mother's life and work:

> She had a magic way of gaining the children's obedience. As a boy said when questioned by the Canadian farmer, 'Now tell us, what sort of woman is Mrs Birt?' he replied, 'Well, she's a very nice lady, but she's the kind of woman that when she says "beans" you daren't say "peas".'
> … Her bright smile and sweet voice inspired poor widows and famishing children in thousands with courage to trust themselves to her care and guidance in leaving their native shores for an unknown land.[38]

Yet it was Rye and Macpherson who were to have the greatest impact on child emigration, and on the organizations that came after them. Whether stirring up controversy, appealing for funds or inspiring others in the field, their relentless commitment ensured their activities became one of the highest profile—and most complex—issues of the day.

Chapter 2

Journey to a new life

Take them away! Away! Away!
The bountiful earth is wide and free,
The New shall repair the wrongs of the Old –
Take them away o'er the rolling sea!
Our Waifs and Strays, August 1887

CONTROVERSIAL as it was, the work of Rye and Macpherson proved extremely influential in the later 19th century. Their high-profile activities encouraged other agencies, desperate for a solution to the increasing numbers of pauper children, to consider emigration, and even the criticisms of Doyle's report ensured that the movement remained in the spotlight. Both Rye and Macpherson were active—and successful—in fund-raising, producing many favourable accounts to impress others, and both developed personal connections with charitable organizations in the field. The hopes and sincere convictions of those running such organizations contrast powerfully with the fragmented stories of the children themselves, left to endure the reality of new lives far from all they had known.

Yet the philanthropists who dispatched children to Canada and elsewhere were prompted by first-hand knowledge of the appalling conditions in Britain's slums.

The brothers Edward and Robert de Montjoie Rudolf, for example, ran the Sunday school in the London parish of St Ann's, south Lambeth, and were driven to action when two regular attendants stopped coming and were found begging on the streets. Edward Rudolf was concerned that the boys might be put in an organization with little opportunity for Anglican religious instruction; he decided it was important to establish a specifically Church of England rescue Home for destitute children. A meeting in May 1881 agreed to set up the

Waifs and Strays Society and money for a Home was duly raised. The
Waifs and Strays had a high profile from its inception. In August the
Archbishop of Canterbury agreed to become president, after which the
Society became the Church of England's officially recognized organization for providing pauper children with homes. It attracted the support of those associated with the Anglican establishment, not least
Maria Rye. She became closely linked with the Waifs and Strays
Society, although she had been sending children to Canada for some 12
years before it was established. Rye was concerned that the Society
should care first and foremost for the girls, since 'they need the help a
thousandfold more than boys', but the Society was to deal with the
housing and emigration of both. Its first Home was opened in December 1881.

'Christian homes in the colonies'

From the start, Edward Rudolf had seen the advantages of child emigration and the Society's first circular had mentioned the possibility of
homes overseas. Religious authorities favoured the moral climate of
Canada, seen as far more wholesome than delinquent cities in Britain
despite its harsh terrain and bleak winters. By 1883 emigration was
under way, with four boys travelling to Canada through the agency of
Miss Macpherson. However, by 1884 the Society was looking to establish its own receiving Home in Canada. An appeal was launched for
this purpose, ultimately raising £1,000; Mrs Henry Hucks Gibbs gave
£250 and the rest of her family contributed smaller amounts. Four of
the Gibbs family became members of the Emigration Committee,
along with other benefactors including Maria Anderdon, the niece of
Cardinal Henry Edward Manning (see chapter 4). The Reverend John
Bridger, who was the Emigrants' Chaplain for the Society for Promoting Christian Knowledge, was asked to look for suitable premises in
Canada, and by the end of 1884 he had purchased a house in Sherbrooke, Quebec. It had accommodation for 36 children, a large dining
room, two kitchens and eight bedrooms; the grounds comprised a
kitchen garden, flower gardens and a lawn for playing. It was named
the Gibbs Home, in recognition of their benefactors' generosity.

The first group of little girls left Liverpool on 23 April 1885 for Quebec in the charge of the Reverend Bridger and the new matron of the

Gibbs Home. They came mainly from homes in Dulwich in southeast London and Mildenhall in Suffolk, with a few from other parts of England.

> At the station their little red hoods attracted considerable attention; and when it was discovered that they were bound for Canada, many of the passengers very kindly evinced great interest in them, one clergyman taking the trouble to purchase dolls for those who were not provided with them… On reaching Liverpool … they were placed in comfortable lodgings for the night; and on the following morning, after a good night's rest, they were ready to go on board.[1]

Rudolf had devised a simple, straightforward scheme for the selection of the girls. They had to be between 6 and 12, or over 16 provided they had spent six months training as domestic servants. They had to be in sound health and of good character. Their nearest relatives must have handed over the girl 'unreservedly into the Society's care', and preference would be given to girls from the Society's Homes; if there were vacancies, girls from Poor Law Guardians, and other Homes and institutions would be considered. The girls were to travel from Liverpool on Allan Line ships, the company favoured by all the migration agencies, accompanied by the Reverend Bridger and a matron. The fee for the voyage was £2 per child.

The first group was followed by others, and in 1887 the Reverend H.D. Barrett went to Canada to report on the Society's work. He met Bridger in Liverpool and took the time to explore the city that was for many their last experience of England. Barrett's impressions of the poorer parts of Liverpool, swollen by over 80,000 Irish families since the great famine, were not favourable; he noted that 'the inhabitants of streets such as Homer and Virgil do not seem to live up to the level of civil nomenclature, as far as I could judge, for several cases of drunkenness met my eye as I drove through, and there seemed to be more neglected gutter-urchins—such as our Society provide for—and shoeless and bedraggled slatterns than one sees even in London.'[2]

Barrett and Bridger, accompanied by a party of 39 'Waifs and Strays', left Liverpool on 28 April (while he does not mention the ship's name, it may have been the *Parisian*). The two vicars held three short services every evening throughout the voyage, and up to half the passengers attended. The children slept in bunks 'in a sardine-like arrangement'; they suffered from seasickness at first, like so many others, but after a couple of days most were 'skipping and playing games' on the deck; only two sisters remained poorly. For those who recovered, the voyage offered a new and exciting experience in which shipboard routine mingled with delightfully unexpected sights and sounds. The rollercoaster is summed up in a letter from one of the young migrants on board:

> We slept on the ship and we got up at twenty-five minutes to twelve. We all thought it was time to get up, and then the Matron told us to get back to bed after we were up an hour, because we made such a noise; but we climbed up on the top and we were eating oranges and lemons, and then we went to sleep until five o'clock, and then we had breakfast at half-past seven, and then we went on deck, and it was very nice, and at eight o'clock started on our voyage, and it was very nice until the next day, when a lot of us was taken ill, but we soon got all right and then we saw icebergs and whales.[3]

The journey was uneventful except for a sea-fog which set in halfway through the voyage, delaying the party for 40 hours. They arrived at Quebec on 9 May and, after a long and tedious train journey, which took 7½ hours to cover only 143 miles, they arrived at Sherbrooke.

Barrett was impressed with the Gibbs Home at Sherbrooke, for its attractive site and its accessibility by rail.

> It stands on the right bank of the St Francis river, on rising ground, with a fringe of trees between it and the river, its grounds being partially devoted to the cultivation of garden produce, and partly laid down in grass. It is ... within a short distance of the railway station ... The Home itself is square with a verandah on three sides, and is in all respects a suitable building.[4]

He also approved the new matron, Mrs Osgood, and her daughter, who helped with the clerical work.

Barrett visited many of the Waifs and Strays children in their new homes, accompanied by the Hon. J Abercrombie who had sailed with them from Liverpool. He was on the whole pleased with their situations. One of the girls, Abigail R., aged 12, had been 'adopted', even taking her new parents' name, despite the fact that she had a father in England. Another, Louisa W., aged 15, had found an excellent position as a servant with the bank manager of Sherbrooke. 'Elizabeth H., aged

11, with Mr and Mrs John Tait, of Merricksville, is doing well and gives no trouble though she is a little deaf. She goes to day and Sunday-school, and was first in her class in the latter of last year.'

Fortunes were inevitably mixed, in part reflecting the different characters of the children themselves. Some were obviously not easy, the effects of a difficult childhood compounded by the strange environment, but there was always potential for improvement, as Barrett was keen to note: 'Ellen T., aged 15, living with Mrs Herman Ryland, Quebec where she has been for two years. Mrs R. has had great difficulty with her as she is stupid and sullen. She is always kind to the children, however, and is now doing much better. She is tall and stout and strong, and declares herself to be happy and contented.'[5]

A meeting at Sherbrooke with the local committee decided that the girls should stay where they were, recommending that quarterly reports should be fuller and more punctually delivered and that the Waifs and Strays' good work should be more effectively publicized. They were anxious to preserve the Waifs and Strays' good name by ensuring all children sent out to Canada were fully trained, aware that British children were acquiring a bad reputation from other agencies sending untrained, ill-disciplined young migrants. A new boys' Home, too, was under discussion, as the Society had received a donation of £500 for this purpose from a Mr Richard Benyon. A house was acquired near the Gibbs Home, to be similarly named after its benefactor as the Benyon Home.

All in all, the Reverend Barrett spent six weeks in Canada and travelled 11,000 miles. The distance included a trip to Winnipeg to see if an Anglican Home could be established out west—a dream that never became reality, although it remained with the Society for many years.

By visiting in midsummer, Barrett avoided the bitter winter cold that compounded the misery of youngsters working on remote rural farms. Bean and Melville cite the experience of a boy of 14 who was sent from the Sherbrooke distribution Home to a farm in Ontario:

> The first year here, the temperature was round forty to forty-five
> degrees below zero … [with] eleven feet of snow … the water froze
> and the wind was dreadful … my two big toes swelled up so bad and
> so [painful, I had to split new shoes in order to wear them … I would
> sit down in the middle of the yard and massage my feet and cry
> with pain.[6]

Another boy of 12 on a Canadian farm describes wading through snow 'almost up to your waist' clad in an incongruous assembly of 'woollen pants, longjohns, flannel shirts and home-made socks.'[7] The climate could be treacherous for children born in Canada, too, and infant mortality was high; a mysterious 'summer complaint' was responsible for the deaths of many Canadian babies into the 20th century, fuelling the need for foreign child labour to assist on the farms.[8]

The Waifs and Strays Society was the charitable arm of the orthodox Anglican Church. Unlike some organizations that emigrated children, it had many homes throughout England and Wales, and sending children overseas was only one facet of its work. Most of the destitute children accepted by the Waifs and Strays remained in the Society's Homes across England and Wales, but about five per cent of them were sent to Canada. The 1894 annual report stated that there were 63 homes, including the two in Canada; during that year 24 children had been sent overseas. Recognition of the Society's work went from strength to strength: Queen Victoria became a patron in 1895, a unique accolade for an emigration organization. That same year, 40 children were sent to Canada, 35 boys and 5 girls. A year later, Maria Rye turned 'Our Western Home' over to the Society and this became the girls' Home. The original Gibbs Home was given up and the new one became the boys' receiving Home.

A Canadian visit

It was not until 1906 that Edward Rudolf made his first visit to Canada, 25 years after he had founded the Society. The party of children he accompanied was small—13 girls from London, joined in Liverpool by four children from northern Homes. The Allan Line had arranged for them to be taken out to the ship, the *Virginian* (p.81), by boat to save them waiting on the quay in the rain. The ship set sail the evening of 17 August and the voyage went smoothly; the girls slept in two cabins reserved for them and the food was good and plentiful. On arriving at Quebec, the girls had to undergo a medical examination before being allowed to disembark. Then they had to take the long journey to Niagara-on-the-Lake; fortunately Mrs Lawrie, who was looking after the girls, had brought a large hamper with her. After five hours, they reached their first stop at Montreal where they changed trains. Rudolf was disconcerted by the fact that they had to step over the railway lines to do so, pointing out that such reckless practices at home would attract a fine. The next stage of the journey was 10 hours to Toronto, when everyone tried to sleep but kept being woken up by the conductor shouting out the name of every stop! At Toronto they changed on to a boat for the 2½-hour journey across Lake Ontario. By the time they reached their destination the thermometer showed 90 degrees Fahrenheit, and it was a weary and extremely hot party of people who were welcomed at Our Western Home.

Rudolf, of course, had not seen the Home before. He thought it spacious and airy, although in need of a coat of paint. His unrestricted admiration was reserved for the grounds, which at that time of the year provided a cornucopia of fresh fruit:

> The Home itself stands in an orchard of apple trees ... and around it are fields of tomatoes, and great orchards of peaches. Melons and grapes flourish out-of-doors, and in the garden of the Home may be seen at times humming-birds and fire-flies—things that one is accustomed to associate with the tropics. Yet in the winter the thermometer is apt to drop below Zero![9]

He was pleased with the life there—that the children spent most of their time outside, where 'tea is spread on the lawn under the huge weeping willow in front of the Home'. And he was delighted that the 'old girls' would come and visit with their children and, sometimes, husbands. A photograph was taken of one of them whose husband was a butler, 'getting £20 a month, so they are very comfortably off. Witness the baby's smart little carriage.'

Rudolf liked Canada and the Canadians seemed to take to him. The *Sherbrooke Daily Record* reported that 'The Rev. Mr Rudolf is a typical English clergyman a little past middle age, endowed with strong common sense, much executive ability, pleasing manners and a delightful English voice. He is thoroughly absorbed in the work of the Society whose prosperity in great measure is due to his devotion.'[10] His first trip to Canada reinforced his conviction that emigration was very worthwhile, associated as it now was with commitment to the Empire. Fund-raising leaflets for the Waifs and Strays proudly described the bond as 'Links of Empire welded by the Church'; new arrivals were identified as 'Links Fresh from the Forge', a potent image of unity and strength. Rudolf's enthusiasm saw children sent out in good numbers.

In 1907, for example, 65 boys and 90 girls were emigrated, including a party of little girls to Winnipeg for 'adoption'. This was one group in which girls outnumbered boys; the number of boys was usually greater. The annual reports show that in 1909, 76 children were emigrated; in 1911, 134 children; in 1912, 132 children; in 1913, 140 children; and in 1914, 125 children were sent out before war was declared. In 1915 emigration was suspended due to the 'submarine menace', but nonetheless one boy and three girls were sent out, and the supervision continued of those already placed in Canadian homes. By 1918 the Society's annual report recorded its largest ever number of Homes—117 in Britain and abroad, a figure that would never be surpassed.

The 'Links' developed strong ties with their new country. During the First World War, some 200 'old boys' joined the Canadian Army and undertook active service. The war also impacted on the old receiving Home at Niagara-on-the-Lake, which was commandeered for military purposes and then sold. Since the days of Maria Rye, thousands of children had passed through Our Western Home; the end of an era arrived with its sale.

To replace the Niagara building, in 1924 the Society acquired a Home for girls in Toronto, soon called the Rye Home. British girls aged between 14 and 18 years were sent there to be trained as domestic servants and then found work in the surrounding area. John Stroud quotes one of the girls who went there; her account seems to suggest that some girls were younger than 14:

> I can still see the name above the door—'Miss Rye's Home for Destitute Little Girls'. I was there a very short time. Mrs Beamer came to the Home and two or three little girls were lined up before her. She seemed to have trouble deciding but she picked the one with the blue eyes. What small things decide our lives! During that same summer the Home sent a lady to visit the home of every child. She travelled with a horse and buggy and a colored boy to drive. She had dinner in my home and she said to me 'I wish I could see every little girl as well placed as you are.' I had a good kind home and received my education in a one room country school which was all we had in those days...[11]

In 1927 the Gibbs Home in Sherbrooke was still going strong, and was honoured by a visit from Lord Willingdon, the Governor-General of Canada. But by 1931 emigration was at a standstill as economic depression began to bite. Mildred Rudolf, Edward's wife, pointed out that at that time Canadian farmers were operating at a loss and farm labourers earned very little; as a result, everyone was trying to find work in the towns. The Society's boys who were already in Canada had little choice but to stay on the farms where they had been placed until conditions improved, but future options looked bleak. The Bishop of Montreal tried to contain the situation by stating that the Waifs and Strays should stop sending boys to Canada. The Society had to take stock of its position and reluctantly decided to close the Rye Home in Toronto. The Gibbs Home was also closed, although it continued as an old boys' club into the 1950s, and the Society, like other organizations, turned its attention to destinations in Australia. Yet the Waifs and Strays left an enduring legacy in Canada, where it had operated with relative success. The last word on its achievements lies in a story recounted by a chief constable, and cited by John Stroud:

> Some years ago, I sent a wire to one of the Waifs and Strays homes, inquiring whether they would take a baby that afternoon. The answer was 'Yes'. In due time one of my constables delivered the most miserable looking object in the world. He was found in an attic of an empty building, lying on a piece of sacking, without a stitch of clothing and moaning feebly. He was only just alive. I gave him a good meal and supplied him with suitable clothing. Thirty years later, a stalwart Canadian, hardworking and law-abiding, joined H.M. Forces. He was that deserted baby.[12]

The Church of England's Waifs and Strays Society was by no means the only Anglican organization to emigrate children. Others, such as the Church Army and the Salvation Army, belonged to the Church's evangelical arm and generally played a smaller role. Some dealt only with young adult migration, like the Church Army founded in 1882 by Wilson Carlile, a curate at St Mary Abbot's in Kensington, London. The organization gave unemployed youths over 18 financial aid to emigrate, which they paid back over time as they earned their keep, primarily by working on Canadian farms. In 1900, for instance, 28 men emigrated, but numbers increased after 1905 when the Church Army was given a 'fine estate at Hempstead in Essex, comprising 740 acres of land'. The site enabled men seeking to go to Canada to have a few months' training in farmwork—a resource that allowed the Church Army to assist more young men find work in Canada.[13] The groups sailed in the charge of an official from the Church Army, and were met on arrival by a Canadian representative who had found them jobs. The figures published in the annual reports do not distinguish between men with families or single men; however, the annual report of 1912–13 stated that there was a much higher demand for single men than married, and many Canadian farmers actually stipulated no children. Between 1905 and 1910, 4,573 persons went to Canada under Church Army auspices. A mere 30 were deported by the Canadian authorities, mainly for reasons of health.

By the early part of the 20th century, the Salvation Army, too, was helping adults and children to emigrate to Canada. William Booth, founder of the Salvation Army, wanted to create his own 'Over-Sea Colony', but this never came to fruition. However, the Salvation Army did start its own Emigration Department and began sending small groups of men from its Hadleigh Farm Colony in Essex to Canada from 1901. Emigration began in earnest in 1903, and by 1905 the Salvation Army was chartering its own ships, such as the SS *Vancouver*, which sailed on 26 April with 1,000 emigrants on board. After the First World War, the Salvation Army helped widows and their children to emigrate. It did not have a separate programme for child migration, and Kohli relates that in 1922 a dispute occurred between the Salvation Army and the Canadian government—the Army was emigrating children and adults together, while the government treated them separately in terms of assistance.[14] By 1926, 1,655 children had come to Canada under the auspices of the Salvation Army; after this date the figures dropped.

William Quarrier's Orphan Homes

While Maria Rye was involved with the Waifs and Strays Society, Annie Macpherson's work became the inspiration for a fellow Scot, William Quarrier. He was born at Greenock, Scotland, in 1829, the son of Annie Booklass and William Quarrier, a ship's carpenter. Quarrier senior died of cholera in Quebec in 1832, whereupon his wife moved the family to Glasgow in the hope of earning a better living. Glasgow was a wealthy and expanding city, but the slums were riddled with overcrowding and disease, and William became acquainted firsthand with deprivation at an early age. Aged about six, he went to work in a factory fixing ornamental heads on pins for a shilling a week, becoming apprentice to a shoemaker two years later. He spent the following years perfecting his trade until, at 17, he found work with a Mrs Hunter. She introduced Quarrier to the Baptist Church and he became a devout and active Christian. In 1856, he married Mrs Hunter's daughter, Isabella. By then, he had started his own shoemaking business, and over the next eight years he expanded this to three shops.

Quarrier was now comfortably off and in a position to help those around him. He was keen to do so, remembering his experience of poverty as a small boy: 'I stood in the High Street of Glasgow, barefooted, bareheaded, cold and hungry, having tasted no food for a day and a half, and as I gazed at the passers by wondering why they did not help such as I, a thought passed through my mind that I would not do as they when I got the means to help others.'[15] Several philanthropists, such as the Rudolf brothers and Barnardo, told of incidents that finally sparked them into action, and Quarrier was no exception. His story was that he came across a distressed young match-seller who just had his night's earnings stolen by an older boy. Quarrier naturally gave him some money, but the episode haunted him. Soon afterwards, on 30 November 1864, William wrote a letter to the *Glasgow Herald* in which he proposed to form the Glasgow Shoeblack Brigade. This was a self-help organization that issued the boys with shoe-shine kits and uniforms, which they had to pay for out of their earnings; they were expected to work by day and attend classes in the evening, as well as Sunday school. Quarrier then went on to start up a News Brigade and Parcels Brigade, which eventually came together as the Industrial Brigade. He also had a night asylum where boys could spend up to three nights.

Annie Macpherson visited Glasgow in 1871 and met Quarrier. They found that they had common concerns, and Quarrier became interested in her work in London and her emigration schemes. Her encouragement helped convince him to open a Children's Home, which he did in November 1871 by converting a building in Renfrew Lane, Glasgow. When this became too small a year later, he bought a mansion at Cessnock, Govan, for the boys and two Homes for girls. These were not simply Homes, but places where the children received schooling and religious training; about half of them were in due course sent to Canada.

Quarrier believed, like the other philanthropists, that the children he rescued 'must have a perfectly fair start in the race of life', and that

Canada offered opportunities that Britain could not. In answer to objections that he was taking away potential workers, he replied, 'Come and see the children as we take them in, and you will perceive that, not the labour market, but the crime market is likely to be affected by our work of rescue.'[16] Arrangements were made for his first party of children to leave for Canada on 2 July 1872, but finances for the operation were problematic; Quarrier was determined that no child should be sent to Canada unless money had been specially contributed for that purpose. As the sailing date grew near, he still needed £70 to send all 35 children from Cessnock.

Only a fortnight before they were due to sail, a large donation was received to make the project a reality. This welcome gift became a feature in many of Quarrier's stories, and was used to illustrate his belief that God would provide. Each boy was given two linen suits, one cloth suit, four shirts, four pairs of socks, boots, a box of collars, a writing case, a Bible, a copy of *The Pilgrim's Progress*, a purse and a pocket knife. The boys from Govan were joined by 10 children from Maryhill and 19 from Edinburgh, so it was a party of 64 children who boarded the *St David* with the Reverend Stobo and Miss Bryson and sailed to Quebec, arriving 16 days later. Stobo accompanied the children to their destination, the Macpherson receiving Homes; many Quarrier children were subsequently emigrated under Macpherson's schemes. The first stop was Knowlton, which he described as 'situated at the head of a pretty little lake, and at the mouth of a beautiful highland glen'; it sounded almost like Scotland, a home from home. He then went on to the Marchmont Home in Belleville, and ended his journey at the farm at Galt.

Quarrier's dream was to set up a Children's Village, where poor children from the urban wastes of Scotland might enjoy a new life in small, personal, cottage Homes, looked after by house fathers and mothers. His vision was reflected in Barnardo's Girls' Village Home at Barkingside (p.96), built in the 1870s, and in the structure of Fairbridge Farm Schools many years later. Quarrier's enthusiasm for a smaller scale in which children could flourish also anticipated Fairbridge's ethos by half a century; he observed that 'I have no faith in large institutions where hundreds are ruled with a stringent uniformity which eats out the individuality of its members, but I have a great faith in a home where not more than a hundred are placed together, and where each individual is cared for and watched over by a motherly and fatherly love.'[17]

In April 1876, with the support of benefactors, Quarrier was able to purchase, for £3,560, 40 acres of land at Bridge of Weir, Renfrewshire, some 15 miles southwest of Glasgow. Here he built the Orphan Homes of Scotland, which were opened on 17 September 1878. (At this time, his only other home was the City Orphan Home in Glasgow.) Up to 30 children were housed in a cottage and attended the village school. Over the following years, Quarrier's dream was realized as the Orphan Homes developed from two cottages and a central building into a Children's Village, which was largely self-supporting, made up of about 40 children's cottages, a church, a large purpose-built school, a fire station, workshops, farms and other facilities. The Village became Quarrier's headquarters and remains so to this day.

In 1882 Quarrier was accused, as was Dr Barnardo a few years later (pp.126–9), of taking in Catholic children, converting them and emigrating them to Canada. A Mrs Kerr had put her orphaned grandson, William Bradshaw, into Quarrier's care, but demanded his return, probably at the instigation of Catholic priest Father Munro, when she discovered the child had been sent to Canada. This was an unusual case as Quarrier made a point of sending to Canada only those children whose relatives had given permission, and we can only assume that Mrs Kerr had been informed of the scheme at the time of admission. She must also have been aware of the fact that the child was being placed in a Protestant religious environment. Quarrier refused the request and it was only when he was summoned to court that he gave the boy back. The *Glasgow Daily Mail* wrote in support of Quarrier and his work, suggesting that the Catholics should start running Homes of their own rather than trying to shut down Quarrier's.

The Quarriers themselves accompanied a party of 80 children to Canada on the *Phoenician* in 1878. Ellen Bilborough, who by now was in charge of Marchmont since Macpherson had relinquished the Home to her, was also on board. It was around this time that Quarrier started sending his children to Marchmont almost exclusively. Bilborough described the children's reactions to their first sight of Canada:

> It was amusing to hear the different remarks of the newcomers as we
> sailed up the river St Lawrence. 'What curious wooden houses!' 'There
> are no hedges!' 'What large hats the men wear!' The sidewalks of wood

also attracted their attention, and the prolonged shriek of the railway engine was likened to the groan of a dying cow. The children attract great attention along the route, especially by the singing of their sweet hymns in their broad Scottish accent.[18]

In Canada, the Quarriers visited many of the children they had sent out and reported:

> We also saw a little boy, who was very low down when rescued, but he is now in a comfortable home, and is so thoroughly Canadian that one would think he had been twelve years out, rather than twelve months... We saw two of our elder boys: one J.G., who used stand on his nose in Jamaica Street for a half-penny; another, J. McC., whose mother left him with us ten years ago, and has never asked after him since. Both of these are now young men, in good homes and doing well.[19]

And the Canadian report of an orphaned boy reads: 'Has a very good character. Is treated as one of the family. Fond of farming, and thought nothing so nice as hay-making that he had ever done before. Will be under excellent Christian training. Sees his brother at church and Sunday-school.'[20]

Quarrier bought his own receiving Home in Canada, called Fairknowe, in Brockville, Ontario, in 1888, and put his daughter Agnes in charge of it with her husband, James Burges. He continued to send out around 250 children each year; the children went in the main in separate groups, a party of boys from March to April and girls from May to June, when the seas were a little less rough. Then, in 1897, the Ontario government passed the Act to Regulate the Immigration into Ontario of Certain Classes of Children. This was to placate public opinion, which at this point felt that Canada was being used as a dumping ground for child criminals and undesirables. By this law, the Homes could only migrate children under licence: it made the rules governing the type of child coming into Canada more stringent and the supervision of them until the age of 18 more careful. The agencies themselves were to be inspected four times a year by government officials. This infuriated Quarrier, convinced that his scheme already conformed to the standards set by the Canadian government, in contrast to other organizations less conscientious about sending healthy, educated children, keeping good records and following up the children once they had been placed. Wagner quotes a letter he wrote to the

Toronto Globe in which Quarrier expressed his angry resentment of the law:

> It lays hold on a voluntary Christian work supported by British money
> and puts it under the control of a Government which does not
> contribute one cent towards its keep. It prohibits any philanthropic
> individual or society from bringing into Ontario a child under eighteen
> years of age without a licence from the Government, while at the same
> time any immigrant — criminal or otherwise — may enter the country
> with his children… I say without fear of contradiction that it was
> hastily enacted, and is the most inquisitorial law that was ever put on
> the statute books of a British colony.[21]

The premier of Ontario, Arthur Hardy, wrote to him to reassure him that the law was not directed at him: 'The Scotch are well known as a most desirable class of settlers and from all we have heard of your good work, both in Scotland and in this country, we have confidence that you would only bring the best class of children into Ontario, even though no law existed on the subject.'[22] In that case, replied Quarrier, why should I be penalized? In disgust, he ceased sending children to Canada.

After Quarrier's death in 1903, his son-in-law Pastor Findlay, along with Agnes and James Burges, re-established the migration programme. Kohli writes that George Bogue Smart, the chief inspector of British immigrant children, reported the arrival of 55 Quarrier boys in 1904 and 102 in 1905, and in 1920 over 100 children went to Canada.[23] The last party of Quarrier children was dispatched to Canada in 1938. Between the years of 1872 and 1900, 4,735 Quarrier children had been sent to Canada, and by the end of the scheme this number had increased to 7,360.

The Children's Home in Hamilton

In 1869, even as Maria Rye and Annie Macpherson were establishing their emigration schemes, a Wesleyan minister, the Reverend Thomas Bowman Stephenson, was opening the first Children's Home. Supported by two Methodist friends, Francis Horner and Alfred Mager, he established the refuge for homeless children in a converted stable in Lambeth, London. Stephenson was new to London, having spent the early days of his ministry in Manchester and Bolton, and the thousands of children begging on the capital's streets and 'living rough in barrels and boxes' horrified him. The 'Children's Home' movement spread throughout the United Kingdom under Stephenson's direction, and became known as the National Children's Home.

In 1871, larger premises for the Children's Home were found in Bonner Road, Victoria Park, in London's East End. Here the children were taught skills to equip them for later life: the boys carpentry and printing, the girls sewing and laundry work. That same year, Mr G.J. Barlow, ex-mayor of Bolton, donated to the organization a farm of 100 acres in Edgworth, Lancashire, where boys could be trained in farming. Along with other philanthropists involved in rescuing destitute children, Stephenson believed that Canada offered children opportunities of a better life away from 'the temptations of the world and the contamination of old associates'. Such 'associates' could include the children's families—Bowman Stephenson was scathing of parents who 'showed only a sort of unintelligent and almost animal affection … prepared to sacrifice nothing for the permanent welfare of the child.'[24] Like several in the emigration movement, his enthusiasm for removing children from squalor blinded him to the emotional scars such family disintegration could cause.

Together with Francis Horner, the secretary of the Children's Home, Bowman Stephenson visited Ontario in 1872. His purpose was to make contact with the Methodist community in Hamilton, Ontario, and to discuss the prospect of sending children from the streets of London to their area. Those he spoke with were keen to accept only children who had been trained, but the idea was generally appealing to them. The Children's Home sought financial assistance from the Canadian government for training in farmwork or other trades before dispatching children to Canada, as well as for appointing a superintendent at the Hamilton Home to monitor children who had left. The government agreed to a bonus of $2 per head, and Lord Dufferin, the governor-general, thoroughly endorsed the scheme, noting that 'nothing could be more excellent'.[25]

A committee was established to raise funds, which duly resulted in the purchase of a 'handsome residence hitherto owned by R.B. Wadell, Esq., adjoining the Hamilton Driving and Riding Park in the east of the city. In connection with this extensive house there are eight acres of land with a magnificent garden and orchard, upon which are innumerable fruit bearing trees of the choicest varieties.'[26] No wonder that

George Bogue Smart considered the place to be 'in every way suitable' and that Barnardo was pleased to use it for his first party of children sent to Canada in 1882 (p.98).

Francis Horner accompanied the first group of 35 boys and 14 girls on the *Polynesian* in May 1873. They arrived in Quebec and went by the Grand Trunk Railway to Toronto, and then on to Hamilton by the Great Western Railway. A journalist from *The Spectator* called to see them at the new home and reported:

> ... it is highly gratifying to see so many healthy and intelligent looking children rescued from the ways that lead to jail and to the gallows, and made good members of society. Their ages average from 14 to 20, the majority being between 14 and 16. Among them are four or five printers, six carpenters and a number of farm hands.[27]

The Reverend W.J. Hunter was made temporary superintendent and all applications for the children had to be made to him. Forms were filled in and references taken up. As usual, the number of applications far exceeded the number of children; one of the city merchants, for example, applied for several boys to work in his warehouse. This was greatly encouraging to Horner, who was at pains to stress the conditions from which the children had been rescued to show just what strides had been made. The *Hamilton Evening Times*, 3 June 1873, reported his stories, which reflected favourably on the organization's achievements to date. One winter night he had seen something dark in the snow and on coming nearer he discovered:

> no less than six little boys all huddled together, everyone of them barefooted and without a whole garment upon them. He asked them what they were doing there and one of them replied that they were getting warm! On examining the place where the children lay, he found that there was a grate in the pavement through which came heat from the kitchen below...'

Between 1894 and 1928 the Home in Hamilton was run by a Mr and Mrs Frank Hills. Letters show that they were much loved by the children, providing for many a stability hard to find elsewhere. One boy wrote to him, 'Dear Mr Hills, You have turned out to be my best friend ...' Mr Hills gave the girls away in marriage, and 400 ex-Home children attended his funeral in October 1927. The Hamilton Home was closed in 1934.

The young people were placed in work, usually on farms, with a signed contract. Records in the Children's Home show they were visited by staff every six months, as well by officials of the Canadian government; time was spent in seeing each child alone, to establish the reality of his or her circumstances. The records include examples of children changing employment if mistreated, so presumably their concerns and complaints were taken seriously by the authorities.

The majority of the children seemed to settle well in Hamilton, and they compared well with those of other organizations. The figures quoted after the tragic death of a Barnardo's child in Canada show that less than one per cent of Bowman Stephenson's children had been in trouble of any kind, and only 17 out of 3,725 emigrated by Quarrier Homes.[28] Most of those brought by the Children's Homes were boys aged over 14, and despite his comments on degenerate parents Bowman Stephenson ensured parental consent was obtained before any children were taken abroad. The young migrants were, perhaps surprisingly, encouraged to maintain some contact with their relatives—presumably the new environment was through a stronger influence than memories of their earlier years.

On occasion younger children, or even babies, came into the Children's Home. A record of 1889 describes the Home's acceptance of an illegitimate baby of three months, who was fostered until he was seven and then sent back to the Children's Home. At the age of 12 he was sent to a farm in Canada, where he enjoyed working, winning the farmer's approval. At 17 he was apprenticed to a harness-maker, and by March 1911 he had apparently set up his own business, since he wrote to Mr Hills on his own headed notepaper advertising the sale of harnesses, whips, trunks, rugs and polishes, with repairs a speciality. He had married a local girl and they had bought their own home but, sadly, had lost their first child. By the age of 22, the boy migrant had made a good life for himself in Canada.

Unfortunately, this was not always the case. One boy who was sent to Canada in 1888 was placed on a farm, but subsequently went missing. The Children's Home, in trying to find him, wrote to his friend, who was surprised that he had left since the farm was a good place. Eventually the youth wrote to the Home, saying that he had been ill and had worked his passage back to England on a cattle ship. He had had an operation on his liver at Leeds Infirmary and was planning to return to Canada in the spring; he needed some of his money for clothes. In fact, the boy joined the Army and was demobbed in 1899. In 1900, at the age of 27, he was back in Canada, but suffering from the liver complaint again. He asked the Home to try and find him some light work, since his illness made it difficult for him to carry out heavy farm duties. The correspondence stops there, so no one knows what became of him.

The stigma of being a Home Child was something endured by many migrants, and often concealed by them as adults. One letter to the Hills reflects this sense of shame, coming from a woman who had arrived in Canada as a girl. She never told anyone but her husband the truth, but he must have told his parents, who said that she came from the poorhouse. This upset the woman and she asked her former guardians for a photo of themselves, to show her in-laws what fine people those who brought her up had been.

The National Children's Home emigration programme ran from 1873 to 1931, by which time economic depression was affecting all organizations. During that 58-year period, 3,200 children were sent to Canada and 85 per cent remained there, the rest returning to the United Kingdom or moving on to the United States.

'The Child's Friend'

Another philanthropist, John Throgmorton Middlemore, was an early participant in child migration. He started to send children to Canada in 1873, not long after Annie Macpherson's first trip, following his own experiences of travel in North America and Canada. However, unlike Macpherson and other reformers, Middlemore was truly non-denominational, and his motivation was not religious: it was to give slum children the chance of a better life.

He was born on 9 June 1844 in Edgbaston, Birmingham, where the Middlemores had lived since the 15th century. A long-standing Catholic family, they had over the years become Anglican, but John's father, William, chose to be a Baptist. Middlemore senior was described as 'a magnificent man of business', who brought the saddlery and leather concern inherited from his father 'to a peak of reputation and prosperity'. His son, unsurprisingly, joined him after he had finished his schooling, and worked there until sent by his parents to an uncle in

Boston, Massachusetts, at the age of 20. Middlemore stayed for four years, impressed by the wide open spaces of Canada and the equality of opportunity it offered; he took a medical degree in Brunswick, Maine, although he never practised.

On his return to Birmingham, Middlemore was struck by the terrible living conditions of the poor. In the slums, families crowded together in filthy conditions, sharing one privy outside. Tuberculosis and pneumonia were rife, and alcoholism commonplace. Children often stole food out of sheer hunger and were imprisoned if caught; young girls were at frequent risk of rape. Middlemore began to ask himself how he could help the children of the slums to a better future; the answer, he believed, lay in emigration to the clean and open countryside of Canada.

He raised enough funds to buy a house, and in September 1872 established the Children's Emigration Home for boys in St Luke's Road, Birmingham. Three months later the determined Middlemore bought another Home for girls nearby. The children he took in were either younger than 10 (not old enough to enter the industrial schools) or about 13 (no longer required to attend school at all). Many, but by no means all, were orphans, and Middlemore chose to admit those he considered to have the bleakest prospects at home. Using a metaphor that reflects his medical training, he explained: 'I am taking away what would only be diseased tissue if it were left in England, but in Canada it grows into healthy flesh and blood and sinew.'[29]

Middlemore's Homes were established from the outset to send children to Canada. The motivation behind his policy—a surgical excision of undesirable influences—is consistent with other emigration organizations. In his first annual report, Middlemore wrote that 'Children are not taken to Canada because they are poor, but to save them from their bad companions, to whom if they remained in Birmingham, they would always be tempted to return. Emigration is the only mode of permanently separating these children from their old associations.'

Despite this belief, Middlemore sought to work within the law. He emphasized that 'before removing a child to an Emigration Home, the responsibility of the parent has always been considered', maintaining that he did not send children to Canada without their parents' permission. Nevertheless, the shock of separation from a familiar existence was felt acutely by the children. Often their lives fell apart with no warning, as in the case of a 14-year-old quoted by Bean and Melville. Although the parents must have given permission for their child to be accepted by the Middlemore Homes, it was clearly a bewildering process that gave the child no influence in decisions about his future life:

> I remember coming home from school one day in England to find the furniture in the back yard and the house locked up. They had not paid the rent. I ended up in the Middlemore Homes. I never saw my mother and father again, although I wrote to my mother. I was not asked if I wanted to go to Canada. There was no choice: you went in and stayed there until they had a bunch ready to go over. One year they sent a bunch to Australia and the next year to Canada.[30]

Yet Middlemore's concern for the children was tangible; he would involve himself closely with their welfare, reading to them and testing their mental arithmetic. He regarded self-respect as essential, 'because most came from homes where there was nothing to respect', and insisted that the children looked presentable. The details of how the Homes were run were important to him and he was not above stepping in and helping to look after the children, earning him the appreciative nickname of 'The Child's Friend'. His kindness and sense of fun was vividly captured by his daughter, as she described the 70-year-old Middlemore seeing off his charges at Birmingham station.

> A great yelling and hubbub arose in one of the big saloon compartments where a crowd of the younger children were, and when I went to quell the disorder, there was my father in among the children playing an imaginary fiddle like mad, using his smart, tightly-rolled city umbrella as a bow and dancing about to his own soundless tune while the children skipped and danced with him and shrieked with joy...[31]

On 1 May 1873, Middlemore took his first party of children to Canada. They sailed on the *Sarmatian*, arriving at Quebec City 12 days later, and took a train to Toronto. Middlemore largely trusted to luck as he had no receiving Home there, nor a system of finding places for the children—curiously he had not requested the help of either Macpherson or Rye, who already had distribution Homes in Canada. Middlemore's account shows his awareness of the venture's risky nature:

> I left for Canada with my twenty-nine children on the first of May 1873. The journey was entirely one of discovery and speculation. I had not a single friend in Canada and did not know what to do with the children when I arrived there. In the course of my enquiries I heard of

the Hon. George Allen and Professor D. Wilson of Toronto, and sent
them telegrams soliciting help. Both these gentlemen interfered most
generously and most cordially on my behalf. They procured temporary
lodgings for my children and treated me with much personal kindness.
My arrival was made known by articles in the Toronto newspaper and
by personal correspondence, and in the course of three or four weeks I
had found good homes for all my children.[32]

The boys were housed temporarily in Newsboys Lodgings, Toronto,
and the girls in a girls' Home, while places were being found for them.
Twenty-three children were settled in Toronto. The rest were placed in
London, Ontario, through the help of two men who had originally
come from Birmingham, Mr Heath and Mr Finnamore.

Patricia Roberts-Pichette has traced these first emigrants to see
what became of them.[33] Of the 29 children, 10 were aged 12 or more,
15 were younger and ages of the remaining children were unknown. In
the first year, there were known problems with roughly one-fifth of the
children: two boys and a girl ran away, two children left the province
with their families and were not heard of again, and a boy of 16 had to
be returned to England. In subsequent years several more children ran
away, but when they were found they were put in new homes and
reports of them showed that they had settled down. The runaways had
all been placed in the city and Middlemore believed that they would
have been better off in the country. From then on, he placed the older
children, in particular, on farms or in country stores, and the rate of
absconding fell considerably.

Other children from that first party included a girl who ran away in
1878 but voluntarily returned to her employer—her mother had come
from England to find her, but she did not want to live with her mother
—and one boy who in 1882 was sent to a reformatory. These were off-
set by successes: within two years, one boy had found his own place
and no longer needed the protection of Middlemore's Homes; and
another boy was earning $150 per year by the age of 18, when most
boys of his age were earning $100 and girls half that.

Middlemore's next trip to Canada was in May two years later, with
a party of 50 children. The children were once again temporarily
housed in Toronto, but this time the city council in London, Ontario,
arranged for Ross Farm to be available to Middlemore as a receiving
Home. Once it had been fitted out for the children, it was renamed

Guthrie House. It was from here that the children were placed, and it was to here they were returned if there was a problem.

The families that took in Middlemore children signed an agreement. This example from 1875 shows the basis of the agreements which were modified through the years:

> I promise to take — into my home, and adopt him/her and to treat him/her in all respects as my own child. I agree that he/she shall attend school and a place of worship. During the year of his/her adoption, I will communicate with you not less than four times as to his/her welfare. Each subsequent year, until he/she is sixteen years of age, I will communicate with you not less than twice as to his/her welfare. If it is necessary for me to part with him/her, I will return him/her to the Guthrie Home, London, Ontario after having given a fortnight's notice of my intention to do so. Respectfully, Signed ——[34]

This agreement was no more legally binding than the ones devised by Macpherson and Rye, and the use of the word 'adoption' is not what is understood today, when children are adopted for life and cannot be returned. Nevertheless, Middlemore had tried to introduce a degree of protection for the children by requiring the family to communicate with the Home a number of times each year. He himself accompanied the children annually from England to Canada for many years, and during his stay in Canada he would go and see all the children he had placed and then write a report. The Guthrie House managers also fulfilled this task, bringing in other people to visit the children as their number grew.

In 1885, Middlemore sent a group of 18 children to be settled in New Brunswick, but the majority of the children continued to be placed in Ontario until 1898, when Guthrie House was no longer available. That same year he opened a receiving Home in Fairview, near Halifax, Nova Scotia. Its fairly spartan conditions did not greatly hearten the young migrants who arrived tired and apprehensive after the long journey. A 14 year old quoted by Bean and Melville described Fairview as 'a big private Home. There was hardly any furniture at all, nothing fancy, just bare boards and some benches that we sat around on and no tables. We ate our meals in the woodshed… I remember us sitting and crying… We were very homesick.'[35] At least their stay there was temporary—from Fairview the children were placed in the Maritimes (although from 1927 onwards none were placed in Nova Scotia).[36] And by the standards of the time physical conditions were deemed adequate; the Canadian inspector Bogue Smart wrote in his 1912–13 report that he had visited Fairview, which he 'found in good order and the children provided with comfortable quarters'. He particularly commended the managers who 'have taken a good hold of their duties and responsibilities and devote as much of their time as possible to visiting among the children', and in 1914 a former Middlemore boy, William Ray, was put in charge of Fairview. Perhaps the desolation among the children would have been inevitable as the uncertainty and stress of living in limbo took their toll.

During 1912 103 boys and 51 girls arrived from England and were placed in homes; 133 children had changed their situations, of which 42 were from the Unions and 91 from Middlemore's Birmingham Homes. On average, 100 children were brought out each year, not only from the Children's Emigration Home, but also from Unions in Wolverhampton, London and Middlesex (plate 5). During the war, dangerous conditions put a stop to child migration, but about 600 Middlemore boys volunteered to fight on the Canadian side. After the war, the first group of children to be emigrated—in May 1919—were from Middlemore Homes.

John Middlemore died in 1924, and in 1935 the Fairbridge Society of London took over the responsibility of settling the children in Canada. The Society had already established farm schools in Australia (see chapter 5) to which they had successfully sent children, and the organization's profile was riding high. In 1935 the Fairbridge Society opened the Prince of Wales Farm School on Vancouver Island, British Columbia, for 150 children between the ages of 6 and 16, and this became the destination of the few Middlemore children sent to Canada after 1935. Others were now dispatched to the Fairbridge Farm Schools in Australia, and others such as the Northcote Farm School run on similar lines (p.157). The Prince of Wales Farm School eventually closed in 1953, by which time Middlemore's organization had brought 5,155 children to Canada.

'Fegan of Deptford'
Unlike Middlemore, the work of James William Condell Fegan was motivated by his religious beliefs. Blending moral and practical concern, he also believed that the destitute boys he rescued needed to be

trained and educated if they were to have a future. As a result, those he emigrated to Canada were mainly older teenage boys who had been taught how to farm before being sent out.

Fegan was born on 27 April 1852, the youngest of four children; his father, James, worked at the Ordnance Survey office in Southampton, England. Young Fegan was brought up as a member of the Plymouth Brethren, which coloured his entire life, and taught by his mother at home; his interests were mainly outdoor pursuits, such as football, cricket and fishing. In 1869 the Fegan family moved to London, and on his 13th birthday James entered the City of London School, before working for a firm of colonial brokers. At this time he had a religious experience, as did Thomas Barnardo, who was starting his work among London's street children at much the same time (p.93).

After this Fegan's spare time was dedicated to preaching and spreading his religious beliefs. He was moved by the plight of the destitute children in London to open a ragged school, and, like several of his fellow philanthropists, he taught there. However, the combination of working in the commercial world by day and teaching in very demanding circumstances by night served to damage his health. Fegan went to Bognor Regis to recuperate, and here he came across Tom Hammond — reputedly the first boy that Fegan helped to find a home. He brought Tom back to London where he was to spend 18 months before eventually leaving for Canada to start a new life.

The first Home that Fegan opened in 1872 was in Deptford, southeast London, earning him the nickname 'Fegan of Deptford'. An industrial school was opened seven years later in Greenwich, after which Homes were opened in Southwark and Westminster. Eventually the most well-known of Fegan's Homes, Stony Stratford, Buckinghamshire (once a school) was purchased in 1900. The boys were sent to school and trained in various trades such as carpentry and making shoes, but later many of them went on to learn farming. Fegan remained keen on the great outdoors, and would take his boys on camping expeditions with equipment bought through donations.

Fegan took an active role in running his Homes. They took in about 140 boys of 5 to 14, and were known for the severity of their regimes. William Tonkin was eight when he went to Stony Stratford, and the experience was a bracing one:

There were no women that I could see. We were ruled by what, for the most part, were hard masters. We slept in large dormitories and if we did not hear the signal to get up, our cots were tipped over and we were on the floor...

Once in a while a boy would run away and we would walk around the playground wondering if he would be caught. He always was, of course, and he would be thrashed before a full assembly — I imagine to put the fear of the Lord in our hearts. He would be beaten across the bare buttocks with a strap or a rubber-soled sneaker. Then he would be put on bread and water for so many days and would not receive any pocket money for some time. At mealtime he was made to stand on the platform where all the boys facing that way would see him.

Every so often ... we had what was called 'Judgement Day'. We boys went one by one into a room where all the masters were and they would judge us. The grade they gave determined the amount of pocket money we would receive...[37]

Piety was a major concern of Fegan, as of other reformers such as Annie Macpherson, Maria Rye and Dr Barnardo. Prayers and Bible readings took place twice a day, and grace was said before and after every meal. Boys sent to Canada were without exception placed in church-going homes. This emphasis on religion sometimes had the required effect, but not always. William Tonkin said that his treatment in Canada made him wary of people who were ardent church-goers. On the other hand, ex-Fegan boy Colin Taylor remarked, 'My training at Fegan's and my fortunate access to a Christian home here [in Canada] have left me with sympathetic views of the Church.'[38]

As Fegan's organization grew, external events began to play their part. Samuel Smith, elected MP for Liverpool, was closely involved with Louisa Birt's work in the city, and a strong advocate of child migration. He campaigned for the Local Government Board to recommence allowing organizations to send workhouse children to Canada, a procedure halted after Doyle's report in 1875, and when this took place in 1883 offered large donations to both Barnardo and Fegan on condition that the money be used to emigrate children. Fegan, like Barnardo, accepted; the migration seed had in any case been sown by Lord Blantyre, one of the representative peers for Scotland in the House of Lords and a close friend. Blantyre suggested that Fegan should make a journey to Canada to see if there were any opportunities for boys in his care to make a fresh life there. Fegan made the journey in 1884, taking 10 boys with him, and was so impressed with what he saw that he made another journey that year, accompanied by 50 boys. Lord Blantyre met the expenses of the boys on the second expedition to Canada, and on this trip Fegan met Dr Barnardo, also travelling to Canada. He seems to have found favour with Barnardo, who attended the evening services Fegan conducted on board ship. In Canada, Fegan visited Ottawa, Toronto and Portage La Prairie in Manitoba, where Barnardo was to establish his farm school in 1887. Fegan established a Home there in Brandon, Manitoba, reputedly becoming the first of the organizations to send children to the west.

In Toronto, Fegan met a wealthy businessman, Mr William Gooderham, who was willing to help the boys who were sent there. It was with his help that a distributing Home was erected in Toronto, where the boys would stay until a place could be found for them within the farming community. Gooderham died in 1889, leaving $10,000 to the Fegan Homes, and the Toronto headquarters was taken over by the trustees. The Homes also received money from the boys themselves, to allow others to be sent to Canada. In his 1907 report, George Bogue Smart noted that $11,000 had been contributed, and the names of donors are inscribed on copper plaques in the Homes.

With the Home established, a yearly journey was made from England to Canada for as many as 130 boys each spring, often accompanied by Fegan himself. It soon became evident that a lot of the boys lacked the skills needed to work on Canadian farms. Fegan had the idea, innovative and highly practical, of recreating a Canadian-style farm in Britain, and in 1911 he bought a farm at Goudhurst in Kent. All the farming equipment was ordered from Canada so that the boys could be fully trained and experienced in its usage before going out to real Canadian farms. Bogue Smart visited Goudhurst in 1914 and reported with approval that all Fegan boys were trained before arriving in Canada. He described the farm in glowing terms: 'an ideal school for London boys... As the stables, farming implements and general equipment are of Canadian model and manufacture respectively, one would imagine it to be an up-to-date Ontario stock farm.'[39]

James Fegan died on 9 December 1925, aged 73, and his wife continued his work until her own death in 1943. By the time emigration to Canada came to a stop, around 3,000 children had been brought to Canada through the Fegan Homes.

The Allan Line

Transporting large numbers of children on a regular basis was big business, and most of the Canadian traffic came to the Allan Line. Its steamships were used by all the agencies and they brought most of the child migrants to Canada in relative safety; accidents were rare, although much comfort on the voyages could not be expected.

The shipping line started in 1819, when a Captain Alexander Allan advertised the fact that he was sailing to Canada in command of a 169-ton brigantine, the *Jean*. This became the first of a fleet of sailing ships owned by the Allan family that plied the North Atlantic. Captain Alexander Allan established an office in Glasgow, and growth under his five sons was rapid. In 1853 the Allan brothers set up the Montreal Ocean Steam Ship Company, popularly known as the Allan Line, in Canada, to be followed three years later by the opening of a Liverpool office, called Allan Brothers. The Montreal Steam Ship Company signed a contract with the Canadian government to carry mail between Liverpool and Quebec, and the first of these voyages was inaugurated by the *North American* on 23 April 1856. The contract was a valuable one, enabling the Allan Line to build more ships and expand.

Maria Rye's first trip to Canada in 1868 was in the 1,888-ton *Hibernian*, commissioned in May 1861, and she sailed on the same ship with her first party of children a year later (p.23). Another party of Catholic children in the care of Father Nugent travelled to Canada in the *Austrian* in 1870 (p.123) — a ship built only three years earlier. Her delivery served to give the Allan Line, for the first time, more steamers than they needed for their weekly mail service to Quebec — an important development as they had lost nine ships by 1864. The Allan Line was under pressure to deliver the mail on time as there were severe penalties for any delays, and this no doubt caused them to take risks, although Canadian waters were acknowledged to be hazardous: the Gulf of St Lawrence had ice floes in spring and autumn, and there was fog even in the summer. Once the ship entered the St Lawrence River, the pilots' inexperience with large ships constituted a danger, since the channel was narrow in parts with shoals and sunken reefs.[40] While this created difficulties for the captain and the crew, it also had a certain beauty which excited the passengers — especially the young ones. Their letters back home and published in the agencies' magazines often mentioned the icebergs and whales and porpoises.

Delivering the mail on time was a big incentive for the Allan Line to order faster ships, although the Canadian government's decision to waive penalties for delays in 1871 was welcomed by the company. There was no loss of ships for ten years after this date, which meant that when child migration started in earnest, their voyages could be considered reasonably secure.

Larger ships, however, were there to stay. The 3,647-ton *Sarmatian* was one of them; in 1871 she was the largest in the fleet and her compound engines made her the fastest, if also the hungriest for coal. The Poor Law inspector Andrew Doyle came to meet Maria Rye, whom he was investigating, as she was boarding the *Sarmatian* with 150 of her charges in June 1874. He checked out the children's sleeping quarters and their food on board and watched the ship's officers' attentive responses to Miss Rye's requests, then came back the next day to see the departure. His report of the Allan Line was favourable.

No voyage was entirely safe, of course, and an explosion in the coal bunker of the Allan Line's *Sardinian* caused alarm on one of Annie Macpherson's journeys in 1878. The ship was at Loch Foyle when the consequent fire broke out; it had to be towed into shallow water, where sluices were opened to contain the blaze. The experience for Macpherson and her party of children must have been a very frightening one, but the behaviour of all was commended by *The Times* of 14 May 1878 as revealing 'no small amount of true fortitude and heroism'. The near-disaster became welcome publicity for Macpherson whose children, according to the same report, 'behaved nobly under the trying circumstances... They kept repeating to one another many of the sayings they had heard from Miss Macpherson about being patient, good and brave.' The lady herself thanked the sailors for their help in rescuing and hanging up the children's sodden garments—luggage was under water for two days—and no doubt appreciated the good reports just a few years after Doyle's trenchant criticism of the whole emigration concept (p.35).

The Allan Line continued to invest in size and speed, and the *Buenos Ayrean* was launched in 1879. She was the first North Atlantic liner to be built of steel, which made her lighter and faster than those of iron. Her first voyage was to Buenos Aires, hence the name presumably, but the ship was to sail mainly across the North Atlantic, making

one voyage a year to South America. In March 1892, 18 children from
the Isle of Man Industrial Home sailed to Canada on the *Buenos
Ayrean*. The Isle of Man Home emigrated children under the auspices
of Quarrier's; they thus started their trip by sailing from Douglas to
Greenock, then taking a train to the Bridge of Weir. They stayed at the
Quarrier's Home and joined 'the feasting day, when all met to enjoy
their parting tea and evening's entertainment, given by the 130 lads of
promise selected for Canada'. The next day they all travelled to Glasgow, where, at the YMCA,

> upwards of 1,000 friends and sympathizers in the work, including
> several ministers of the various Christian churches, met with and
> commended the boys and those going in charge, Mr. J. Thompson, of
> Cockenzie, an evangelist; Mr. S. Campbell, of the Isle of Man; and Mr.
> Boyd, who accompanied them, to the care of God. Busses conveyed the
> boys to the St Enoch's railway station, Glasgow, and then, on arrival of
> train at Greenock, to the SS *Buenos Ayrean* (Allan Line) by tender. At
> 7 p.m. Mr and Mrs Quarrier and other friends bade the final good-bye,
> and, amidst hearty cheers, left for home. Steam being up, Captain
> Vipond got under way, arriving in Loch Foyle at six o'clock next
> morning (Friday).[41]

The other travellers in steerage, or third class, were a mixture, including 200 Irish and 200 Russian Poles 'in a most destitute condition, and
filthy looking in their person'. Whatever the immediate discomforts,
the boys' first dinner on board—Irish stew, rice dessert, coffee and
bread and butter—seemed wholesome enough. A daily routine was
quickly established to maintain morale and discipline during the long
days ahead: 'Boys up at 6-30 a.m., wash and dress, then, weather per-
mitting, a run on deck; breakfast at 7-30; prayers at 10 a.m.; lunch at
12 noon; dinner at 5-30; prayers at 7-15. Hot gruel at 8, and bed at 8-15
o'clock; interspersed with a romp on deck, tug of war, watching for
whales, ships, icebergs, &c.' Whether the routine could be followed
every day is doubtful, as the ship encountered appalling weather in
mid-Atlantic, with little relief from the wind and rain.

> Tuesday 29th: At 4 a.m., nearly all pitched out of our hammocks by the
> rolling of the ship. Glass gone down quickly; severe gale blowing. At
> breakfast the tables were entirely swept of dishes, food, globes, lamps
> &c., smashed to pieces; everyone holding on by anything they could
> catch. 12 noon, passed a steam tramp and the ship *Charles Eustace* of

Glasgow, outward bound. Reader, just imagine yourselves comfortably seated at tea—and we in mid-ocean, 1,000 miles from land, engines full speed head on, not registering two miles for the last hour, sea running mountains high, and our decks being continually swept from stem to stern by the rolling wave—you will then have some idea of what a storm is in mid-Atlantic.

However, on 5 April they landed at Halifax, Nova Scotia, on a beautiful morning; the journey had taken 12 days. It had been a success despite the weather. Mr Campbell had nothing but praise for Captain Vipond and the Allan Line's arrangements for the children.

The rolling of the ship which caused so much seasickness among the children was improved in part by the Allan Line's flagship, the *Parisian*, launched in 1881. Middlemore travelled on her that year, leaving on 9 June and arriving 10 days later at Quebec, and in April 1882 Maria Rye sailed on her with a group of girls to Halifax. The ship was also used over the years by Barnardo, Birt, Macpherson, the Waifs and Strays organization and the Catholic emigration societies. At 5,359 tons, the *Parisian* was the line's largest steel ship, but her importance lay in the fact that she had been built with bilge keels—two fins attached lengthways along the outside of her bilge, which reduced her rolling motion. She was also very fast, breaking the record of sailing from Liverpool to Montreal in 1898 by achieving the distance in eight days, 21½ hours.[42] The *Parisian* made history again in 1902 by becoming the first steamship to have a wireless radio fitted.

By 1891 the Allan Line was the most successful transatlantic shipping line with a fleet of 37 ships. The company abandoned their original title in 1897, changing their name to the Allan Line Steamship Company, and in the early 1900s they ordered two state-of-the-art steamers of over 10,000 tons, the *Victorian* and the *Virginian*. Both were propelled by the modern steam turbine engine, invented in 1884 by English engineer Charles Parsons. The ships broke speed records in crossing the Atlantic, and they were used by Birt, the Waifs and Strays, the Catholic Emigration Association and some smaller organizations.

Both the *Victorian* and the *Virginian* served as mail ships, racing to fulfil the contract that had brought the Allan Line financial success. Edward Rudolf, founder of the Waifs and Strays Society, described the drama of the mail delivery he witnessed on the *Virginian* in November 1906: 'At Rimouski a tender with its characteristic "walking-beam" engine came alongside to take off the mails; and it was interesting to see the countless sacks of letters and huge baskets of parcels being shot down to it.' For J.C. Maillard, master of a Church of England Home in Somerset, the speed of the *Victorian*, and the efficacy of the operation, were most impressive: 'In due course we reached Morville [sic], in Ireland, on the Friday morning, about 8 o'clock. At 1 o'clock the mails were brought aboard by a small steamer from Londonderry, which also brought a number of passengers; and within half an hour we steamed away, and by 6 o'clock we were out of sight of land.' The ships were transferred to the Canadian Pacific company in 1917.

In 1903, the Canadian Pacific Railway bought the Elder Dempster Line, but the threat posed to the Allan Line did not immediately materialize. However, by 1909 Canadian Pacific had bought the Allan Line —a fact not made public until 1915, when a Canadian Bulletin stated that the Allan Line and Canadian Pacific were going to combine under the title Canadian Pacific Ocean Services Ltd. In fact, the two companies continued to operate separately under their own names until 1917, when the Allan Line was finally and officially absorbed. The *Victorian* and the *Virginian* were transferred to the Canadian Pacific Company in 1917.

A more problematic cargo than mail, the children who went to Canada had little idea of what to expect. Accounts of how individuals came to be crossing the Atlantic reveal a touching hope and imagination rather than real information or hard facts. Both voyage and destination could easily be given a rosy glow, enhanced by the desire of the children for adventure and change. When Mr Quarrier was making his list of children to be sent to Canada, for example, he told a young Scottish boy 'what a wonderful place it was and that I had a sister living not far from Belleville, Ontario. You can imagine the thrill, the excitement, the enthusiasm of such a prospect: to cross the mighty ocean, travel miles by train to meet an unknown sister, see new people and new lands. It was all too much for a 10-year-old boy to contain, so I said "yes".'[43]

There were many children who wanted to go overseas because a close relative, usually a brother or sister, had gone before. Boys who had been fed on a diet of tales from the Golden West, full of cowboys, Indians and Canadian Mounties, were longing for adventure; others were attracted by the idea of working with animals. Many were persuaded that their chances for a good life abroad were greater than if they stayed at home, and many of them eventually found that to be true, even if most of them were subjected to very hard work at a young age.

The journey began on a train from the place where the children were living to, usually, Liverpool for the English or Glasgow for the Scots (plate 6). In *Our Waifs and Strays* Rudolf describes his first journey to Liverpool in 1906 with 13 girls from the Home. They left Euston Station on a dull, damp morning, and quickly:

> busied themselves with appropriating corners in the four comfortable corridor compartments reserved for the party, and in stowing themselves and their thirteen little bags therein, while their thirteen boxes, each marked with a conspicuous red cross were taken off to the guard's van. There were a few tearful farewells, though not many of the children had relatives affectionate enough to be concerned in any way at their departure... But soon after the train had glided out of the station, punctually at 10.30, the children settled down either with books or at a spelling game... The train was a fast one, and the journey was pleasantly enlivened by luncheon, vast quantities of fruit and sandwiches being produced by Miss Bailey, conjuror-like from sundry small parcels... Liverpool was reached at 2.20... A wagonette was waiting to take the children, and a wagon to take the luggage down to the wharf.[44]

The children were taken to the ships by tender and boarded before the other passengers. At that point they underwent a medical inspection, and if a child did not pass—for example, if there were signs of ringworm—he or she would be returned to shore. The children had never been aboard ship before; many were unprepared for what lay ahead and completely bewildered, while seasickness—almost ubiquitous in the early stages—compounded their distress. One eight-year-old described their terrible apprehension: 'I had never been out of England before. I remember the sun was going down and it seemed so lonely. I remember crying.'[45] Slightly older children, young teenagers of 13 and 15, were often unescorted, simply placed in the captain's charge for the most traumatic journey of their lives.

Part of the problem was accommodation, which was always the cheapest—steerage, or third class. Bean and Melville quote a 13-year-old boy, one of a party of 35, who sailed from Liverpool on the SS *Montclare*. 'We were kept aboard for two or three days before finally sailing ... I will *never* forget the smell of paint and the close quarters.'[46]

And another boy, travelling on the *Mongolian* in 1910, also remembers
the smell vividly:

> My cabin was in steerage; six wood bunks to a cabin, each bunk with a
> straw mattress and a grey blanket. The cabin was over the works of the
> ship and the clank of the steering gear together with the whine of the
> propeller shaft, the smell of hot oil and steam, and no ventilation,
> drove me out. I spent my nights hidden in a corner on deck against a
> ventilator shaft for warmth.[47]

Sometimes the children slept in hammocks as well. These were described in an unpublished report by Alfred de Brissac Owen, a clergyman's son and Barnardo's agent in Canada. (The philanthropist Dr
Barnardo had sent his first group of children to Canada in 1882.)
Owen took a party of 155 boys to Halifax on the SS *Circassian*
between March and April 1885. 'The hammocks were assigned to the
bigger boys but did not at first meet with popular approval until a day
or two at sea convinced them that in rough weather a hammock is a far
superior "doss" to a bunk.'

Owen gave detailed descriptions of the food served aboard the *Circassian*—essentially plain, unvaried and with no choice. Breakfast was
usually coffee and fresh rolls with butter, plus porridge occasionally
sweetened with treacle. Dinner (lunch) consisted of soup, fish or beef
and potatoes, and plum or currant pudding. Tea was at 5 pm, when
rolls, or bread and butter, and tea were served. Whatever food was
available, very little of it was eaten on the first three days of the trip as,
without fail, the children were seasick during this time. Owen describes
their first day at sea:

> The poor lads were all very seasick and the breakfast of coffee with hot
> rolls and butter was turned away from with utter disgust. I sent them
> all up on deck in order that the whole place below might be thoroughly
> cleaned up but the poor fellows were glad to avail themselves of the
> first opportunity of crawling back to their bunks.

Harry Dickenson, a boy who sailed with another Barnardo's party, this
time on the *Corinthian* in 1911, described how waves 40 or 50 feet in
height came crashing down on the deck during a storm, while the children were confined to the berths: 'We would rock and toss around ...
you would be so sea-sick you would have a terrible time to last a couple
of days... The boys had to get into a bath which was made of canvas

and filled with ocean water. Then we would line up and they would turn the hose on us…' One of the boys was killed by a wave smashing him on to the deck, and Dickenson describes the funeral at sea:

> They said that sharks followed the ship and that they knew when
> a dead body was on a ship, so they put lead weights inside the coffin.
> They placed the coffin on the rail of the ship and proceeded with the
> burial service for the dead; the band was there. The coffin was covered
> with the Union Jack. All the time the fog horn was blowing we could
> not hear a thing when the body was committed to the deep. The sound
> stopped and all we could hear was the band playing, 'Abide With Me'.
> Finally the fog lifted and we proceeded on our journey.

Several of the boys became ill on Owen's voyage: a few had sore throats, one child had a swelling on his wrist that had to be poulticed, some had to be dosed with a 'little aperient medicine', and many of them had ringworm, which was difficult to prevent in crowded conditions. One boy became very ill with what seemed like dysentery and died within a very short space of time; he also was buried at sea. An accident occurred towards the end of the voyage when the ship lurched suddenly and three boys descending a ladder fell off it. The boy who landed underneath the others fractured his thigh bone, but fortunately the ship's doctor proved 'a most efficient surgeon, especially considering that everything had to be done with the vessel rolling and pitching to such an extent that it was sometimes difficult to keep foothold'. Obviously the surgeon had some experience of setting legs aboard ship.

After a few days getting used to their surroundings, some of the children started to enjoy life on board. When the weather was good, they played games on the deck or made themselves useful by taking on easy tasks. One girl travelling on the *Sicilian* in 1912 wrote, 'We were happy on board with the other girls. We played games and were allowed some money to buy candles. The sailors and the Captain were very good to us.' In general, the captains and crews of the ships seem to have put themselves out to accommodate the children. One, Captain William Smith, was mentioned several times by those involved. The Reverend Barrett, who travelled to Canada on the Waifs and Strays behalf in 1887 (possibly on the *Parisian*), praised the captain in his account of his voyage:

> Went round the ship with the captain in the morning, inducing the
> sick, when possible, to go on deck. Captain Smith, who is commodore

also of the Allan fleet, takes the greatest care of all his ship, from his
most distinguished saloon-passenger to the smallest baby-emigrant.
He visits them daily, and tastes the food provided before the dinner is
served. It is not to be wondered at, therefore, that it is of excellent quality, and that there is a very good feeling prevailing all through the ship.[48]

Smith captained the *Peruvian* when Maria Rye travelled to Canada in
1870, and Kohli describes his kindness to the children on board. After
the sea voyage he accompanied the party to the railway station to see
them off, and had the foresight and generosity to bring with him
enough provisions to ensure that they were well fed on their journey to
Portland, Maine.

Captain Joseph Dutton was another who won praise. Known to be
a religious man, he was described in the autobiography of the Reverend
William Bowman Tucker, who was emigrated aboard the *Prussian* in
1871, at the age of 12.

He was introduced to us, Captain Dutton, and he expressed to us his
great interest in the young lives that he was assisting in transporting.
He assured us of his dependence upon God, and I for one was relieved
of fear as I thought of our Captain looking to God for safety and guidance. I observed later that this Captain did Christian work among the
older passengers by assembling them for Bible studies and for Sunday
services.[49]

Owen praised the attentiveness and care of all the staff on the *Circassian*. By the time the ship had reached Halifax on 6 April 1885, two of
the boys in his charge were unfit, in particular the one who had slipped
off the ladder and broken his leg. To move the boy to the train, the legs
were taken off the table on which the boy lay, and he was carried on the
table-top out of the ship and into the carriage, where the makeshift
stretcher was laid across two seats. Owen wrote:

The greatest kindness was shown in this matter by the officers and
men, in fact throughout nothing could exceed the attention and kindness of all on the ship. The Chief Steward was unfailing in his efforts to
supply everything that could contribute in any way to our comfort and
I was repeatedly told that I had only to ask for anything I wanted for
the boys, and I should have it.

The captain also came in for praise. He had consented to a steward
accompanying Owen and his party on their train journey, and Owen

was grateful for the assistance: 'I knew that he [the steward] would be a great help to us on the train when otherwise my hands would be altogether too full with the constant care of the two sick boys and all the other arrangements to attend to. T. and E. were useless and incapable.' Destinations for the children included Quebec City or Montreal, Quebec, and St John, New Brunswick (plate 9). Arrival, after days of suspense on board ship, often proved an anticlimax to the nervous, excited children on board. A 12-year-old boy describes the bleak impression made by St John:

> We were ... marched off into the customs building, which closely
> resembled a huge barn... The interior was no more comforting than
> the exterior, and if it was designed to make immigrants feel warm
> and comfortable about Canada, it failed miserably... The furniture
> consisted of rows of low benches and two long wooden tables at which
> the customs people worked. The lighting consisted of single light bulbs
> suspended in two rows from the ceiling which gave the whole atmos-
> phere an eerie effect.[50]

The train journey to Owen's final destination, Hazelbrae Barnardo's Home in Peterborough, was a long one. On 7 April the party travelled all day on the Intercolonial Railway, having a meal of dinner and supper combined at 4.30, consisting of stewed meat, bread and butter and tea. The chief steward had provided 'turkey beef tea' for the invalids and '3 barrels of more substantial fare for the others'. They went to sleep at 7.30 pm on very hard bunks, and were woken early up the next morning (8 April) at 7 am, for a breakfast of biscuits and cheese. Four hours later the party arrived at Point Levis, the landing across the St Lawrence from Quebec City, and changed on to the Grand Trunk Railway. Here they had a substantial meal and a doctor came to see the patients, who were thought to be progressing well. At 1 pm they were off again, arriving at Montreal at 11.15 pm, where they were fed in the Immigration Sheds. The journey continued at 1 am—by now it was 9 April by now—and they reached Belleville at 12.20, when they 'were detached from the emigrant train and shunted into a siding until the departure of the Peterborough train at 4 pm. The siding was in the vicinity of a pump and the lads all washed thoroughly and cleaned their boots.' At 8 pm they arrived outside the gate of the home at Peterborough, where they were given a good meal and must have gone to sleep exhausted. The journey had taken three whole days. Many thousands of Barnardo's children took that particular journey over many decades. Other children would have endured very similar journeys.

What did they see, the children, as they pressed their noses against the carriage windows and looked out on Canada for the first time? Bowman Tucker, arriving in September 1871, was struck by the orchards:

> loaded with 'bright red, rosy apples'... There were other things to see, such as the large fields of what we were told was 'Indian corn', and between the rows of which were many very bright yellow things lying on the ground and that somewhat in shape reminded us of our English marshmallow ... but we soon learned that these plentiful objects were 'pumpkins', and that were good for pie-making, and that the cows were fond of them. As for cows—we had never seen so many![51]

One Barnardo girl wrote, 'The little narrow streets of Quebec, cobbled and very steep, seemed very foreign to me as did the people. Surely we were in a strange world!' A Fegan boy wondered 'about all those pails tied to trees. We had never heard of maple syrup.' Edward Rudolf succinctly summed up this first experience when he commented on the Canadian train journey of the children whom he brought over: 'Everything was new to them—the people (for in Quebec there are far more of French descent and tongue than of English), the houses, built bungalow-fashion of wood with broad verandahs, and the country, with its rocky hills and woods of maple and fir.'[52]

And how did they feel about this new experience? Most of them were very homesick: they might not have had much of a home back in England, but at least there was familiarity; they knew what to expect and they had friends. In Canada, once they had left the distribution Home, they were on their own in a strange place.

The stay at the receiving Home was a short one, as it was important to settle each child in his or her new place quickly—and to make room for the next party. As a general rule applications had been made to each agency, forms had been filled in by the farmers and recommendations from a clergyman or priest and sometimes another from a respected person in the area were sent in; all that remained was for the children to be chosen. This was often a haphazard arrangement, as one woman related to Phyllis Harrison. Phyllis had come to Canada in the early 1900s and described how she was chosen while staying at a home in St Ann's Parish in Montreal:

We were called inside—12 boys and 12 girls—and lined up on each side of the room. There were four people there. The woman who was later my adopted mother came over to the little fair girl beside me and said 'I like this one.' My adopted father kept watching me. Every time I looked at him he was smiling at me. He said to my mother 'I like this little dark one' and patted my head. So my mother said 'Well, I guess that's it.' And that was all that was said.[53]

The system, if it can be called such, was weighted entirely in favour of the adults; the children were never asked their opinion and their feelings were ignored. Many felt the process of selection to be humiliating, almost as if they were animals being purchased, and a demoralizing end to a long trip over sea and another journey on land. Other adjustments were demanded, too. They had been part of a noisy group of children, sharing new experiences, and the people in charge of them were at least familiar. Suddenly they were parted from friends and, very often, siblings, and taken to a remote farm to live with strangers. Sometimes these strangers turned out to be kind, sometimes not. Whatever the circumstances, and much of this depended on luck, the anticipation of the journey was over—the new life was about to begin.

Chapter 3

Barnardo, the biggest player

What was needed in order to give them the opportunity they
had missed ... was, in a very real sense, a new heaven and a
new earth—the fresh conditions of a colonial life.
THOMAS BARNARDO quoted in *Memoirs of the Late
Dr Barnardo*, 1907

THOMAS BARNARDO was the biggest player of them all when it came
to sending children to Canada, and the achievements of his organization were to extend far beyond his own life. He became the leader in
the field, and by the early 1900s Canadians were calling all child
migrants, no matter where they originated, 'Barnardo boys'. At the
turn of the century more than a thousand children a year were being
emigrated by Barnardo's, and an article on his funeral in 1905 by the
Illustrated London News reported that he had sent nearly 16,000 children to Canada. In fact the figures were higher—18,172.[1] Like other
organizations, the emphasis switched to Australia in the 1920s and
30s, but Canadian roots went deep. By 1939, a significant tally of over
30,000 children had been dispatched to Canada by Barnardo's.

It was a remarkable achievement by a remarkable man—especially
one who came late to child migration. Barnardo began his reforming
work on city streets, as did fellow evangelicals Annie Macpherson,
William Quarrier and James Fegan, and like them he was horrified by
the scale of deprivation that he saw. The hopeless situation of children
surrounded by poverty and vice particularly appalled him, and he was
brought close to despair in seeing 'Young men and women crowded
together in pestilential rookeries without the least provision for
decency'.[2] Barnardo came to dominate the child migration field, not
least through his talents for fund-raising and promotion, and his
relentless determination was to arouse both admiration and controversy in those who witnessed his dramatic rise.

Barnardo's early years

Thomas John Barnardo (plate 7) was born in Dublin on 4 July 1845 to a family of nine children. His ancestry was shrouded in mystery, including rumours that his 15th-century forebears were Italian aristocrats, and that over the centuries his family had wandered through Europe, making and losing fortunes, until John Michaelis, Barnardo's father, settled in Dublin, acquiring British nationality and dealing in furs. This story persisted until the late 20th century, when genealogical research revealed a less romantic background. Gillian Wagner, Barnardo's biographer, discovered that Barnardo's origins were Jewish — not Lutheran, as was believed at the time (perhaps to authenticate his Protestantism) nor aristocratic nor wealthy. Barnardo's mother was his father's second wife, the sister of his first one, and she was in fact Catholic.

As a child Barnardo disliked school and seemed to be a natural rebel. The final institution he attended was St Patrick's Cathedral Grammar School and he hated it, not least because of the Reverend William Dundas who ran it. Barnardo reacted with such hostility to Dundas, describing him as 'the biggest and most brutal of bullies ... the most cruel as well as the most mendacious that I have ever in all my life met'[3] that it instilled in him an enduring loathing of cruelty and violence, particularly towards the young and vulnerable. And yet the schoolboy Barnardo was described by fellow student Robert Anderson, who later served on the Council of Barnardo's Homes, as a self-centred person, one who was unlikely 'to do anything for anyone else, particularly for a dirty or diseased child'.[4]

At 17 Barnardo declared himself an agnostic, much to the consternation of his mother, and professed more interest in the works of Voltaire, Rousseau and Thomas Paine than in conventional religion. However, the family's life was changed in the 1860s by the great Evangelical Revival in Dublin in the 1860s, with meetings drawing thousands of people; many speakers were converts who urged their audiences to come to God. The Revival was inspired by a belief that the Bible could arouse faith and courage in the poor and a sense of responsibility to those less fortunate than themselves in the rich. Religion had become the impetus to social reform, prompting people such as Elizabeth Fry to improve prison conditions and William Wilberforce to crusade against slavery.

Barnardo's mother went to such meetings regularly, and her sons George and Frederick became members of the Open Plymouth Brethren. Through their influence, Barnardo became a dedicated convert, choosing to be baptized, and to reject Voltaire and Paine in favour of the Bible. His adolescent diary illustrates his new commitment, describing 'a holy calm as if the Lord Himself were speaking with me', and quoting extensively from the Psalms. Although he continued to work in his father's fur business, religion now informed everything he did in his free time, including giving Bible classes at one of Dublin's ragged schools in the evenings and on Sundays. Here, in a dingy building crawling with bugs, he observed dire poverty first hand and was appalled: 'Had I a dog I would not kennel it where I found these immortal souls...' Barnardo also preached three evenings a week — a courageous thing to do to when faced by jeering, drunken crowds — and looked for work in which he could serve God all the time.

In 1866 an opportunity seemed to arise when Hudson Taylor, a missionary, came to Dublin. He had founded the China Inland Mission and sought people to serve in China, immediately inspiring Barnardo to go to London and train for missionary work. Taylor's missionaries were due to sail on the *Lammermuir* in May, but Barnardo, much to his disappointment, was not to be among them. He was advised instead to train as a doctor, so that he could go to China with a skill and help the people there. Hudson Taylor himself had studied to be a doctor and Barnardo signed up at the London Hospital, once attended by his mentor.

The hospital had a good reputation for surgery. Barnardo spent much time in the dissecting room learning anatomy and watching the surgeons at work, operating on what looked like a kitchen table with a washtub filled with sawdust underneath to catch the blood. He had progressed to assisting the surgeons when the cholera epidemic struck, and the London Hospital was swamped with patients. The disease raged through the capital; and within three months nearly 4,000 people had died. While qualified doctors tried to treat the sick in hospital, the medical students were sent out to visit patients in their own homes; on just one day Barnardo was present at 16 deaths. His visits to the sick and dying in Stepney opened his eyes to the desperate conditions in which the poor lived; he later observed that, 'But for the epidemic, I should never have known Stepney and all its horrors.' If the physical poverty was a revelation, so was the moral degeneration he witnessed, of people 'steeped in ignorance and sin ... whose souls needed the illumination of the Gospel'.[5] Barnardo began to preach and to distribute copies of the Bible.

While studying, he also taught in a ragged school in Ernest Street, Mile End, an experience prompting him to start a school of his own. Assisted by two medical students, Barnardo rented a donkey stable in Hope Place, Stepney, where despite their limited resources the companions managed to put down flooring, limewash the walls and furnish it with some benches and a couple of lamps. 'Into this old, disused, and transmogrified donkey-shed ... we gathered a crowd of idle, ill-washed children, on two nights a week and on Sundays ... it was there that I had my first indication of and inspiration towards what proved to be my life's work.'[6]

Barnardo told a story which he called his 'inspiration' and, although unverifiable, it plays a part in the Barnardo hagiography. One evening when Barnardo was ready to leave Hope Place (an excellent name for his first enterprise), a young boy called Jim Jarvis asked if he could stay there. When Barnardo enquired further, he discovered that the urchin had no parents and slept in the gutter of a roof, night after night. Nor was he alone—hundreds of children had no home and slept rough, some of them very young. Jim Jarvis took Barnardo to where some of these children were sleeping so that the horrified teacher could see for himself. Some weeks later, so the story goes, Barnardo was invited to the home of Lord Shaftesbury, who questioned him about this story. Barnardo took him to where he knew young children were sleeping rough and showed him. According to Barnardo, Lord Shaftesbury was shocked by the scene, but the great philanthropist was by then in his sixties and had been a social reformer for many years. He was very familiar with the East End, and it could hardly have come as a surprise to him that children were sleeping in gutters.

Responding to what he had seen, Barnardo soon managed to buy three small houses near his donkey-shed. Funded by donations, they provided a refuge for young teenage, destitute boys and became the East End Juvenile Mission. Barnardo knew Annie Macpherson through the ragged school and, when she told him that she planned to take a party of boys over to Canada, he selected some to join her first group of children to be emigrated in May 1870. One was Jim Jarvis who, like the others, was sent to a farm in Ontario; it is not known what became of him.

Barnardo tells the story of Jim Jarvis partly to explain the change of direction in his life. The plight of the boys affected him so deeply that he decided not to go to China, but to concentrate instead on helping destitute children in the slums of London. However, it was a choice made simpler by the donation of £1,000 by Liverpool philanthropist and Member of Parliament Samuel Smith, supplied on condition that Barnardo abandoned any idea of missionary work in China and continued his rescue work in the East End. In giving up China, Barnardo lost the little enthusiasm he had for his medical studies and left the London Hospital unqualified, although he continued to use the title 'Doctor', enjoying its kudos. This small vanity was one of the things that his enemies later held against him, but the matter was solved by him going back to his studies, taking the exams and indeed becoming 'Doctor' Barnardo.

In the summer of 1870, Barnardo rented a large house in Stepney and converted it into a Home for boys. Accompanied by a helper, he would search the streets for ragged urchins and bring them back to the Home. However, he was initially very wary of getting into debt and would limit himself to numbers that he could afford to support. This practice changed after a destitute child called John Somers, whom he had had to refuse, was found dead a few days afterwards. The inquest found that he died from exhaustion, cold and starvation, and Barnardo felt himself to blame; he wrote, 'I dare not, because of either lack of funds or the fear of debt, cease for one hour that work of God to which I have been called...'[7] And a notice went up outside the Stepney Home, saying, 'No destitute child is ever refused admittance.'

Such an open-ended commitment spurred Barnardo on to raise more funds. He founded the City Messenger Brigade to deliver circulars and public notices, charging 3d per hour or two shillings a day. When it proved successful he formed a second brigade of wood choppers, supplying householders with firewood at a cost of four shillings per 100 bundles. This was so successful that Barnardo had to start importing wood, and by 1878 the brigades were earning £2,000 per annum. His friendship with Richard Morgan, editor of the weekly journal *The Christian* that Macpherson wrote for so effectively, enabled him to write human interest stories arising from his work, and at the same time ask for donations. He also appealed directly for funds when preaching. Photographs of the children—first wearing the rags in which they were found, and then neat, clean and busily engaged at the Home—were another useful source of income, sold singly or in packs. Although this was not a new idea—Macpherson had sold photographs privately to her supporters—Barnardo's approach was boldly commercial, and proved very successful.

Barnardo's flair for publicity also extended to the temperance movement, active in the East End at the time. Barnardo directed part of his indomitable energy into fighting the demon drink, and in this he scored a great coup and gained huge publicity. One of the largest gin palaces in the East End was the Edinburgh Castle, and when it eventually came up for sale Barnardo determined to buy it, conducting a successful fund-raising campaign which allowed him to purchase the building. He transformed it into a mission church and then—with a leap of the imagination—encouraged those who had once drunk gin there to return for—coffee! The former gin palace was redecorated, newspapers provided, meat pies could be bought alongside coffee and mugs of cocoa, and the Castle became a meeting place for all the working men in the area. The change from gin palace to church and coffee house was a clever move in the battle against alcohol, and Barnardo's reputation was assured when the Castle was opened by Lord Shaftesbury.

In the summer of 1873, aged 28, Barnardo married Syrie Elmslie, a teacher two years younger who ran a small school for boys. A year later their son, William Stuart, was born. Marriage gave Barnardo the opportunity to realize a plan that had not been practicable for a single man: he wanted to provide a Home for girls. John Sands, a fellow member of the Plymouth Brethren, had given the Barnardos the generous gift of a 21-year lease on a house in Barkingside, and Barnardo embarked upon his plan by converting a coach house adjoining his house. In one of his fund-raising articles in *The Christian*, he declares, 'I hope to train up a band of kitchen-maids, housemaids, parlour-maids, laundry-maids, dairy-maids and cooks to meet the great demand existing everywhere for cleanly and instructed female servants.'[8] This was an ambitious project—unlike Maria Rye and her trained workhouse girls, Barnardo's street children were, in his words, 'criminals in embryo, the offspring of degraded and vicious women'.

He had the sensitivity to understand that the girls would be better off in small groups of different ages, like a family, looked after by a housemother, rather than being placed in a large impersonal institution. Large sums were received from benefactors, and Barnardo oversaw the planning and construction of 14 mock-Tudor cottages round a grassy area with a church, school, infirmary and a farm. In another example of how far Barnardo's star had risen, the Village was opened by the highly influential evangelical politician Lord Cairns. Each cottage had four bedrooms, a playroom, kitchen and private rooms for the house mother. The bold enterprise captured the public imagination and inspired other philanthropists—Kingsley Fairbridge and his wife visited over three decades later, on their way to establish a farm school in Australia (p.145). A reporter from *Chambers Journal* wrote in July 1877:

> The older girls take it in turn to help cook the dinner, to lay the cloth, to keep the house in order … Each small domestic duty is performed over and over again till each child learns to be quite adept at cooking potatoes, or cleaning out a room, or washing and dressing a younger one … to do thoroughly all the commonplace duties which are likely to fall to her lot as a servant …

Most importantly, the Girls' Village Home was remembered fondly by many of the girls who were sent to Canada and made their lives there.

Barnardo's success was viewed with scepticism by some people, including the Charity Organisation Society, who did not like the way he operated. He was accused of dishonesty in handling money, of taking children from their parents and treating them cruelly, and of raising money by selling falsified pictures of the children. Eventually a court of arbitration was set up in 1877 to look into these allegations, a stressful time during which donations fell to an all-time low. Barnardo was vindicated and, along with him, the whole evangelical philanthropic movement that encouraged his work and supported him (including funding a young, brilliant and expensive defence lawyer). However, from that time on, to prevent anything like this happening again, the Barnardo Homes were to be run by a Board of Trustees to whom Barnardo was accountable.

1 (*above*) A party of young girls brought to Canada by Maria Rye in the mid-19th century. They were housed in 'Our Western Home', a converted gaol and court-house situated at Niagara-on-the-Lake, until they were found jobs, usually domestic work on farms.

2 (*right*) A photograph of Maria Rye (1829–1903). Well educated and from a professional family, she first used her entrepreneurial flair to set up businesses to give women employment. By 1869 her main interest was sending pauper children, usually girls, to Canada.

W. Bond

NORWICH.

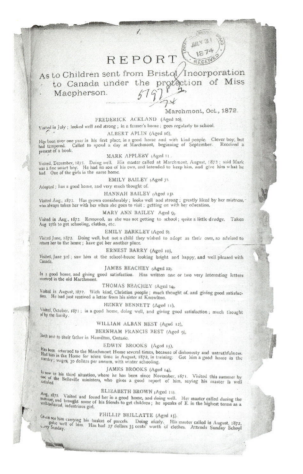

REPORT

As to Children sent from Bristol Incorporation to Canada under the protection of Miss Macpherson.

JULY 31 1874 RECEIVED

5797

Marchmont, Oct., 1872.

FREDERICK ACKLAND (Aged 10).
Visited in July ; looked well and strong ; in a farmer's home ; goes regularly to school.

ALBERT APLIN (Aged 16).
Has been over one year in his first place, in a good home and with kind people. Clever boy, but had tempered. Called to spend a day at Marchmont, beginning of September. Received a present of a book.

MARK APPLEBY (Aged 11.)
Visited, December, 1871. Doing well. His master called at Marchmont, August, 1872 ; said Mark was a fine smart boy. He had no son of his own, and intended to keep him, and give him what he had. One of the girls in the same home.

EMILY BAILEY (Aged 7).
Adopted ; has a good home, and very much thought of.

HANNAH BAILEY (Aged 13).
Visited Aug., 1872. Has grown considerably ; looks well and strong ; greatly liked by her mistress, who always takes her with her when she goes to visit ; getting on with her education.

MARY ANN BAILEY Aged 9.
Visited in Aug., 1872. Removed, as she was not getting to school ; quite a little drudge. Taken Aug. 27th to get schooling, clothes, etc.

EMILY BARKLEY (Aged 8).
Visited June, 1872. Doing well, but not a child they wished to adopt as their own, so advised to return her to the home ; have got her another place.

ERNEST BARRY (Aged 10).
Visited, June 3rd ; saw him at the school-house looking bright and happy, and well pleased with Canada.

JAMES BEACHEY (Aged 12).
In a good home, and giving good satisfaction. Has written one or two very interesting letters received in the old Marchmont.

THOMAS BEACHEY (Aged 14).
Visited in August, 1872. With kind, Christian people ; much thought of, and giving good satisfaction. He had just received a letter from his sister at Knowlton.

HENRY BENNETT (Aged 11).
Visited, October, 1871 ; is a good home, doing well, and giving good satisfaction ; much thought of by the family.

WILLIAM ALBAN BEST (Aged 12).

BERNHAM FRANCIS BEST (Aged 9).
Both sent to their father in Hamilton, Ontario.

EDWIN BROOKS (Aged 15).
Has been returned to the Marchmont Home several times, because of dishonesty and untruthfulness. Had him in the Home for some time in August, 1872, in training. Got him a good home in the country ; wages, 30 dollars per annum, with winter schooling.

JAMES BROOKS (Aged 14).
Is now in his third situation, where he has been since November, 1871. Visited this summer by one of the Belleville ministers, who gives a good report of him, saying his master is well satisfied.

ELIZABETH BROWN (Aged 11).
Aug., 1872. Visited and found her in a good home, and doing well. Her master called during the summer, and brought some of his friends to get children ; he speaks of E. in the highest terms as a well-behaved, industrious girl.

PHILLIP BRILLATTE (Aged 15).
Often see him carrying his basket of parcels. Doing nicely. His master called in August, 1872, spoke well of him. Has had 27 dollars 35 cents' worth of clothes. Attends Sunday School every Sunday.

3 (*left*) Annie Macpherson migrated children to Canada from Poor Law Unions as well as her own homes. This report on children from Bristol Incorporation, now in the National Archives, reveals their mixed fortunes. One child is described as 'a fine, smart boy', but another was returned to Marchmont several times because of his dishonesty (MT 32/20).

4 (*below*) A photograph of Marchmont, Annie Macpherson's distributing home, in 1886. The first house, offered to her by the Mayor of Belleville, burnt down in January 1872 and the citizens of Belleville raised money for a new one.

5 (*opposite*) This poster from the National Archives lists names of children who the Poor Law Union in Poplar, London proposed to emigrate to Canada in September 1884 (MH 12/7698). The oldest was 16 years and the youngest only a year old.

POPLAR UNION.
DESERTED CHILDREN

NOTICE IS HEREBY GIVEN that, on the 12th day of December next, the Guardians of the Poor of the Poplar Union will proceed to consider the question of the expediency of assisting the

EMIGRATION TO CANADA

Of such of the following children as may be then maintained in the District or other School chargeable to this Union by reason of their having been deserted, or otherwise abandoned, by their Parents, and who by age, physical capacity and otherwise may then be found to be eligible for such emigration, namely:--

NAMES.	Ages	NAMES.	Ages.
BYFORD, WILLIAM	11	HAGERTY, ELLEN	11
„ FREDERICK	9	HEWSON, GEORGE	11
BROWNING, SAMUEL	7	„ JOSEPH	10
„ FREDERICK	5	HODGE, EVA	8
BERRY, ALFRED	12	MAKER, GEORGE	5
„ FREDERICK	8	„ ELIZABETH	4
BRIGHTWELL, ELIZABETH	11	MEREDITH, EMMA	10
BROWN, DOLLY	12	„ „ CHARLES	8
BRIAN, JAMES	9	„ „ WALTER	7
„ MARY	6	MONK, MARY ANN	11
„ PATRICK	8	„ ELIZA	3
BRITTAIN, ADA	9	„ RACHEL	6
„ „ CHARLES	3	MARTIN, FREDERICK	8
„ „ WILLIAM	2	„ HENRY	7
BOLTON, BERTIE	5	„ AMELIA	4
„ EDITH	8	NEWBERRY, ALBERT	11
CAVERLEY, ARCHIBALD	10	„ „ WILLIAM	9
CRAWLEY, ANN MARY	13	OLDING, SUSAN	7
CALLAGHAN, MARGARET	9	OXHALL, RICHARD	5
„ ELLEN	6	„ EDWARD	3
DEELY, LOUISA	4	PRATT, ROBERT	9
ELLICK, SARAH	16	ROWBOTHAM, WILLIAM	5
„ LOUISA	14	SOUTH, CATHERINE	11
HOLMES, CHARLOTTE	12	„ GEORGE	8
„ JANE	9	SHERVILLE, PERCY	8
HAMILTON, ARTHUR JOHN	11	SHACHL, ALBERT	11
„ „ WILLIAM	7	SILK, HARRIET	10
„ „ GEORGE	4	WHITWROWE, JENNIE	4
HARVEY, RICHARD	10	WHITE, AGNES	12
„ GEORGE	6	„ MARGARET	4
„ MARGARET	2	WILLIAMS, JOHN	11
HUGHES, ALBERT	13	WARD, MARY ANN	14
„ FANNY	12	WILKINSON, THOMAS	11
HANCOCK, ALICE	12	„ „ SARAH	10
„ „ ARTHUR	10	„ „ HENRY	6
„ „ HERBERT	8	WILLMOTT, JEFFREY	10
„ „ ALBERT	5	„ „ SARAH	4
„ „ OLIVE	3		
„ „ HENRY	1		

BY ORDER,
JAMES R. COLLINS, Clerk.

Union Offices: High Street, Poplar.
September 12th, 1884.

J. WILLIS, Steam Printer, Dewberry Street, St. Leonard's Road, Bromley, E.

Painswick 1886

Miss ~~Potts~~ Laver	8		14	
~~Teresa~~ Davies	9	Mr Steel	15	
	10		16	
	11	Eliza Harris	17	
			18	

Yours sincerely, in the children's cause, Thos Barnardo

6 (*above*) An early photograph of children preparing to leave Painswick, Gloucester, in 1886. The young migrants, with their few belongings, were to travel to Liverpool, from where they would sail to new lives in Canada.

7 (*left*) A photograph of the philanthropist Dr Thomas John Barnardo (COPY 1/ 492 f212). Although he came late to migrating children, Barnardo's Homes became a major player, sending over 30,000 children to Canada between 1882 and 1939. His Canadian homes were at Toronto for the boys and Hazelbrae, Peterborough for the girls.

8 (*right*) Decisions to migrate children were not always clear-cut. This Home Office document from the National Archives lays out the case of two sisters aged 13 and 9 (HO 144/1118/203442). It was proposed to send them from Dr Barnardo's to Canada; their father — who objected — was in prison for their neglect.

9 (*below*) A chilly group of Barnardo's children disembark at the landing stage at St John, New Brunswick, *c.*1920s. A maritime province in Upper Canada, New Brunswick was one of the first destinations for British children in the 19th century.

ROWE,

EVA MAY SELINA, now aged 13.
HILDA KATE, now aged 9.

Committed on 26th November 1907 under 4 Edward VII Chapter 15.
Father living.

Committed at Southampton, at Petty Sessional Court, by Magistrates for Borough and County.

203442

The mother died in November 1905. The father, a painter, was said to be of lazy and drunken habits. In March 1906, he was sentenced to three months hard labour for having neglected his children. The neglect, however, was subsequently resumed, and in November 1907 the father was sentenced to six months hard labour for having neglected his children, who had undergone the severest privations, and were found to be living under the most wretched conditions and in a state bordering on starvation.

Memoranda.

A notice - copy attached - of the proposed emigration of these girls was sent to the father on the 20th inst., and the accompanying letter has been received from him in reply. It is hoped, that, in view of the facts mentioned above, the Secretary of State will see his way clear to sanction the emigration of the children, notwithstanding the father's objection.

10 (*above*) Young boys harvesting at the Philanthropic Society Farm School in Redhill, Surrey, 1898–1910. Formed in the 18th century, the Society sought to rehabilitate young offenders; its Redhill Farm became an agency providing training for young migrants. The 300 boys there learned trades such as brickmaking, shoemaking and carpentry, as well as agricultural skills. Many boys who trained on the farm went abroad to work in various parts of the British Empire.

11 (*left*) Work on Canadian farms was very hard for migrant children, often requiring heavy physical labour in harsh weather conditions. This photograph shows a young Barnardo's migrant, one E. Lanbridge, loading a timber cart with his employer, a Mr Dorlan.

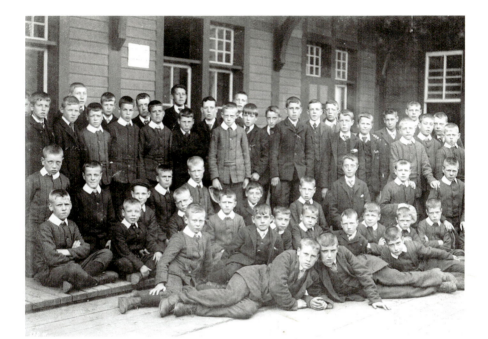

12 (*above*) A party of well-dressed boys photographed on the way to Stratford, Ontario, where Annie Macpherson bought a home after selling the Galt farm in 1882. It was run by her sister and brother-in-law, Rachel and Joseph Merry.

13 (*below*) A group of girls from Barnardo's travelling to New Brunswick, Canada with their chaperone in the 1920s. A Barnardo's girl, Kathleen Rourke, observed: 'Some of us had the very devil in us, causing many headaches for our minders.'

14 (*right*) This report on young Francis Allen is held in the National Archives (HO 144/524/X76100). He eventually was sent to Canada as a child migrant because the Catholic home in which he was placed did not want to release him to the care of his aunt, a staunch member of the Salvation Army.

15 (*below*) This photograph of Catholic boys en route to Canada dates from March 1929. The Catholic Emigration Association had sent large numbers of children each year to Canada, often to French-speaking homes, earlier in the century. But the Association's activities were curtailed in 1925 by the Canadian Government's ruling prohibiting unaccompanied migrants under 14.

P Y.

☞ Form for Report to Industrial Schools Rota of Cases under the Industrial
[I.S.]   Schools Acts.   Sent to St. Vincent's.

Division _____ Southwark (Mr Robinson) _____ † See S. A. and A. Code, Art. 71 (P).   [FORM No. 1.]

* For use at Head Office.   Index No.* __46125.__

Date of Rota _____ July 5th. _____ ,1897.   Age __6__ years __8__ months

                                                 Date of Birth __4/11/__ 1890.

Name _____ Allen, Francis. _____   Place of Birth ___ " ___

Address · _____ No settled place of abode. ___ " ___

Religious Persuasion? _____ Roman Catholic. ___

Who gave the above Information ?

Charged with _____ Wandering, etc., _____ before Mr. Slade.

Where Charged _____ Southwark _____ By whom _____ Rescue Officer.

Date of hearing _____ July 3rd.   Remanded to _____ July 10th.

Names of Parents }   Father.   Mother.
or Guardians   } _____ Dead. _____   _____ Louisa. _____

Occupation of Parents or Guardians _____ " _____

Number and ages of other children } _____ 3 - 10 - 5 - 3. _____ Questionable.
in the family   }

School (if any) child is attending _____ None.

Standard in which working __0__ Attendances for last six months? __none.__   Parent's Statement, Visitor's Report.

Have the Parents been sum- | Parent's Statement. | No, not in | Visitor's Report. |
moned and fined for the | | | Under Bye-Laws. | Under Education Act.
non-attendance of this child ? | a place long enough. |

Are any children of the family in Truant, Industrial or Reformatory Schools ? ___ no. ___

Have you seen the child ? __Yes.__ _____ If so, where ? _____

[Is the child [if a boy] on licence from a Truant School ? ___ " ___

[If so, give School _____ " _____ and attendances since licensed (Possible and Actual) ___ " ___

Condition of Home. ___ · · ___

General Remarks :— _____ No Home. _____ Found wandering and not having any Home or settled place of abode, or proper guardianship, or visible means of subsistence. Mother was turned out of her lodgings a fortnight ago, since then has been sleeping in lodgings houses. She has not been seen for several days. Her character very questionable. Previously lived in Chelsea and Battersea.

Emigration as a solution

When the court case was over, Barnardo set about fund-raising again with renewed vigour, by the 1880s receipts were improving again. He also began to think of other ways of enabling him to bring more and more children into his care without a huge increase in cost. One obvious way was to move the children on so that others could take their place: 'to secure the open door in front it must maintain its exit door in the rear.' But it was becoming difficult for him to find work for all his boys and girls once they were ready to leave the Homes. As he explained: 'We in England, with our 470 inhabitants to the square mile, were choking, elbowing, starving each other in the struggle for existence; the British colonies overseas were crying out for men to till their lands, with few ties to bind them to the mother country, and at an age when they were easily adaptable to almost any climatic extreme.'[9]

As with other organizations, emigration offered a solution. Barnardo had been impressed with the example of Annie Macpherson, who had taken her first party of boys to Canada in 1870 (see chapter 1). He had already sent children to Canada under her auspices and was familiar with her system of emigration, but now he felt the time had come for him to set up a system of his own. An article in *Night and Day* served to outline his way of thinking:

> With about 1,100 children under my care, and with fresh and harrowing instances of child anguish and neglect brought to our doors daily, a very natural desire has often pressed itself upon me, to find … channels by which those who have been trained in our Homes might be safely and speedily sent out upon their life's work, and so make room for some of those little ones yet unreached… Neither ignorant of or indifferent to the grand work being done by Miss McPherson [sic], Mr Quarrier … and others, the idea of Emigration often came to me in the night watches and during hours of perplexity as one solution… Yet, unwilling to follow in 'another man's line of things' … I have been slow to move in organising methods for the transplanting upon a large scale the young life of our streets and alleys to the virgin soil and pure atmosphere of our colonies.

In 1875 Doyle's 'Report on the Emigration of Pauper Children to Canada' had brought the emigration of workhouse children to a halt. Samuel Smith, Member of Parliament for Liverpool, was a supporter of child emigration, believing it to be a good way of reducing high unemployment among young people and an effective social safety valve. He and others urged the Local Government Board to reverse their decision, which they did in 1883, and workhouse children were once again allowed to be sent overseas. Samuel Smith then offered a large sum of money to both Barnardo and J.W.C. Fegan, another evangelical philanthropist (p.76), on the condition that it be used to emigrate children from their Homes.

Having embraced the idea of emigration, Barnardo organized his first party, consisting of 51 boys between the ages of 14 and 17. These children were selected by the Reverend Fielder, governor of the Stepney Home, and he accompanied them when they left Liverpool for Quebec on the *Parisian*. The party sailed on 10 August 1882—late in the year to send children to Canada since the harvest, when the farmers most needed help, was nearly over. However, the Reverend Thomas Bowman Stephenson of the Children's Home (later the National Children's Home) had offered the boys accommodation during the winter at his receiving Home in Hamilton, Ontario. In the event, only 16 boys out of the 51 were not placed on farms straight away. Reverend Fielder was delighted with the success of the enterprise; not only had there been many applications and children placed out within a fortnight, but Canada had 'a beautiful climate and an immunity from the vices and want' which beset the children back home.

Barnardo was filled with enthusiasm for this new venture and 10 months later sent out another, larger group of boys. Then, in July 1883, Barnardo went to Liverpool to see off the first group of 72 little girls—the youngest only four years old –who sailed to Canada in the *Sardinia* in the care of Miss Emilie Morecroft. He records: 'The girls wore plain, though comfortable clothes ... with a stout ulster, travelling jacket and pretty red hood.'[10] They had their own Home to go to, a rent-free house called Hazelbrae in Peterborough, Ontario. It had been given by the mayor of Peterborough, George Cox, a wealthy Canadian businessman with interests in railways, real estate and banking; in 1898 he became a senator. Hazelbrae proved to be an elegant brick mansion of three storeys, set in grounds of about six acres, containing a huge lawn, vegetable gardens and an orchard. Here the girls shared the housework and helped to tend the kitchen garden; destitute children from Peterborough were also admitted. The house had been arranged to accommodate 120, but those involved were confident that 'so large a number would not remain as the demand for these children has hitherto proved so great as to warrant the belief that it will not be necessary for the permanent maintenance of more than fifty'.[11]

In the December 1883 issue of *Night and Day*, Barnardo celebrated the popularity of his initiative: '"Please may I go to Canada?" is the most popular sentence just now on the lips of our girls.' In that same year Miss Milly Sanderson, a teacher and the new secretary of Hazelbrae, visited the Girls' Village Home in Barkingside for a few months to be trained in their methods. She wrote, in the June 1884 issue of the same magazine, of how she tried to help the girls form realistic expectations about life in Canada: 'I told them of short summers and weary winters, when all the poetry of life seems to be either parched with heat or shrivelled with cold; and then I spoke to them of work—not slavery—but honest, intelligent labour... Good hard work, is the order of the day, and commands good wages.' Then, in a pointed way—perhaps directed at Barnardo himself?—she sounded a cautionary note for over-optimistic philanthropists. 'Canadian sunshine is bright and Canadian air is pure, but I never yet have heard that they have the power to renovate corrupt hearts or reform evil lives.'

Applications for domestic and farm servants flooded in. The Canadian applicants had to describe their personal and financial circumstances and their religious affiliations, and each application had to be accompanied by a reference from a minister or a magistrate. If they were accepted, they had to sign an agreement to keep the child for a certain period and provide him or her with board, lodging and clothing. Boys and girls between 13 and 17 were placed as servants and were paid wages and their keep. Very young children were treated as part of the family, although not strictly adopted as the legal process of adoption in Ontario and Quebec was only introduced in the early 1920s.

In selecting the children from his Homes in Britain, Barnardo stipulated the following: 'As to physique, that they should be thoroughly sound and healthy in body, and without predisposition to disease, having besides no disablement in limb and no failure of intellect that would interfere with their progress in life.'[12] To ensure this, the children had to undergo a medical examination before leaving England—and they were inspected again on arrival by the Canadian authorities. The rigorous policy could bring about devastating decisions for children hoping to be sent together. One Barnardo girl, Louise, wrote:

'My sister and I were picked to go to Canada together, but they found something wrong with her eye. They wouldn't let her come with me. My heart was broken.'[13]

Barnardo also required that the children should have an elementary standard of education and some degree of training. For the boys, this focused upon an industrial pursuit of some kind, while girls were instructed in domestic service, with the intention of rendering them immediately useful to the households acquiring them.

As a religious man, however, Barnardo had other concerns about the children who would represent his organization. He required that they should be 'honest, truthful, and decent, as well as industrious and capable', as might be expected. The children's moral character, however, was of the utmost importance—especially given their often unpromising backgrounds. It could only be guaranteed if they had been 'brought under religious influences, taught to love and reverence the Bible as God's word, and trained in the faith and love of the one Saviour for sinners'.[14] Barnardo wanted to be sure that this religious education was continued, and one of the conditions of employing one of his children was to undertake to send the child regularly to church and Sunday school.

For his part, Barnardo guaranteed to ensure that the children were being looked after in their new homes by continued supervision comprising 'systematic visitation' and regular correspondence. He believed that 'young emigrants must not be cut adrift', but although he regarded this as a vital principle it was a difficult one to maintain. The long Canadian winters and the great distances to be covered made travelling difficult, with the result that children could remain isolated for over a year and any bad treatment stay undetected. Nonetheless, visits were made and recorded, and many of those who were discovered to be ill-treated were eventually moved.

Barnardo himself often made the trip to Liverpool to see the children off. He was not alone, since the Boys' Band also accompanied the children on the train journey to the port. Each child had his or her own 'Barnardo trunk', made of wood and covered in leather; it had been designed at the industrial school. Inside was the standard issue outfit for Canada—each child had the same. A full list of the boy's kit was published in *The Pall Mall Magazine*. It included overcoat, suit, blue jacket, jersey, pair of blue trousers, ties, shirts and three caps—blue, tweed and 'storm'. Underwear was limited by modern standards—only two pairs of woollen pants and undervests—but the clothes were at least tough and made to last. Two pairs of new boots were issued, one for arrival and one for travelling, plus accessories such as brushes (for hair and clothes), a satchel or haversack, a packet of stationery and handkerchiefs. Each boy, unsurprisingly, received a Bible and a New Testament, as well as a Text Card featuring verses from the 29th Psalm, but there was other reading material too—a book of True Stories, a Traveller's Guide and a volume of Historical Tales. Each boy thus embarked on his voyage fortified with examples of courage and good conduct, as well as reminders of the country to which he was unlikely to return.

Departure itself, inevitably, was an emotionally charged moment. As the children leaned on the rails and watched the land recede, the Boys' Band—who had travelled to Liverpool for this purpose—began to play. The ship moved slowly out to sea to the sound of hymns wafting over the water.

Visits to the Maple Leaf

In 1884 Barnardo made his first trip to Canada, lasting three months. He wanted to learn more about Canada, as well as to see Hazelbrae and visit some of the children. He started in Toronto, where he had been offered a building—214 Farley Avenue—at a nominal price by a group of sympathizers. This soon became his Canadian headquarters and distributing Home for boys, remaining so for the next 30 years. During his time in Toronto, Barnardo visited prisons, schools, churches and the homes of rich and poor. He welcomed the humanitarian attitude with which those in charge of the jails treated their prisoners, and approved 'the kindly, religious feeling of the great body of working people'.[15] The campaigner against alcohol was particularly struck by their 'powerful sentiment in favour of temperance', noting in his diary that when he visited people in their homes he was never offered a drink. It did not occur to him that people might not have wished to offend him by doing so, although he did notice that there was not much consumption of alcohol in hotels either.

Barnardo visited the Girls' Home at Hazelbrae and was impressed by 'the charming house situated a little outside of the town, upon a hillside, commanding a view of the country round about'.[16] Once there, he drew up a list of the girls he was going to see in the next few weeks, though how much he managed to achieve in such a short time over the long distances is difficult to know. The country certainly appealed to him and he maintained that Canada was 'a fair garden-like country, yielding abundantly, where children could only benefit from interests in animals, flowers and gardens and where a child would flourish in the grand "Canadian air"', but then Barnardo was a good publicist. He had to be—his funding depended on it.

Children such as William C., admitted to the Stepney Home aged eleven and a half, were a valuable example for Barnardo's cause. His parents were alive but struggling to make ends meet, and he spent two years at the Boys' Home before being selected for the 1884 Canada party. William proved to be a strong-willed and disciplined child, offering to forfeit his winter wages during his first year in Canada if his employer would allow him to attend school. He obviously put his sacrifice to good use, as by the summer he had passed the examination for a second-class teacher's certificate. Barnardo appears to have been interested in this exceptional boy who continued teaching until he had repaid the money Barnardo had lent him and earned enough to attend the University of Toronto. By 1900, only 16 years after his arrival, he had become a highly paid official at the Chatham National Bank in New York and a 'promising business man' with excellent prospects.[17]

Such good examples were needed, as the enthusiasm which had greeted the first child migrants from Britain was beginning to wane. Among the most vociferous critics were the Canadian trade unions, alarmed that the wages of their members were being undermined by child labour. The *Toronto Globe* took up the baton, querying the process on moral grounds: 'Street waifs and inmates of reformatories, refuges and lodging houses ... are not the classes with which to build up a strong nationality,' it declared.[18] There were accusations of criminality, of health risks and of bad blood coming in to contaminate the good Canadian families who took them in. Many of the rumours about the children were unfounded, but they did not improve their image, and many became seen as second-class citizens. As the need for cheap child labour remained high, however, the confidence of the emigration agencies was unshaken, and their work continued.

Barnardo was a new player in child migration and he was deter-

mined to distinguish his children from other agencies, such as Maria
Rye's. He wanted to ensure that people in Canada appreciated that the
children selected for emigration were the best in his Homes. He therefore drew up a list of assurances designed to set the public's mind at rest.

> *First*: That no child shall be sent out manifesting criminal or vicious
> taint.
> *Second*: That no child is to be sent out who is not at the time in excel-
> lent health, and without tendency to disease.
> *Third*: That all such children (excepting, of course, the very young
> ones who go out for 'adoption') must have been passed through a
> period of the most careful training, not only in industrial pursuits,
> but also of a moral and religious character.
> *Fourth*: That as regards all children who come up to the standards of
> the three previous conditions, only the flower of our flock are to be
> sent to Canada.
> *Fifth*: That upon reaching Canada, all children are to come under the
> care of properly qualified persons connected with our institutions on
> the Canadian side, by whom they are to be distributed carefully into
> well-selected homes; and that even then our work is not to be consid-
> ered complete, but that regular communication shall be maintained
> with these children for years by personal visitation of experienced
> assistants, and by a system of written reports from the child and its
> employers. That careful statistics shall be kept showing frequent
> reports of their whereabouts, progress, and general welfare, until they
> have reached an age when they no longer require our supervising care.
> *Sixth*: That if, in spite of all these tests, precautions and safeguards, it
> is found by experience that some particular child, after having been
> placed out in Canada, becomes definitely immoral or criminal, then
> every legitimate means is to be adopted to recover possession of that
> child, and to return him or her at the earliest opportunity to the old
> country.[19]

Barnardo's trip to Canada in 1884 had another purpose—to explore
the feasibility of establishing an industrial farm in the newly accessible
northwest. He had chosen Manitoba as a location, following the
opening up of a railway terminal in Winnipeg a few years earlier, and
had tirelessly campaigned for a grant of land. He had written to Sir
Charles Tupper, the Canadian High Commissioner in London, asking
for between 3,000 and 5,000 acres of good-quality land, suitable for
training in mixed farming. He also requested that they be given free

railway transport, as without it his plan could not work. Tupper's response was positive, reflecting the still supportive attitude of the Canadian government towards child migration schemes, and he said that a grant of land was a possibility if the Canadian Pacific Railway was co-operative.

In 1884 Barnardo was able to set out the foundations of his plan. He explored various prairie locations and visited key cities, talked to officials and discussed the project with the railway company leaders—those of the Grand Trunk and the Canadian Pacific proved particularly helpful. Negotiations were successful, and by 1887 the purchase of what was eventually a 10,000-acre farm through grants and donations was made in Russell, Manitoba.

In 1887 Barnardo returned to Canada, full of enthusiasm for his new project. The farmhouse at Russell, built to accommodate 200, housed 90 young men over 17 in its first year. It was a severe wooden building with a large dining hall on the ground floor; dormitories were placed above and a small barred room acted as a jail. Barnardo wrote that 'from the windows of the hospital-rooms on the second floor is a view as charming as any that can be seen in the North West'.[20] By the end of 1888, the first wheat crop had been harvested and a 'creamery and cheese factory' started. Although it was reported that the 'lads ... have weathered their first winter admirably, and have proved their pluck and suitability in a most encouraging degree', this does not tell the full story of what the boys must have suffered in the extreme cold of a Canadian prairie winter, or how bleak the farm must have been as a base. At least time there was relatively short—each group of youths stayed for a year and then moved on to work as labourers on other farms. The Russell farm was a forerunner to Kingsley Fairbridge's Farm School in Australia, although it had to close through financial difficulties in 1908, four years before Fairbridge opened his first farm in Western Australia (p.145).

Barnardo made a third trip to Canada in 1890, contributing an account of the farm's progress to the 25th Annual Report of the same year, now held in the National Archives (HO 144/310/B6159); he wrote that the farm stock had done well and the creamery had increased its output. By that time another most important step had also been taken, one that would give the boys something of their own and help them to a better start in their adopted country. Barnardo had submitted a 'Scheme of Colonization' to the Ministry of Agriculture and it had been approved.

New plans in Canada

The Colonization Scheme was a new development in the story of child emigration as it enabled young men to be sent from Britain to Canada to be trained in animal husbandry and crop management—with the express aim of settling the land. The Canadian government had an allotment scheme in place, offering every young man over 18 a small farm of 160 acres, and Barnardo planned to link this in with his training programme at the farm. Every year several allotments near the farm were chosen, and a house and stables built on each one, the cost of the buildings being part of an advance to the settler.

An example of expenses illustrates the costs involved.[21] It is interesting to note the relatively small cost of the house and stable, and that further expenses have been incurred by the presence of a second person:

HOMESTEADING EXPENSES 1896

First expenses	$	Subsequent expenses	$
Transportation to Russell	30	Expenses while backsetting,	
Expenses of entry	11	repairs, contingencies	30
Provisions for one month	15	Clothing etc.	25
One yoke oxen	120	Wintering oxen	10
Plough	16	Seed	25
Repairs	3	Additional furniture	25
Cart	25	Provisions 6 months,	
Harness	14	2 people	96
House and stable	16	Harrows	16
General household outfit	25	Plough	16
		Cow	32
TOTAL	275	**TOTAL**	275
To be met by:		To be met by:	
Deposit	150	Six months' work with team	
Advance	125	on Home Farm, after	
		completing one month's	
		breaking on Homestead	150
		Further advance	125

Each Barnardo boy assisted to a plot had to pay $150 to the manager of the farm, with the entry being recorded in the Land Office. On the deposit of this sum the settler was provided with oxen, a plough, a wagon, harness and provisions; the cost was to be paid back over a number of years. Other things he needed, such as seed, implements, etc., could be bought at the lowest cost, or repaid by helping out on the Home Farm at busy periods. It was calculated that after 18 months, the settler would be self-sufficient and might even be able to support a wife or another Barnardo boy on his property. Barnardo, innovative as ever, was very keen on this plan, 'as many of my older lads are eager to take advantage of its provisions, its effect will be to make our Farm a colonizing centre of very considerable importance in the near future'.[22]

The scheme gave unemployed boys from the city slums a new chance in life and, supported by good training, they were able to take advantage of it. Although it was a very hard life, it did give the boys a sense of purpose, as can be judged by many of the letters sent to Barnardo's, such as this one from W.C.R. in the Northwest Territories: 'This year I shall break 15 acres and next I shall backset ten, and harrow and seed it, and if I get a good crop, I shall have about 800 dollars... Dr Barnardo's farm at Russell is not far from me, so I shall also be able to have a look at some of the Youth's Labour lads at work.'[23] (The Youth's Labour House was a training institution in London which the boys attended before emigration.)

Joseph T., one of the early youths to be trained at the farm, offers a philosophical view in a letter published in *Ups and Downs*, October 1900: 'I have not had it all sunshine ... but still, for all that, I cannot complain, for I will have, when my time is out on November 5th, the sum of $850 saved up, and, in another year, if the crops are good, I will settle down on a farm of my own.'

One problem of settling in the northwest was a lack of women. The *Canadian Gazette* pointed out that if more girls were not emigrated, farmers would not stay in Canada but move to the United States. Not one to miss an opportunity, Barnardo wrote, in *Ups and Downs*, that girls in Ontario should consider travelling west. To do so would give them a chance of escaping domestic service and of becoming in charge of their own household, with an attractive young husband. 'There are many young men out there whose stockings are never or poorly darned,

whose bread is soggy and weighty ... and whose hearth is unswept.'
However, Barnardo neglected to mention that the weather and farming in that part of the country were so hard on women that some men
had to abandon farming or go south for the sake of their wives. It is
interesting to note that most Home girls left the farms for the towns
and cities when they reached 18. They turned their back on the domestic
service for which they had been trained, preferring to work in factories,
restaurants and shops before marrying. Only a few married farmers.

Another initiative was 'boarding out', a process established in
Britain, where the local Poor Law Guardians were permitted to place
children with foster parents on the rates. Barnardo tried this with
some of his children who had not been emigrated. When it proved a
success, he decided to board out large numbers of his boys and girls in
carefully selected country villages. Local committees in the area were
set up to help choose the foster parents and oversee the children. The
foster parents received five shillings a week, and had to sign certain
guarantees in respect of their charges. Barnardo called boarding out
'the golden key that opened the closed door' and was keen to apply it
to children sent abroad. The practice of boarding out Barnardo children
in Canada began in 1891; children under 12 were placed with foster
families, who were paid to look after them. When the children turned
12 they were able to work, but most left their families at the age of 14.

In 1896, Barnardo opened a new home in the northwest in Winnipeg. This was for boys aged between 10 and 13 years, younger than
those sent to the Russell farm. It was opened in response to a demand,
seemingly without end, from farmers for younger boys to work on
their farms. The boys sent there were relatively established in Canada.
They had arrived as small children and had been boarded out on farms
in northern Ontario where, growing up in a family, they naturally
learnt about Canadian farming and went to local schools. Barnardo's
superintendent in Canada, Alfred de Brissac Owen, believed that:

> the 'boarding out' department of our immigration work has proved
> one of its most useful and, in the results accomplished, one of its most
> valuable features... They [the children] commence life in Canada at an
> age when they have scarcely begun to form habits or permanent attach-
> ments ... and they become acclimatized and reconciled to the conditions
> of country life with a facility that would be impossible in children of
> more advanced years.

He went on to say that 'it would be difficult to obtain better material for successful settlers on the western prairies than the little lads who have gone up there [to Winnipeg] after serving their apprenticeship in Ontario farm homes'.[24]

Statistics show that Owen's latter statement proved incorrect. Young men did not stay in farming; they made their way to the towns as the girls did, but later, when they were in their late twenties. Joy Parr's sample of Barnardo boys reveals that only eight per cent of them tried farming, with an even smaller percentage actually staying in farming all their lives. There was little economic incentive to do so and even less of a social one: living on a farm was lonely. At first many of the boys took up working in the seasonal labour market, spending summers working on the lake boats or the land and winters clearing tracks. But—generally before hitting 30— the men moved to towns and smaller cities. They took jobs in factories manufacturing everything from biscuits to agricultural machinery, and in the service industries, and it is there that the majority spent their lives.[25]

The industrial farm at Russell, Manitoba continued until 1908, three years after Barnardo's death, when the farm land was sold to raise money for the organization. In a way it did remain in Barnardo hands, at least in part, since several of the buyers were men who had come to Canada as Barnardo boys. Barnardo's particular vision had come to an end, however, and the Home itself stood empty and abandoned for many years.

A fresh start in Canada

Barnardo was a prolific writer and he used this talent to raise money for his work. His tone was always upbeat, emphasizing successes and portraying his work in Canada as a valuable exercise in transplanting 'the flower of his flock' into new, clean soil, where they could breathe the purest air. Photography was another promotional tool, and Barnardo took a camera on his Canadian visit of 1893 to record those who had established themselves creditably. One picture he took was of Lavinia T., described as a 'sensible girl who has evidently flourished in Canada'; she had arrived at Barnardo's Homes as a disconsolate three year old, and had been emigrated to Canada at 12. She now had some savings behind her and good future prospects,[26] while another boy who had been rescued from the streets aged 15, William J., had become a Sunday school teacher.[27]

Many letters published in the Barnardo magazine *Ups and Downs* —circulated to Barnardo children in Canada to keep them in touch with the old country and each other—show that the children were establishing themselves overseas and that they were grateful for the opportunity to do so. Such letters, naturally, were the ones that Barnardo chose his readers and supporters to see, but they were not the whole story, of course; another side to emigration emerges in reports and other letters. Yet it is also important to remember the circumstances in which Barnardo and his helpers found his waifs and strays. Some children were sought out by the Homes and actively rescued from destitution on the streets, or from gangs of thieves. Some children referred themselves, or were recommended by magistrates, charitable ladies visiting the poor or ministers of religion; the NSPCC also became involved after its foundation in 1884. Parents who brought their children were usually driven by economic necessity, aware that the Homes could offer them a better future and were an improvement on the dreaded workhouse.

The issues were often far from straightforward, even in the harsher moral climate of the time, although Barnardo was well known—sometimes criticized—for his determination to intervene. The following accounts describe the backgrounds of some of the children rescued by Barnardo's Homes; they were featured in the 25th Annual Report, held by the National Archives:

> *Minnie L. (13)* Mother who had sunk to the lowest depths of sin, was at the time of application, a common prostitute ... and was believed to be supporting, not only this girl, but the degraded stepfather, by her infamy. No relatives to assist.
>
> *Alice T. (15)* Father died in an asylum. Mother lives by rag-sorting, and is a confirmed drunkard. This girl has been grossly neglected... Suffering from hunger, she recently stole two cabbages from Covent Garden Market... Whilst under remand a City Missionary interested himself in her case. The poor girl was at first unwilling to enter the Homes. 'Poor mother,' she said, 'has no one but me to pick her up when she falls down drunk.'
>
> *David S. (14)* Father, a non-commissioned army officer, became so intemperate that he was dismissed the service. Mother also gave way to drink. Home became a veritable pandemonium, and the culmination

was at last reached in the suicide of the father. Mother became a
vagrant, oscillating between workhouse and streets. David and his
brother lived on the streets 'as best they could'...

Frank H. (6) A hunchback. Had a fall which resulted in injury to spine.
Father died of consumption. Mother has tried to maintain her children by shirt-making but can't earn enough.[28]

These entries reflect the attitude of the times in their moral condemnation of the 'undeserving poor', in particular women who often had no
other means of keeping their family together save by prostitution. The
bald accounts reflect poignant stories of desperate circumstances,
despite which some affection shines through. Minnie's mother might
have been a common prostitute, but she was trying to support both her
daughter and husband. Alice did not want to desert her mother. The
strength of family ties is there to be seen, but these were links that the
philanthropists wanted to break so that the child could make a fresh
start, often in Canada.

In his keenness to save children from moral and physical danger,
Barnardo indulged in what he called 'philanthropic abduction'—an
illegal practice and one which others in the child migration field
eschewed. In an article in *Night and Day*, he justified the practice of
taking children away from parents who were either ill-treating their
children or who led immoral lives, asking the critical question 'is
judicial law always to be co-extensive with *moral* law?' He confessed
that, under his auspices, 47 children had been abducted illegally to
save them from their circumstances. Some children were sent to
Canada to distance them, quite literally, from their families; between
1882 and 1908, six per cent of boys and eight per cent of girls were sent
to Canada without their parents' consent.[29] In this, Barnardo revealed
himself as more ruthless than other organizations; Macpherson, Birt
and Quarrier, for example, refused to emigrate any child without the
consent of their parent or guardian. Barnardo became involved in two
high-profile court cases (see chapter 4) where children were abducted
and emigrated to Canada. They resulted in the 1889 Prevention of
Cruelty to Children Act, in which guardianship was removed from
parents committed for trial or convicted of wilful neglect. In 1894 the
Act was extended to allow children whose custody had been transferred to be sent abroad with the permission of the Home Secretary.

The National Archives contains the case of two young girls, Hilda

Kate R. and Eva May Selina R., who were selected for emigration to Canada without their father's consent (HO 144/1118/203442). The story of the girls, aged 9 and 13 respectively, illustrates the complex situations surrounding many of the children emigrated by Barnardo's (plate 8). In a letter dated 20 January 1911, the father was informed by Barnardo's that his two daughters were to be sent to Canada; he was also given details of where they could be contacted in Peterborough, Ontario, through the organization. The father, who was in prison, wrote a piteous letter protesting against the emigration, ending, 'I think it is most cruel for two children to be sent so far away from there [sic] Father & Friends that loves them so dear.' However, in seeking the Home Secretary's permission to emigrate the girls, Barnardo's included their case history which casts a different light on the situation: 'The mother died in November 1905. The father, a painter, was said to be of lazy and drunken habits. In March 1906, he was sentenced to three months hard labour for neglecting his children.' Over a year later, he was jailed again 'for having neglected his children, who had undergone the severest privations, and were found to be living under the most wretched conditions and in a state bordering on starvation'. There is no record of the outcome, but the girls probably went overseas, leaving their father—inadequate but with some affection for his daughters—unable to see them again. There was no hint of how the children felt.

Half of the children emigrated by Barnardo were from one-parent families, usually widows unable to support their children. Once her husband had died, a widow found herself in difficult circumstances. If she received any help at all from friends or relatives, or if she moved from her husband's parish, she was likely to lose poor relief. And the kind of work available to her as a woman would not provide the income needed to support herself and her children. Eventually she and her children would find themselves in the workhouse, or the mother would reluctantly have to ask a Home to take in some of her children. Once a child was admitted, it was difficult to keep up family connections since the Home actively discouraged this—visiting rights were restricted and pressure to sign an 'emigration clause' was often intense. When a child was emigrated, Barnardo would send out before-sailing notices to 'respectable' relatives and after-sailing notices to 'disreputable' ones. Children of 'respectable' parentage were encouraged to write to their mothers and fathers and 70 per cent of Barnardo's girls kept in touch with their families. Yet, surprisingly, the figure among the 'disreputable' families who kept in contact was not much lower, at 60 per cent.[30]

Brothers and sisters who came to Canada together went to different homes, but kept in touch and looked out for each other. There are many stories of a brother or sister coming to the rescue of a sibling who was in a home that treated them badly, or of a sister looking after another sister who had become pregnant. And if the longing to see family back in the old country became too strong, they would save their money and visit Britain; 16 per cent of Barnardo's child migrants returned home to live as adults.

Sometimes it worked the other way and the family came over to Canada. Edith H. wrote a letter in 1909 in which she said that Barnardo had brought her mother and little brother David to Canada. She and her sister worked in a factory so that they could earn enough money to support the family and allow their mother to stay at home and look after David. Other Barnardo men and women also saved up to bring members of their family to join them overseas. Considering the attitude of the Homes, the distances and the difficulties of keeping in contact, it is amazing that a great proportion of separated families managed to stay in touch.

In his book *Something Attempted—Something Done*, Barnardo tells the stories of some of the children who were sent out to Canada. One of them was:

> Louisa J. (14) Rescued from a wretched home. Mother has been one of the vilest characters on the streets of East London… This girl and her younger sister had already had their young lives scorched, and were veritably 'saved so as by fire'. Is now doing well in the family of a Methodist Minister, and writes now and again bright little letters to her unhappy mother.

The children were not always white or Christian, for among them were a 'Zulu' and two young Jewesses. The 'Zulu' was placed with a farmer in Canada, but entered a training college because he wanted to return to his country as a missionary. The mother of the Jewish girls died and the children were sent to Canada as 'bright attractive children, and likely to make their way in their new surroundings'.

Many young people wrote to Barnardo saying that their lives had been improved by emigration. Although most went to English-speaking families, some were sent to homes where German or Polish was spoken.

F.H. (*Parry Sound, Ontario*) … I have been put in a Swiss family. I do a
little of everything. I like it well here. I have a chance to learn German
and farming. I am going to Sunday school. I have plenty to eat and in
the winter I went to the school until spring… We have twenty acres
cleared and about 170 acres of bush to clear yet. It is on a lake. We are
fishing sometimes. It was very cold when I came here, and there was
lots of snow. I am glad I was sent over here. I am thankful to you… I
will pay you back for what you have done for me.

A.J. (*Waipanee, Ontario*) I like Canada very much. But it is very cold in
winter. We have a beautiful view of the river, but when the snow
comes it is all ice, and we have skating and sleigh rides; and in summer it is hot and we have a lot of fruit.

F.C. (*Smith's Falls, Ontario*) I like my new place twenty times better
than my other place. We have all our crops in now. We had two very
rough storms of thunder and rain, and it blew a lot of our fences
down, and it took us the greater part of the morning to fix them. It
has been the worst storm that I ever saw since I been in this country.[31]

The letters give a flavour of life in Canada: the winters were very cold,
but the children could derive some enjoyment from the snow. Work
was hard, and bad weather made it harder, but the boys were taking a
certain pride in what they could do. Many of them listed their achievements in their letters, from harnessing and driving horses to taking in
the crops, milking, thrashing grain and constructing buildings.

However, records do reveal that some children were treated badly.
Unlucky ones among them could be whipped and beaten, or even sexually assaulted; some had accidents with farm implements and machinery because they were unused to them, and poorly trained. Employers
could be very unsympathetic: one nine-year-old boy was returned to
the Home because of the 'breakings out on his feet which appear to be
caused by frostbite', and even as late as 1929, when far fewer children
were arriving in Canada, the Barnardo's manager's response to a child
accused of dawdling would strike us today as unduly severe: 'It is
absolutely necessary that you strive to realise that you are no longer a
little boy of eight or nine years of age who may be excused for playing
around… You were not brought to Canada to spend a holiday nor yet
to have a life-long vacation … no matter where you go *you must
work*'.[32] Hugh Caesar, a Barnardo boy, wrote of two Barnardo boys
that he knew: 'Billy hanged himself and Johnnie was found on the stable floor, his stomach full of strychnine.' He knew of another boy,

Fred, who had drowned himself. That one boy should know three others who committed suicide shows the desperation that some of the children experienced. Helen Gough's childhood had been unhappy and lonely. Later, she wrote: 'When I was 18, I was advised by the Home that I was on my own. I came directly to Toronto. I have had my troubles since I have been "on my own" but I have been much happier.'[33]

Whatever kind of life each child migrant led, adapting to it must have been hard. All were poor and came from the city streets of Britain, where they had experienced loss, separation, hunger, neglect, lack of love, sometimes abuse, to various degrees—all of which had left an indelible mark. They had been placed in institutions requiring them to behave in particular way and were used to living in a noisy, crowded community. This did not prepare them for country life in Canada in isolated farmhouses where there was hardly any social life and where the long winter evenings were dull, quiet and could be frightening, if the child was left alone. Girls with little experience of home life were expected to be masters of domestic chores, and work on the farms could be physically exhausting for those barely into adolescence. A 12 year old boy, quoted by Bean and Melville, explained his day of continual labour:

> The farm was a hundred acres and there were three horses, about six head of cattle, pigs and chickens… In the morning we would get up anywhere around 4.30 am and we would go to the barn, milk the cows and separate the milk and then have breakfast, groom the horses, put them on a wagon and mow the hay or cut the grain. Eleven o'clock would be our dinner time and then out to the fields again and then at 4 pm it was supper time. Then we worked on bringing the grain in and the old chap would stand in the barn door with the lantern and that was eleven at night… In the winter … you had to wade through snow almost up to your waist.[34]

Mostly, the children were regarded as servants—that was why they were there—and, despite the pious hopes of emigrating authorities, they were seldom made to feel part of the family. Some employers had scant regard for young migrants, and they often did not trouble to conceal it. One girl who was out with her mistress overheard a comment reflecting this, and it haunted her through later life:

The man who was helping her [the mistress] said 'Who is that you have
standing there?' And she said, 'That's just the girl from the Home.'
And he said, 'They're pretty poor trash, ain't they?' And she said, 'Yes,
they are.'[35]

Their lives were in the hands of people who did not care about them,
and the uncertainty of how long they might stay in a place and what
was to happen to them next must have been a constant anxiety—
understandable reasons why some children appeared despondent or
bad-tempered. One Barnardo boy who arrived in Canada in 1915
describes his time there in bleak terms: '... I realised we were just chat-
tels for Canadian farmers. We were never allowed to forget that we
were lucky to be alive; you really were a nobody... Their attitude was I
was there to work, not sit around in school, so I was doomed to be just
a labourer.'[36]

Their status as servants was not what the children were accustomed
to and they did not always meet the expectations of their new masters
and mistresses, so there were complaints of rudeness, 'black looks'
and insolence. Lack of cleanliness (sometimes due to bed-wetting) and
coarse manners and language were also a concern, with employers
anxious that their own children might pick up bad habits. Even if they
were stubborn, lazy or slow, the farmer could often not afford to
employ anyone else, and so resorted to punishment to frighten children into changing their ways. Discipline by employers was always
problematic, and Joy Parr maintains that nine per cent of boys in her
Barnardo sample were subject to excessive punishment. The Home
came to expect that their charges ran the risk of ill-treatment, but their
limited resources meant that there was not much they could do. When
the inspector did visit a farm, it was difficult for him to discover what
was happening—a child might prefer not to reveal that he was being
beaten in case it happened all over again. In extreme cases, children
died from ill-treatment, and the people who perpetrated the crimes
were prosecuted. Sometimes justice was done, sometimes not. The
most famous case was that of George Everitt Green in 1895.

George Green was of limited intelligence and was handicapped by
defective vision. The first farmer with whom he was placed sent him
back because his bad eyesight made it difficult for him to work, despite
which he was then sent to the farm of Miss Helen Findlay. Six months

later he was found dead in an upstairs room, emaciated and covered in welts. At the trial, neighbours testified to the terrible abuse that George had received from Miss Findlay, but in her defence lawyers pointed out his condition, claiming that he had come to Canada suffering from a constitutional defect that could have caused his death. The jury could not come to a decision and the trial was dropped.

This case did not help improve conditions under which child migrants worked, as might have been expected. The *Toronto Evening Star* gave voice to Canadian concerns: 'There is a general belief and strongly defined suspicion that Green was not a solitary instance of children with tainted blood having been brought to Canada ... and no law too strict can be framed to prevent these waifs, handicapped by heredity, from mingling with the pure and healthy children of this country...' The Trades and Labour Council, always opposed to child migration on economic grounds, seized their moment and declared that the philanthropists made 'Canada a common dumping ground for large numbers of the vicious, the lame, the halt and the blind'. The Ontario legislature made a bid to reassure the public and passed an Act in 1897 to regulate the immigration of 'certain classes of children', making it an offence to emigrate children with any physical or mental defect or a criminal record. The work of the agencies was to be inspected four times a year and John Joseph Kelso, a man in favour of child migration, was appointed Inspector of Juvenile Immigration Agencies.

As Canada became more uneasy, Barnardo began to consider other destinations for the children in his Homes. He had received requests from Australia, South Africa and New Zealand through the 1890s but had generally resisted them, concerned about the long voyages and his inability to support children if they did encounter problems half a world away. A few unofficial parties were allowed to go, and in 1896 the appointment of Lord Brassey—president of the Barnardo Homes—as Governor-General of Western Australia led to discussions about financial backing for more official schemes. However, a debate in Parliament questioned whether Australia really needed cheap child labour when many other migrants were arriving. A possibility of sending out girls instead was mooted, but no official emigration took place until after the First World War.

By then, Barnardo was dead. He died in 1905, in the year that emigration reached its peak and 1,300 children were sent to Canada. Sixty boys followed the hearse through the crowded East End streets to Liverpool Street station. He was buried in the Girls' Village at Ilford.

Barnardo's wife carried on his work and between 600 and 1,000 children annually continued to go out to Canada until 1915, when the First World War made transporting them dangerous. A few years before the First World War a new political mood embraced child migration, seeing it as an imperial work supplying human 'Bricks for Empire-Building'. On the ground, however, the prospect of emigration among the Homes and their wards was starting to meet with reservations. In 1910 the Executive Committee of the Girls' Village was informed by the governor that the girls were not keen on going to Canada, and that they were supported by their relatives in this. The Council minuted that the opinions of 'respectable parents ... should not be disregarded' and that the objections of a girl in her teens should be taken into consideration. In 1912 the Governor of Stepney Causeway highlighted some of the problems with emigration: 'So let me say in all frankness that Canada ... is not to many of us the bright and joyous world that you would fain paint it. Your Canada parties break across our Home Life. The schoolmaster laments his cleverest pupils, the shop masters lose their top boys ... and all because of the detestable "Canada List".'[37]

In Canada, while public opinion was growing cooler towards child migrants, the department overseeing the programme was all in favour. George Bogue Smart, the Inspector of British Immigrant Children and Receiving Homes, had been appointed in December 1899 by the Canadian Department of the Interior. He attended conferences in Britain and was sympathetic to the aims of British philanthropists, although he did criticize their methods. He succeeding in tightening up the system by, for example, ensuring that the Canadian inspections of the children in their homes were more careful and that health examinations of children entering the country were more rigorous.

In 1915 Barnardo's dispatched 293 children to Canada. Many Barnardo boys had enlisted to fight in the war, and so more help was needed on the farms. However, this was the last group until 1920, when another batch of 581 children was sent out by Barnardo's. By that time, the direction of child migration was changing. The Empire Settlement Act of 1922 included money to support juvenile emigration to any of the colonies, and Australia became a viable option.

In 1924 the British government sent out a delegation headed by Margaret Bondfield to investigate child emigration. Their conclusion was that while they generally approved the work and believed that a child's prospects were better in Canada than in England, children should only go out when they were of working age. In reference to Barnardo's, they pointed out that the children were worked too hard on the farms. A year later, the Canadian government temporarily banned children under 14 unaccompanied by their parents from emigrating—a ban that was made permanent in 1928. This did not stop those over 14 coming to Canada, but the Depression in the 1930s saw the need for child labour sharply diminish.

As the goalposts of child emigration shifted, Barnardo's had become the dominant organization in the field. The early 1920s had been a period of acquisition, as Barnardo's took over the operation of the Liverpool Sheltering Homes as well as the work of Annie Macpherson and the Marchmont Home at Belleville (p.29), although the latter was to close in 1925. In the years after the First World War and before the Canadian government's ban, no less than 43 Boards of Guardians had used Barnardo's to emigrate children, as had several other organizations.[38] Even after 1925 some children continued to be sent to Canada, such as J.W.H. who arrived in April 1931; confronted by practical farmwork, he noted the limitations of the training offered by the Liverpool Sheltering Homes: 'We used to go to the Corporation Stables of Liverpool City to learn about Horses and Cattle, but we really did not learn that much not even how to milk a cow.' The annual report stated that 79 boys had been sent to Canada in 1930, but emigration appeared to have stopped in 1933. The final minutes of July 1933 discussed repairs, but made no mention of emigration.

As the Second World War approached, Barnardo's activities in Canada were drawing to a close. Both the Hazelbrae and Toronto Homes shut in 1939, and an aftercare facility was established instead, which stayed open until 1963. Shortly before war broke out the last party of Barnardo's children arrived in Canada, and the end of an era seemed to have been reached. Not quite, however—the very last Barnardo's boy, aged 18, arrived by air in 1948, following a special request by a former Barnardo boy for someone from Barnardo's to help on his Canadian farm.

Chapter 4

The Catholic emigration movement

Many of our children are sent to Canada, where a prosperous
career is opened before them... But the children are rescued
chiefly from the crowded courts and alleys of the city, with
knowledge and associations of the pavement and the gaslight
rather than the field and open sky... Patient study and scientific
treatment of the children are needed ... [to awaken] the love
of such things as are to form their environment; failing which
they may lose heart in the great lone land, and drift back to
the squalid life of crowded cities.
St Peter's Net, 1904

IN THE 1870s the organizations that rescued children from the urban
slums and sent them to Canada, such as those of Annie Macpherson,
William Quarrier and James Fegan, were mainly run by evangelical
Protestants. Catholic children were among those emigrated to Protestant homes, which meant that they were brought up to adopt non-
Catholic religious practices. The Catholic Church was deeply
concerned about this loss of faith, and desperately needed to establish
well-organized and well-funded institutions to deal with the poor and
destitute among its flock. Yet it had suffered from centuries of discrim-
ination and was struggling to deal with enormous growth in its congregation and the social problems that came in its wake.

The scale of the increase showed the challenge facing the Church.
Government figures show that the Catholic population increased ten-
fold between 1767 and 1851, from 80,000 to 800,000. Sheer weight of
numbers was not the only factor—the nature of the congregation also
changed from rural to urban, immigrant and poor.[1] The Irish Potato
Famine of 1845–9 resulted in a huge influx of Catholic Irish immigrants to the mainland, especially to the major western ports. A plaque
on the gates to Clarence Dock in Liverpool is inscribed: 'Through
these gates passed most of the 1,300,000 Irish migrants who fled from
the Great Famine and "took the ship" to Liverpool in the years 1845–

52.' Many of them travelled on to other continents, but many others did not, and by 1851 nearly a quarter of Liverpool's population was Irish. The migrants came to Glasgow as well, increasing the Irish population by two per cent compared to Liverpool's five per cent between 1841 and 1851.[2]

The winds of change

The Church had been gaining ground in Britain for several decades. The gradual improvement in the restrictions against Catholics had begun in the late 18th century, when a series of acts were passed allowing Catholics to own land, inherit property and join the Army. They culminated in the Catholic Relief Act of 1829, which lifted most of the remaining restrictions and enabled Catholics to stand for Parliament. This new freedom needed to be reflected in the Church through stronger administrative structures and more manageable diocesan territories. The pope reinstated the Catholic hierarchy in 1850, and bishops responsible to their own dioceses replaced the vicars apostolic, primarily responsible to the pope. The Church now had the freedom to address the problems in each diocese and could put in place an administrative network to assist the improvements it needed to make.

Nicholas Wiseman was appointed cardinal in 1850 and became the first Archbishop of Westminster, the Catholic primate of England. Formerly Vicar of the London District, he had spent much of his time at the Vatican, sparking alarm in the Anglican Church with his new and powerful position as archbishop. To reassure the Protestant nation Wiseman wrote an Appeal, stressing that his main concern was not with power but rather with the socially deprived:

> Close under the Abbey of Westminster there lie concealed labyrinths of lanes and courts, and alleys and slums, nests of ignorance, vice, depravity, and crime, as well as of squalor, wretchedness, and disease; whose atmosphere is typhus, whose ventilation is cholera; in which swarms a huge an almost countless population... This is the part of Westminster which alone I covet, and which I shall be glad to visit, as a blessed pasture ... in which a Bishop's godly work has to be done, of consoling; converting and preserving.[3]

Wiseman was determined to act on his word. He began setting up reformatories and schools, such as St Stephen's Reformatory, Blyth

House, Hammersmith, in 1855 and St Nicholas' Catholic Industrial School for Boys, originally founded in Walthamstow in 1862 and later moved to the former home of Elizabeth Fry, the Quaker social reformer, in Ilford.

Following Wiseman's death in 1865, his successor, Cardinal Henry Edward Manning, continued this work with great vigour, believing that 'the care of children is the first duty after, and even with, the salvation of our own soul'.[4] Due to Manning's insistence, Catholic children in the workhouses had instruction in the Catholic faith, but much negotiation with the Poor Law Guardians was needed before the Poor Law Acts of 1866 and 1868 were passed, legally requiring Guardians to send Catholic children to Catholic schools. The Church for its part made this easier for the Guardians by charging them less than the usual amount given from the rates to educate a child—a viable proposition as many Catholic schools were run by religious orders whose members gave their services free. For example, the Sisters of Mercy, founded in 1840 and the first religious house in Birmingham since the Reformation, opened its own school, St Mary's, in 1850 at Handsworth; for a short time it ran a teachers' training school there as well. The Sisters of Charity of St Paul, whose convent was founded in 1864 in Selly Park, have run St Edward's School since its opening, while The Sisters of Notre Dame, founded in France as an order dedicated to the education of girls, opened their school in Plymouth, Devon, 150 years ago.

The Westminster Diocesan Educational Fund gave funds to establish and maintain industrial schools, reformatories, orphanages and rescue homes. As Archbishop of Westminster, Manning worked together with the diocese of Southwark, then comprising Surrey, Kent, Sussex, Berkshire, Hampshire and the Channel Islands. A committee selected individuals to enter the rescue homes, basing its decisions primarily on whether a Catholic child or children were judged likely to be lost to the Church. A typical case at the end of the 19th century appears in *St Peter's Net*, the Westminster diocese magazine:

> CASE E. 280. B___ Two girls, 9 and 7. Father (non-Catholic) deserted family five years ago. Mother (Catholic) has struggled on, trying to keep home together by charing. Finds she cannot manage to do so any longer. If she enters the Workhouse with the children, they will be sent to non-Catholic schools as their father is a non-Catholic. She appeals

to our Society ... the Committee accept. As no payment can be made towards maintenance, this means an outlay of £26 a year. It is in such cases as these that we see the evils of a mixed marriage.

The same motivation lay behind emigration. The Catholic authorities, along with all child-rescuers, believed that Canada would give pauper children a better chance of improving their lives, and that emigration was a practical response allowing more children to be taken in at home. However, keeping children in the faith was their primary concern. Leaving emigration solely to non-Catholic organizations would inevitably result in Catholic children leaving the church of their birth. The Catholic organizations recognized they had to offer opportunities abroad for their own children, 'to come to the front and protect at all and every sacrifice, these treasures of the Church of God'.[5]

The early years of emigration

At the start of Catholic child emigration, each diocese was in charge of sending its own children to Canada. The organization of this was amateur and uncoordinated, relying as it did on individual priests, Catholic orphanages and convents, plus other sources of help that the Church in Canada could provide. Nevertheless, it was an attempt to respond to the children's particular circumstances, and it began at a very early stage. The very first Catholic priest to take children to Canada, a contemporary of Rye and Macpherson, was Father Nugent.

James Nugent was born on 3 March 1822 in Liverpool, son of an Irish Catholic and a mother who had converted into the faith. He trained at the Catholic seminary Ushaw College, Durham, and then studied in Rome, returning to Liverpool in 1846 to be ordained. The city at that time was flooded with Irish immigrants escaping the famine. They lived in overcrowded slum conditions where illness was rife; many children were orphaned and left to live on the streets. Nugent worked across the city to set up Catholic orphanages, mother-and-baby homes and hostels for single men and women. He was particularly keen on establishing schools, convinced not only that education was the way out of poverty, but also because, as he said, 'genius and talent runs to waste in the gutters of our large towns in England'. Realistic about the temptations and dangers of the streets, he also spearheaded the campaign to 'Save the Boy' by setting up a refuge at Soho Street. Here boys were taught to read and write, as well as being trained in shoe-making, tailoring, woodwork and even printing—the *Catholic Times* was printed there each week. In 1869 the refuge was moved to larger premises, yet—as all the philanthropists were discovering—there was never enough room. Moral and practical concerns were a powerful imperative, and so Father Nugent decided to emigrate some children to Canada.

This was a new idea at the time as the later 19th-century phase of emigration was only just beginning. Maria Rye had taken her first group of children to Canada in October 1869, followed by Annie Macpherson in May 1870. Father Nugent was as much a pioneer as they were, and in some ways he was more astute; he was anxious, for example, to keep the Liverpool authorities on his side. At a meeting of Poor Law Guardians, magistrates and other interested parties, Nugent explained his plans to take children to Canada for 'adoption' into Catholic families and then to go on a lecture tour to raise money for his scheme.

Father Nugent left Liverpool with his party of children on 19 August 1870. They sailed via Londonderry to Quebec on the SS *Austrian*, arriving on 28 August. Nugent is quoted in Canon Bennett's biography as saying that he brought out 24 children, but the passenger list published on the internet by *Olive Tree Genealogy* actually shows 35.[6] It reveals that several of the children may have been related, with probable sisters of 10 and 14, brothers of 14 and 11 and two possible pairs of twins, aged 13 and 14 respectively. Two of the girls, Catherine D. and Ellen B., were only eight, and there were other emigrants of 19 and 21, but the majority were aged between 10 and 16. The children were taken to Montreal where homes and work were found for them in the area, but aftercare provisions appear slight, having much in common with Maria Rye's. Nugent's intention was 'to secure, if possible, in each locality I visit, two or three gentlemen, large hearted men, men of intelligence, who will take an active interest in this work: who will be the means of communicating between me and those who are prepared to receive children, and who will further report to me from time to time upon the conduct of these young settlers.'[7] In reality such limited supervision left the children isolated, their only contact with those who had placed them dependent on a chance visit from a benevolent gentleman. Optimism and confidence about their future would not prove adequate, and as child emigration became more established their deficiencies were to be regularly exposed.

Father Nugent continued to send children to Canada for another 20 years, sometimes under the auspices of other organizations. Of a group of children sailing to Quebec on the SS *Sarmatian*, for example, 15 were assigned to Father Nugent on the passenger list and the rest of those on board to Maria Rye. Nugent's emigration work won approval from the Catholic press, and in 1896, the golden jubilee of his ordination, the *Catholic Fireside* acknowledged his enduring success: 'Many of those whom Father Nugent found homes for years ago in the United States and Canada are now owners of houses, cattle and land, besides being persons of position in the town and city in which they reside.'

Father Nugent's emigration of children encouraged the archdiocese of Westminster to follow suit. It started its own emigration programme in 1874 with the formation of the Canadian Catholic Emigration Society, appointing as secretary Father Richard Seddon, also secretary to Cardinal Manning. Seddon accompanied the children to Canada, where they were sent to families in the eastern townships of Quebec and the Ottawa area. Aftercare provisions, in the manner of Rye and Macpherson (see chapter 1), were limited, lacking a coherent system and relying on visits by the local clergy. Like Nugent he sent groups— never very big—with those of other organizations. In July 1881, for instance, he took out 11 children on the *Circassian*; in the same month, Father Nugent accompanied 12 children, but Miss Rye's party of girls numbered 49. The Society had no receiving Home in Canada so the children were housed in Catholic institutions, such as St Nicholas' Institute, Toronto—run by the Sisters of St Joseph—until they were placed. Father Seddon continued this work until September 1898 when, escorting a party of 31 children and a matron on the *Numidian*, he died of a heart attack on the voyage.

The organization of Catholic child migration improved with the formation of the Liverpool Catholic Children's Protection Society in 1880. Founded by Bishop O'Reilly of Liverpool, the Society had its own hostel in the city to accommodate Catholic children emigrating to Canada. On arrival in Canada the children went to a receiving Home in Montreal, where an agent was responsible for them. Kohli says that some children went to St Vincent's, Montreal, where a Miss Agnes Brennan was in charge of arrangements; others went to the Reverend

G.M. Godts of St Ann's Church in Montreal.[8] The party was accompanied by Margaret Lacy, who worked for the Society, and the well-structured system allowed more children to be dispatched at one time, making the journeys more efficient. In September 1887, for example, Lacy accompanied a party of 99 children on board the *Circassian* to Quebec. Financial pressures were always acute, however, and they finally caused the Liverpool Society to stop emigrating children in 1902.

The 'tug of faith' children

Despite the work of Father Nugent and others in sending children to Canada, many of the young and destitute remained in Britain, their futures as Catholics the subject of increasing concern. In the autumn of 1884 Dr Herbert Vaughan, Bishop of Salford, decided to discover just how many children were being lost to Catholicism through parental neglect, the workhouse system and the intervention of evangelical societies. He instructed his clergy to put into effect a house-to-house census of the whole Catholic population of Manchester and Salford, then estimated at 100,000, and to account for every child.

By May 1886 the census was complete: three-quarters of the Catholic population had been registered and 8,445 children under 16 were deemed in danger of losing their ties to the Church.[9] In response, Vaughan established the Salford Catholic Protection and Rescue Society, explaining his action in a pamphlet called *The Loss of Our Children*. In this he said that while he gave the proselytizing institutions credit for their dedication, he saw their anti-Catholicism as a threat; English Catholics must consequently not 'be behind the times, but ... found their own associations for educating their waifs and strays'. Innovative ideas were welcomed. One Catholic institution, for example, St Joseph's in Manchester, was originally established as a boys' Home, but Vaughan changed it into a Home for both boys and girls — a novel scheme for the time which enabled siblings to keep in contact and prevented family break-up. In 1892 Vaughan succeeded Manning as Archbishop of Westminster, and in 1898 he founded the Crusade of Rescue to provide homes for destitute Catholic children. Administration for this later passed to Father Bans, who in 1903 established the Catholic Emigration Association, the organization involved in emigrating children to Canada and Australia.

As well as actively promoting the establishment of schools, the Catholic Church began to resist attempts by evangelical philanthropists to rescue Catholic children. One of their targets was Dr Barnardo, the rules of whose Homes prohibited him or his officials from removing children on religious grounds. Barnardo's reluctance to hand over Catholic children led to some high-profile court cases, including, in 1888, those of two children, Harry Gossage and Martha Tye, who had been emigrated to Canada. These and the other Barnardo cases described here are found in the 25th Annual Report held by the National Archives (HO 144/310/B6159).

Harry Gossage was an 11-year-old boy whose mother had sold him to two organ-grinders she met in a public house in the spring of 1888. They took him around the country with them for a while, then abandoned him in Folkestone. The child was found wandering the streets and put into the town's workhouse; he was discovered there by the local vicar, who asked Barnardo's to take him in. Mrs Gossage was traced and signed a formal agreement with Barnardo's, allowing Harry to stay in the home; his father was dead and she could not keep him. However, she did not sign the 'Canada' clause, which would have formally allowed for Harry's emigration.

In November 1888, a wealthy Canadian, Mr William Norton, visited Barnardo's, and a chain of events began to unfold. The Times wrote a scathing article on 2nd December in which Dr Barnardo was quoted as saying, 'His object in seeing me was that he was anxious to find a nice-looking boy not older than 10 or 11, one who was not likely to be interfered with by his relatives, as he wished, if he liked him, to adopt him as his son.'

Mr Norton was 'an absolute stranger' who to avoid any interference withheld his address. However, he had brought with him a letter of introduction from a clergyman, and on the strength of this and his own impressions Barnardo accepted the offer. The Times commented that Barnardo should have ensured that this nice-looking boy was wanted 'for good purposes and not for bad', and he certainly deserved criticism for allowing a stranger to take a boy away without a follow-up address. Harry Gossage was the chosen boy and he was taken by Norton to Canada.

Harry's mother was a Catholic, and not long after he had been sent to Canada Barnardo received a request on behalf of Mrs Gossage that she wanted her son to be transferred to St Vincent's Catholic Home. Barnardo replied that the Homes' rules forbade them from removing children on religious grounds, only later revealing that Harry was actually abroad. Supported by the Catholic Church, Mrs Gossage eventually issued a writ of *habeas corpus*, giving Barnardo three months in which to produce her son. But Barnardo no longer knew where Harry was, and under these circumstances there was no way in which the court could force him to produce the boy.

The other court case occurred at the same time and involved a girl of 14 called Martha Ann Tye. She had approached Muller's Orphanage in Bristol of her own accord, and the orphanage asked Barnardo to take her in. She had been sexually assaulted by her mother's lover, who had been sent to gaol for the offence, but after his sentence was served he married Martha's mother. The child's life became intolerable, hence her desire to escape from her home. Martha's mother agreed to her daughter's staying at Barnardo's for two years, but—crucially—she did not sign the 'Canada' clause. Later she changed her mind and sent a letter asking for her daughter to come back, eventually threatening legal action. Only then did Barnardo disclose that, like Harry Gossage, Martha was now in Canada.

Barnardo's story was that a widow called Madame Gertrude Romande had come to the home and taken away a few girls to train for domestic service, one of whom was Martha. The widow was never traced and some doubt has been cast on the story. Madame Romande may never have existed at all, and Martha may have been hidden at a secret address before being emigrated to Canada.[10] Whatever the truth, Martha, like Harry, was never produced, and the court concluded that Martha had been emigrated to avoid her being returned to a Catholic institution.

Emigration was the defining factor in both these cases, as officials were simply unable to trace the children. Other cases, where the children were still in England, had a different outcome. One of them involved a boy of 10, John James Roddy, who was admitted to Barnardo's in June 1888. According to Barnardo, he 'lived in a chronic condition of misery and want. He was constantly observed late at night in the streets while, it was alleged, his mother was in public-houses; he was insufficiently clothed and fed; his mother ... spent nearly all her earnings in drink.'[11] His mother signed an agreement leaving him to

Barnardo's care for 12 years, and gave her religion as Protestant. She subseqeuntly applied for her son's return through the solicitors conducting the Gossage and Tye cases, saying that in fact she was a Catholic. The case came to court, and as Barnardo had not sent the child overseas and there was nothing to impede the mother's rights, Barnardo was duly ordered to return him.

Another case was that of a 13-year-old orphan named William Murphy. His mother admitted to being a Roman Catholic on her deathbed, although she had called herself a Protestant throughout her life and had brought her son up as one. William was accepted by Barnardo's, but an application was made to the court 'to appoint as the boy's guardian a well-known Roman Catholic nobleman'. The judge spoke to the boy to find out what he would prefer, to which William replied that he wanted to be brought up as a Catholic. He went on to complain about Barnardo's, bewildering the Home's authorities as he had previously stated that he was happy there. When the Home's chairman asked William why he had changed his mind, it transpired that the boy had been punished for a misdemeanour by being deprived of his dinner just before the judge spoke to him. Barnardo commented wryly on how such an accident of timing could determine an entire future: 'And so, with a keen, though passing, sense of dissatisfaction, sharpened by an eager appetite, he had expressed himself in such an emphatic manner as to convince the learned Judge that it would really be the best thing to hand this Protestant boy of 13 ½ years of age over to the care of a Roman Catholic guardian until he ceased to be a minor!'[12]

Despite the criticism and adverse publicity such cases aroused, Barnardo was unrepentant. He denied the charge of proselytism and vigorously defended himself in the 25th Annual Report:

> The return of the children has been refused (with two exceptions) *not upon the ground of the religion of the applicants*, but solely on account of their *character*. It was to save the boy Gossage from a cruel and immoral mother that he was sent to Canada; it was to guard the girl Martha Ann Tye from a weak and silly woman, who had grossly neglected her, and from the influences of an immoral man, that she was sent abroad.[13]

The press coverage of these cases raised awareness of the parental neglect and cruelty that some children suffered, and the sordid conditions that they had to endure. Voices of authority entered the fray: the Assistant Commissioner of Police for London railed against 'the divine right of vicious and brutal parents to make their children brutal and vicious'. In 1891 the Custody of Children Act (known as the Barnardo Act) was passed, in which parents' rights were restricted for the first time. Parents considered 'unfit' had to prove they were not so in a court before a child could be restored to them; and the child was also to be consulted. This was an important step as far as the rescue homes were concerned, giving them some legal power over the children in their care.

However, litigious relations between Barnardo and the Catholic Church continued, with neither side willing to concede. Only in 1899, when an agreement was reached between Barnardo and Cardinal Vaughan, who had succeeded Manning in 1892, did relations begin to improve. As part of the arrangement, Barnardo undertook to notify the Westminster diocese of all applications he received on behalf of Catholic children. When Barnardo died in 1905, his obituary in the magazine *St Peter's Net* generously praised his achievements. Headed 'A great philanthropist', it paid warm tribute to his life and work: 'However theological differences may divide, in charity all men can unite, and we offer out tribute of ungrudging praise to one who has devoted a whole lifetime of singular energy and concentrated enthusiasm to the noble work of rescuing the friendless waifs of our cruel cities.'

Nor were the Catholics themselves above refusing to return children in their care. A particularly sad case documented in the National Archives (HO 144/524/X76100) concerns a young boy, Francis Allen (plate 14). In 1897, when he was six years old, his mother asked his aunt Rhoda Coles to look after the six-year-old boy, but when Mrs Coles became ill she returned Frank to his mother. She promptly handed him over to a cousin, Joseph Allen, a Catholic, who failed to care for the boy. After he was found wandering in the streets, Joseph Allen agreed that the child should be placed in a Catholic institution, St Vincent's Industrial School. A report on Frank for St Vincent's gives his religion as Catholic and describes his circumstances in a bleak light:

> Found wandering and not having any Home or settled place of abode, or proper guardianship, or visible means of subsistence. Mother was turned out of her lodgings a fortnight ago, since then has been sleeping in lodging houses. She has not been seen for several days. Her character very questionable.[14]

When Coles recovered, she wanted to offer Frank a home. The records show that she was interviewed by the Southwark Divisional Superintendent who found her and her husband, a plumber, quiet and respectable; they were comfortably off with a six-room house and they had a son who regularly attended school. The Superintendent recommended that the child be returned to his aunt, but Canon Edward St John of the Southwark diocese refused to do so as the family were devout members of the Salvation Army. Neither St John nor the aunt would give up, and the case was sent to the Home Secretary to be resolved. Eventually a compromise—not necessarily in Frank's best interests—was reached. His elder brother Alfred, who had been placed with the Lambeth Poor Law Guardians, had been sent by them to Canada, and in the end St John agreed to release the child if he were sent to his brother in Canada. In January 1901 the Home Office decided that this was the best course of action for the now 10-year-old boy. Catholic intransigence had denied him a good home with his aunt, where he would have been cared for and educated; instead, he was sent abroad to work.

Putting down roots in Canada

The Southwark Diocesan Council and Rescue Society that played a large part in Frank Allen's life was formed in 1887 by Bishop Butt. The emigration arm was called the Southwark Catholic Emigration Society; it was run by Canon Edward St John, who personally accompanied Catholic children to Canada over many years. At first his work was confined to emigrating children between 10 and 14 from Catholic orphanages, but in April 1893 he took a party of 40 older boys, aged between 16 and 20, to Quebec. This St John believed was the 'first attempt as far as I know in which any Catholic organization had tried to help big lads to start afresh on the other side of the Atlantic', and again his motivation was the fact that older boys were finding their way to Canada through Protestant agencies.

As Catholic organizations became more involved with emigration, the needs of the process became more pressing. In 1895 the Southwark Catholic Emigration Society decided to open a receiving Home in Ottawa, a favoured location and 'the centre of a splendid country in Ontario, where we can place a large number of children with prosperous Catholic and Irish Canadian farmers; it is essential that the children should be with men fairly prosperous, otherwise they will be made to do labour for which their age unfits them...' New Orpington Lodge was opened in October of that year in Hintonburg, now part of Ottawa, and two parties of about 30 children stayed at the receiving Home in the first year. The Lodge was then bought for £600 by the Society and remained in their possession until the 1940s. It was the Catholics' main—and later only—receiving Home.

St John returned six years later to see what had become of his 'big lads'. He found that a quarter of them were earning wages that they would never have had a chance of getting in England. Another 10 boys had moved away from the area in which they had been placed, so although St John did not visit them he heard that they had work. Another 10 had not done well and had returned to England or gone elsewhere; and two had died, leaving a few unaccounted for. He felt that he was glad something had been done by a Catholic charity, 'even if it was not perfectly done'.

However, St John had realized early on that the area round Montreal was 'not at all a good centre from which to place them', and resolved to look for a more appropriate location. When Father Archibald Douglas, manager of the St Vincent's Home in Harrow, London, joined St John in his search, they decided to set up a farm out west—a place where their London boys could work for a year and get used to Canadian life. They did this despite the fact that there were not many Catholics in that part of Canada.

The farm, called New Southwark, near the new town of Makinak, Manitoba, was opened in 1897. The land belonged to the government and Father Basil Gaisford was put in charge of the boys. St John described it in *Boys and Girls*, the diocese quarterly journal, in glowing terms:

> The farm is situated in a lovely spot, a few miles north of the Riding
> Mountain which is covered with good timber and forms a lovely view
> from the new home... There is also abundance of dead timber on the
> farm that will serve for fuel for many years. This dead timber is the
> remains of a former forest which was cleared by a great fire some five
> years ago. The soil, deep and black, is extraordinarily fertile, and is
> well suited for grain, while there are also some hundreds of acres of
> beaver grass... This abundance of hay will we hope be of great value as

our stock, as [sic] beasts increase. The uncleared ground is covered with ground fruit of almost every description. Raspberries, currants, gooseberries, cranberries, wild cherries, blueberries, hops and wild strawberries grow in the greatest profusion. The country is full of game, which can be had for the shooting ...[15]

From this description it is easy to understand why the unspoilt land and its abundance was so appealing to the priests who wanted to give their London boys a clean break and a new start in life. The farm had all the ingredients of what St John calls a 'boy settler's paradise', and some of the letters from those emigrated there reflect the excitement of the new environment. Two from boys emigrated to the New Southwark farm were published in *Boys and Girls,* January 1898. Arthur M. described haymaking in this wild country with obvious relish:

> The wolves still continue their evening concert. There was one the other day pretty daring in our hayfields; he stood behind a haycock playing with the mice, taking no notice of us pitching hay, till the rifle was sent for, one bullet grazed him and caused him to jump and bound into the bush... We have some wild geese and shot plenty of (prairie) chickens since you left.

And his friend W.C. O'C. vividly conveyed the strangeness of the new land in his letter to Father St John: 'while out hunting, we heard the cry of a mountain lion ... it is horrible, it is more like a human being in great distress; they say it is like a bear only more fleet and fierce; once they used to run after the great herds of buffalo...' These new and sometimes wondrous experiences were only possible because of the opportunities that emigration provided, creating links to a new homeland to replace ties left behind. The resilience and courage of young migrants undoubtedly contributed to their success, enabling them to establish new roots in the unfamiliar, often inhospitable terrain.

As St John was praising New Southwark, the needs of girl migrants were also being addressed. The same edition of *Boys and Girls* reported that a Miss Proctor had been appointed to supervise the emigration of Catholic girls from a base at St Ann's Home, Montreal—both a Home and a distribution centre. The Local Government Board in England had approved the Society's emigration scheme for girls for a year, requesting a full report at the end of that period. Part of this approval seemed to be based on the aftercare arrangements that Proctor had made with the Children of Mary, Sisters from the Sacred Heart

Convent, who had taken on the role of visiting the girls after they had been placed out. The Society became the legal guardian of the girls who came to Canada, a status confirmed in a contract signed by their employers. The contract also dictated the amount of each girl's earnings, and stated that she had to be returned to the home after 15 days' notice when the engagement terminated. Each girl's wages were to be paid to Miss Proctor and put in a bank account, enabling the authorities to keep control of individual finances: 'the money placed in the bank cannot be spent either by me or by you without the consent of both.' Out of this the girls had to pay their expenses, which were kept as low as possible. 'The charge for staying in the Home is two dollars a week (8/-) or ten cents (about 5d) a meal. It is made as low as possible for the sake of our younger members. There are only three rules, about cleanliness and order, reasonable quiet morning and evening, and attendance at mass.'

Miss Proctor had ambitious plans for her Home, as she noted, 'I hope next year for a better sitting room, and I hope this same year for a piano.' Thriftiness was a perceived virtue, and the girls were encouraged to save—a habit that officials hoped would sustain them in later lives.

> One-half the misery, debt, and some of the sin comes from wasteful habits. If a girl who is only earning three dollars a month, just puts by something every month, it enables her to buy good clothes which last longer, and are nicer and more becoming at the same time. The habit of saving once formed, you will all go on with it…

The letters from children in Canada chosen for publication in the diocesan magazines told, naturally, of the positive side of emigration. Yet they also give real insights into their lives there, and the challenges that boys and girls faced in settling into their new lives. Willingness to adapt was the real key to success, and it could take some unexpected forms. Violet McM., writing in *St Peter's Net* in 1906, appears a resourceful 12 year old, about to embark on learning a new language to bring her closer to the people in her new world.

> I live in a country place near the sea… There are cows, horses, pigs, sheep and chickens. There are three cows that we milk. We have different money in Canada, we have cents and dollars; a dollar in English money is four and twopence … I am going to learn Gaelic after a while. Gaelic is the Scottish language; nearly all the people speak it in Canada. We call shops stores, and trams trolley cars, and carriages teams.

The Catholic Emigration Association

The Southwark Catholic Emigration Society merged with the Canadian Catholic Emigration Society, keeping the latter name, after Father Seddon's death in 1898. In 1903 Arthur Chilton Thomas, barrister and manager of Father Berry's Homes in Liverpool, and Father Emmanuel Bans of Westminster, London, founded the Catholic Emigration Association. The organization aimed to provide an umbrella for various Catholic diocesan welfare agencies wishing to undertake child emigration, and the Society acted as the children's legal guardian in Canada until they reached 18. Father George Vincent Hudson of Birmingham, active in work with destitute children in Coleshill, a parish of the city, became the secretary. Hudson's work with pauper children became celebrated in the Midlands, and the Rescue Society he established was known as Father Hudson's Homes. The name was officially recognized as a tribute after his death in 1936.

The Catholic Emigration Association was set up in direct response to a recommendation from Father Bans and Chilton Thomas. Their report, entitled 'Child Migration to Canada', was produced in 17 November 1902, after a three-month fact-finding visit to Canada the same year. They had gone to Canada 'in order to satisfy ourselves as to the advisability of child emigration from a spiritual, moral and material point of view' and they were thorough in this task, personally visiting 302 child migrants. They described how the Catholic children sent to Canada fell into four distinct groups:

Helpers (aged 10 to 13 years) The boys and girls helped on farms and the girls also acted as domestics.

Workers (over 14 years) Farm work done by boys. This group had the most failures due to problems in adjusting to farm life after their previous city life.

Placed in families as though adopted (up to nine years) Educated and treated as one of the family, with maintenance paid and regular visits. It was argued that the younger children were the most successfully placed as they soon forgot England and grew up as Canadians.

Boarded out (up to nine years) Placed with farmers at a cost of £1.1s.0d per month or in an institution from £12 to £15 a year. The children were educated and trained, becoming helpers at the age of 11.

The situation of the children under 18 seemed satisfactory; none were in police custody, and priests spoke well of them, with few exceptions. In fact, some of the priests themselves were criticized for their lack of sympathy towards the children. Migrants aged over 18 proved more difficult to trace; out of these, five had entirely given up the faith, three were considered 'mentally deficient', 10 girls had gone 'morally wrong', one boy was in prison and seven had been or were in reformatories.[16] This was only a very small proportion of those who had been emigrated, however, and the majority were establishing themselves well.

Bans and Chilton also interviewed Canadian bishops, priests and nuns, as well as government ministers, magistrates, police and people involved in child emigration, both Catholic or Protestant. They concluded that the policy to emigrate children was a good one because 'at home they are at a disadvantage; in Canada they have grand advantages'. They went on to explain what these advantages were:

(1) Spiritually, because in Canada the Catholic Church is stronger, the Priests are more numerous, the number of Catholics is greater, and a more Catholic atmosphere prevails.
(2) Morally, because in Canada the standard of life even in the cities is much purer than in England, and the inhabitants are more temperate.
(3) Materially, because in Canada there are great and innumerable openings for boys and girls. There is no difficulty in getting work, there is no slackness, and anyone can get work at good wages.

Two years later, Bans and Chilton visited Canada again, seeking to effect a joint scheme between themselves and the Canadian child migration agencies. On 31 October 1904 they reported that this had been accomplished successfully, under the auspices of the Catholic Emigration Association. New Orpington Lodge in Hintonburg was enlarged, redecorated and renamed St George's Home, perhaps after the cathedral in Southwark, and the Association's agent in Canada, Cecil Arden, moved in. St George's Home became the Association's headquarters and a focus of Catholic child migration for the new century.

Bans and Chilton also wanted to see whether the system they had advocated two years previously was working. The problems experienced by the over-18s had been helped by the establishment of a Catholic Emigrated Old Boys and Girls Society. Members could keep in touch with the Society and each other for moral and practical support—and probably help further emigration by donations, since Father Bans had reported that they had seen many old boys and girls and 'cannot recall one who is not in comfortable circumstances, although we made a special effort to find such'. He did not make the point that the successful ones might be those who wanted to keep in contact, while those struggling or who had undergone traumatic times might prefer to lose touch with the organization that had sent them to Canada. George Bogue Smart, the Canadian inspector, was invited to the reunions of the Old Boys and Girls Society; he was full of enthusiasm, describing them as 'splendid institutions, beneficial to all'.

The 1902 report had also recommended a formal system of visiting agents, and this had been put into action. The figures reveal that by 1905 there were 1,147 Catholic children on the register in Canada, of which 301 had not been visited.[17] That same year, a number of boys who had 'given considerable trouble' were sent to lumber camps by Arden, under instruction from the Catholic Emigration Association. In 1907 the care of the St George's Home was moved from the emigration office's management and given to nuns from the Sisters of Charity of St Paul, which was consistent with practice in Britain. Mother Evangelist O'Keefe was put in charge, remaining until 1926; by 1909 she had a staff of 10: five Sisters, two clerks and two gentlemen who visited the children, although the Sisters themselves also helped in this respect.[18] The changes drew the attention of Bogue Smart who in 1913 praised the Association's work, calling it 'eminently useful... There are 1,600 children under supervision and visited regularly. From personal inspection and a perusal of their visitors' book a small number only were not doing well.'

However, the visiting system did not always protect children from ill-treatment, vividly revealed in an account written by one William Francis Conabree.[19] He was emigrated, aged 14, from Liverpool in 1904 and was sent to a farm, replacing a boy who was so thin and ill that Conabree wondered if he survived the trip back home. He also wondered why he had been sent to the same family, since this boy had been treated so badly. In his first year, he was 'without a soul to turn to for help, no writing paper, no money even to buy a stamp. I was forbidden to go outside the front gate by this farmer, for if I did he said he would horse whip me to death, and meant it.'

Conabree was whipped regularly and experienced appalling treatment for no other reason than being a 'dirty Englishman'. All the clothes he had brought with him had been given to the family's children and his letters destroyed (including, presumably, the notepaper and stamped addressed envelopes which the Association should have provided). He had no bed but slept in the kitchen, and was expected to work all day in the fields. At night the farmer and his wife would go to bed leaving him to wash all the dishes, scrub the floors and bake the bread: '… she would say "pity help you if you let it burn".' A visitor came after a few months and he had hopes of being taken away, but the visitor was related to one of the neighbours and so nothing happened. Winter time, as for so many children, was a severe trial. The farmer made him put his feet in ice-cold water, with the result that they froze and then swelled up, splitting open in places; his toenails even fell off. Conabree could not put on his shoes and had to go round with his feet tied in rags; another visitor came while his feet were in this condition and this time castigated the farmer. Unfortunately he did not take the boy away because he had to write a report first, during which time the farmer forced the boy to send a letter retracting his accusations. In the end Conabree had to run away to escape his hated employer. Eventually he was placed with an elderly French Canadian farmer who treated him much better; he stayed there for three years.

The issue of placing children with French-speaking families, since a large percentage of Catholics in Quebec and Ontario were of French origin, was a perennial concern. The 1902 report of Bans and Chilton had recommended that placing children in French-speaking families should be the exception, not the rule, and proposed printing the Association application forms in English only to discourage French applicants. However, it was felt that placing children under seven years of age in French homes was acceptable, as they would adapt more easily to the new customs and culture. The report, written after Bans and Chilton's second visit, stated:

> We are quite clear that in the majority of cases the children are better treated with the French than with the English, and that it is certainly of great advantage for a girl to be placed with the French on account of the extra refinement that she acquires. It is, however, certain that there is a prejudice here in England against placing with the French — simply because they are not English. We think on account of this prejudice it will be necessary to make a practice of not giving children who are sent for emigration by the public authorities the advantages of these better placings with the French.

As a result, children emigrated through Poor Law Guardians were placed only with English families, while those from Catholic homes continued to be sent to French-speaking ones. It is interesting to note that the report regarded French family life so favourably, and that it made no comment on how learning a foreign language would compound the difficulties of settling into a new land for a disorientated city child.

The quality, as might be expected, was variable. Some French Canadians gave good homes to children, others did not. The story of George Robbins, emigrated to Canada in 1905, was told by his grandchildren. Unhappy at his situation, he ran away to America, escaping

> the harsh conditions he found himself in by no choice of his own. He at times shared with his own children & grandchildren of his journey, running away crossing the ice (we believe the St Lawrence River) & arriving in New York, USA. By God's good grace he was united with the wonderful Benjamin family of Tupper Lake, NY, some time between 1905–1914, who raised him. He referred to this French Canadian family as his mother & father. Finally a place to call home. Parents to love, nurture & support him.[20]

In *Home Children*, George Sears tells of a different life with a French-speaking family, in which language difficulties only increase the alienation felt by the young boy:

> For some reason or other the mistress took a dislike to me... It seemed to me that every day when he (the farmer) got home, there was always a tale to be told about me. Although I did not understand the lingo at the time, I sensed the talk was about me at the dinner table. One fine day I'd had enough and I pointed a finger at her and said, 'You, *cochon*', and I made a dive out the back door...[21]

Placing children with French families continued to be a problem throughout the time of Catholic child emigration. Money was always a concern, mainly because the children were underpaid. In his article, Frederick McEvoy states that the French farmers of Quebec and eastern Ontario were known for paying low wages and Mother O'Keefe—the manager of St George's Home—was accused of tolerating this.[22] George Sears' description of his life shows the nature of the problem:

> From Ottawa I was sent back to a French farmer who had two big farms ... I worked there for nearly two years—no doubt for nothing.

When the nuns saw the money was not coming I was taken away to Ottawa again. The food was very good, but as elsewhere I was considered an outsider—an immigrant d'Angleterre… I was near 18, so I came to Ottawa to claim my fortune. I had written to Father Banns [sic] about the nuns having left me to work on some farms without pay. To my surprise the good man thought it his duty to send my letter to the Mother Superior in Ottawa. She wanted me to contradict what I said but I wouldn't. I told her she could keep my fortune made in six years of labour, but she gave it to me. If I recall correctly it was $70.[23]

When Mother O'Keefe's successor, Mother Francis, took over in October 1926, she said, 'I have no love at all for the homes around the Gatineau and had fully made up my mind to recall every boy gradually from that district.'[24] However, she was to prove no more successful than her predecessor since, in 1928–9, Smart reported that French-speaking farmers were paying only $4.00 a month when they should have been paying $10.00. In no uncertain terms he told Mother Francis, 'the only way I know of preventing your boys from being exploited is to refuse to give employers boys on terms which permit it'.[25] Nonetheless, she found support from the Deputy Minister of Immigration who acknowledged the fact that trying to persuade farmers to raise wages after they had been used to cheap labour was difficult and that Mother Francis had 'accomplished wonders with the work'. Yet in 1934 the same complaint of low wages was being made, in addition to the fact that an English boy had to make huge adjustments in his behaviour in order to live comfortably with a French family. Religion was still the deciding factor, and children were placed with French families, despite the difficulties this posed, because they were Catholic. However, at this point the problem was short-lived; St George's Home was to close in 1934.

During the First World War the number of children sent to Canada significantly declined, and by 1917 the British government had prohibited emigration. After the war, the Canadian government wanted to encourage the emigration of children once again. A meeting of the prime ministers of Canada, Australia and New Zealand in 1921 considered the following proposal put forward by the British Overseas Settlement Committee:

[That] His Majesty's Government in the United Kingdom co-operate with the Overseas Governments in a comprehensive policy of empire land settlement and empire directed migration extending over a period of years, and to this end to contribute up to a maximum of £2 million a year in any year in respect of schemes of land settlement, assisted passages and such other kindred schemes as may commend themselves to Governments concerned.[26]

This became part of the Empire Settlement Act of 1922, in which the UK and Canadian governments agreed to pay $40 per capita each towards the cost of sending children to Canada under the auspices of the voluntary agencies, so long as they were accepted as medically fit by the Canadian authorities.

The Catholic Emigration Association responded to this by sending over 400 children annually to Canada; St George's Home was enlarged to deal with the increase in numbers, helped by a Canadian government grant. Despite both governments' attitudes, however, child welfare organizations in Canada began to object to taking in the slum children of Britain. A further milestone was the 1924 report of Margaret Bondfield (parliamentary secretary to the Minister of Labour in the British government), who sensibly recommended that children who came to Canada to work should be of school-leaving age, which was 14. Shortly after, in 1925, the Canadian government banned entry to children under 14 unaccompanied by their parents. The focus of emigration began to shift, and Cardinal Bourne started the Catholic Emigration Society in 1927–8 to deal with emigration of families and adults. The Catholic Emigration Association remained independent, dealing with children under the age of 17; even five years after the ban, in 1930, St George's Home still had nearly 400 young people in its care.

The Depression impacted rapidly upon child migration, and the Deputy Minister of Immigration wrote to Mother Francis in May 1931: 'Every care should be taken not to bring in more boys that can be properly handled. There is no doubt that the falling returns from agriculture mean less employment and lower wages.'[27] In 1932 a hundred boys were allowed to go to St George's, but in April 1932 only 80 made up the quota—the last group of boys to be accommodated at the Home. Mother Francis returned to England and informed the Canadians that the work was to be run from Birmingham, signalling the end of an era that had transformed thousands of young lives. The Minutes of the Select Committee of the House of Commons on Health, 11 June 1998, estimates the total number of children emigrated to Canada by Catholic agencies to be over 10,000.

Yet the enthusiasm for child migration continued, and Catholic organizations began, like the others, to consider alternative destinations. Australia was a natural focus of interest, and in 1937 the Crusade of Rescue, the British Catholic organization for finding homes for destitute children, unveiled a proposal at its annual general meeting. Canon Craven suggested a migration scheme for British boys, aware that the Christian Brothers, a Catholic teaching order, were developing a farm school in Tardun, Western Australia (p.210). The scheme was endorsed by high-placed Australian politicians, such as prime minister Joseph Lyons and the premier of Western Australia, both of whom visited Britain that year. The following year saw the plans come to fruition when 37 Catholic boys were sent from Britain to Western Australia. They were welcomed with official receptions and warm greetings, the first of many young Catholic migrants sent to carve out new lives for themselves on the other side of the world.

Chapter 5

Farm Schools and Kingsley Fairbridge

Train these children to be farmers! Not in England. Teach
them in the land where they will farm. Give them gentle men
and women for their mentors and guides, and give them a farm
of their own where they may grow up among the gentle farm
animals, proud of the former, understanding the latter. Shift
the orphanages of Britain to where farmers and farmers' wives
are wanted, and where no man with strong arms and a willing
heart would ever want for his daily bread.

KINGSLEY FAIRBRIDGE, *Veld Verse*, 1909

BETWEEN 1869 and 1935, Britain sent over 100,000 children to Canada
through the child migration movement. As attitudes there began to
change, the 20th century saw other players entering the field—Australia, Rhodesia (now Zimbabwe) and the former destination of South
Africa, favoured by Brenton in the 1830s, all received child migrants of
varying ages. Many were sent under farm school schemes whose popularity reflected the growing emphasis upon improving the land, people
and prosperity of the British Empire.

The original idea of using farm schools within child migration
schemes came from Andrew Doyle, the Local Government Board
inspector who had investigated the projects of Maria Rye and Annie
Macpherson. His highly critical report, published in 1875, had encouraged the Board to suspend any emigration of workhouse children,
effectively curtailing Maria Rye's activities for two years and causing
much bitter recrimination between herself and Doyle. However, his
report also recognized that children trained in Canada by locals, gaining gradual familiarity with the country's people and climate, could
provide a very effective labour force for the Dominion. Doyle perceived
that many of the problems experienced in the schemes of Rye and

Macpherson were caused by the arbitrary selection and placement of unskilled children who were then left to cope as best they might. Although training children was clearly not without cost, he believed the end result would be much more valuable to the Canadian farms and homes where they were to work.

Perhaps the closest thing to Doyle's idea had been the industrial farm in Russell, Manitoba, established by Thomas Barnardo in 1887 (p.104). However, this was designed principally for older boys aged around 17 who would only stay there for a year before taking up labouring jobs on farms (they were obliged to accept any situation offered after receiving training at Manitoba). The investment was considerable, but Barnardo was ambitious for his school, envisaging it becoming noted for 'the character of its inmates and the thorough quality of the work done by them'. It was also well placed for the boys to gain farming experience, encompassing both river valley and prairie grassland.

Manitoba was in many ways a successful experiment: its buildings were well maintained and it gained a good reputation locally for dairy products. The school won recognition further afield too, receiving an official visit from the Governor-General, Lord Aberdeen, in 1897, but like many subsequent farm schools it ran into financial difficulties and finally closed in 1908 — a year before Kingsley Fairbridge's Child Emigration Society was founded. Later known as the Fairbridge Society, this was to become interlinked with the farm school concept and to impact upon thousands of children's lives.

The concept of farm schools emerged in various forms as different enthusiasms took hold. In 1902 Elinor Close founded a migration agency to develop the unusual idea known as the 'scattered farm system'.[1] In this, she sought to bring workhouse children aged between two and three years of age from Britain to farms in the western parts of Canada. Close's plan (not dissimilar to that of Fairbridge) was that 20 young children would be raised at her farms and sent to local schools. After leaving school, they would be placed on local farms to gain experience. Not surprisingly, she had problems convincing the Canadian authorities that bringing children as young as two years old to work on farms was a viable proposition, but the government of New Brunswick did agree to work with her to start a farm in that province with older children. In 1904 the government accordingly granted her 200 acres of land at Nauwigewauk, near Rothesay, to operate the Elinor Close Farm Home. In 1906 the first of Close's children came to Canada, though the scheme ended eight years later with the outbreak of the First World War.

Fairbridge had himself met Elinor Close and broadly supported her scheme, though the two did come into conflict and their desire to develop Canadian farm schools acquired a sharp competitive edge. Fairbridge, something of an innocent in charity fund-raising waters, was bitter over Close's jeopardizing of his plans for a farm school in Newfoundland—the first of his projects, and one that never material-ized. Accustomed to battling against the odds, however, he was not to be deterred.

The vision of Kingsley Fairbridge

Kingsley Fairbridge was to become the name most closely associated with the farm school movement, and he has been described as the founder of child colonization. He was born in Grahamstown, South Africa, in 1885, the elder son of Rhys Seymour Fairbridge, surveyor to the government of Cape Colony and later to the British South Africa Company. His parents moved to Rhodesia in 1896 and Fairbridge came to London five years later, aged 16. Here he witnessed the capi-tal's deprivation and poverty at first hand—children running wild in slums and gutters, women fighting and men beating their wives. As with Barnardo, it made a profound impression.

In 1906 Fairbridge was awarded a Rhodes scholarship to Oxford— no mean feat for a largely self-educated man—on his fourth attempt. At Exeter College, Oxford, he was able to refine his vision of how white settlers could cultivate and improve large areas of land in Rhodesia and his homeland, South Africa. This belief was combined with his acute awareness of the plight of destitute children in towns and cities across Britain. A logical solution—to emigrate some of the children in the slums to healthy farm lands in the Dominions—saw the creation of the Child Emigration Society, founded by Fairbridge at Oxford in 1909.

In the mould of Barnardo, Fairbridge was determined to pursue his plans overseas, but he was unable to establish a farm school in Canada. In 1912 he went instead to Western Australia, accompanied by his young bride Ruby Whitmore, in response to the offer of land from Sir John Scaddon, Premier of Western Australia. A local committee of the Society was formed in Perth, and a small farm of 160 acres (plus one horse, one cow, two pigs and about 70 poultry) near Pinjarra became the humble starting point of the farm school. Under pressure from the Oxford Committee to show quick results, Fairbridge constructed some simple accommodation for the school. It reflected the basic 'cottage home' plan that he and Ruby had seen in Barkingside before they left England, and which was to recur on many more Fairbridge sites. The hot summer was draining and demanding for the couple—Ruby was pregnant and Fairbridge suffered recurring bouts of malaria—but nevertheless the school was officially opened on 7 August 1912 (plate 16).

From the start, Fairbridge's commitment to his project was total. He drew on practical skills acquired in Rhodesia to serve as labourer, lumberman, gardener, poultry farmer and dairyman, and his wife acted as matron. In January 1913, 12 workhouse boys from London's East End came to live at the first school established at Pinjarra, 60 miles southeast of Perth (plate 17). Ruby, whose first child had been born four months earlier, was moved at the sight: Wagner quotes her as saying that it would have been hard to imagine 'a more incongruous, desolate little bundle of humanity'.[2] Clad in cheap suits and thick-nailed boots and clasping identical canvas bags, the children were also blistered and sunburnt—the result of Fairbridge's decision to let them swim at Fremantle in the baking summer heat.

As the Western Australia government provided no teachers for the migrant boys, Fairbridge also took on the duties of schoolmaster, entertainer and trainer. Among other things he taught the children practical skills of self-defence, how to wash their clothes and crockery and how to make packing cases for fruit. Perhaps most importantly, Fairbridge sought to inculcate in his charges habits of cleanliness and self-respect.

In 1913 another 23 workhouse boys were sent to Pinjarra under the care of the Child Emigration Society. Records in the National Archives show that they were aged between 7 and 13 and came from a number of parishes including Droitwich, Islington, Kingston, Petworth, Rye and Taunton (MH 102/1400). No more boys arrived until after the First World War, which seriously impacted on Pinjarra. Fairbridge tried

to join up, only to be rejected on health grounds; however, three of his
staff died in the conflict and funds dried up as the war continued.
Struggling in the increasingly difficult conditions, the Society still tried
to promote its philosophy and achievements—of which Pinjarra was a
major part. On 3 November 1915 Miss Dorothy Poole, a member of
the Child Emigration Society's Executive Committee, described the
school and the Society behind it in a letter to Malcolm Jones from the
Emigrants' Information Office. Now in the National Archives
(MH 102/1400), the letter strikes a determinedly optimistic note:

> *Dear Sir*
>
> We have a Farm School near Pinjarra, Western Australia. Its head is Mr
> Kingsley Fairbridge, once a Rhodes scholar from Rhodesia and among
> the original promoters of the scheme. His wife is Matron, and he has
> two young men to help—one an Australian, the other an Englishman
> resident in Australia (both medically unfit for active service). There is a
> school building attached to the place. There are 32 young boys who are
> being trained, pari passu with their ordinary schooling, for agriculture
> on scientific methods. Mr Fairbridge has the support of a local com-
> mittee, which includes Sir Edward Stone, Lieut-Governor, and various
> influential persons: and the Government of Western Australia makes a
> grant to the Farm School.
>
> Of course the financial position is not very hopeful, and the Society
> has been exceedingly hard hit by the war; but we hope to be able to
> carry on. Every possible economy is being practised in working and I,
> a member of the Executive Committee, am acting as Honorary
> Secretary to save office expenses.[3]

With no further children being sent to Australia it became ever harder
to raise money, and the Oxford Committee of the Society advised clos-
ing the school for the duration of the war. The Perth Committee perse-
vered, however, and the school remained open while Fairbridge battled
to make financial ends meet. He took on responsibility for maintaining the buildings and accepted a lower capitation fee for each child as
politicians wrangled over subsidy, but such measures could only stave
off the inevitable. The school was running on borrowed time.

As the war waged in Europe, the boys at Pinjarra grew up. Mindful
of the deficiencies of earlier schemes, the Local Government Board
requested reports from the school on the progress of individual children. The National Archives holds several, including those sent in

December 1915, some 18 months after the children's arrival (MH 102/ 1400). Their success in settling clearly varied from one to another. Walter A., aged 10, for example, was described as making 'fair' progress and having 'fair' ability; he had recovered from a broken arm and was now in good health.

> PHYSIQUE: Light, active and wiry. Well grown and well developed. Very good runner and keen on all sports.
> CHARACTER: A keen fellow, shaping well.
> APTITUDE FOR FARMING: considerable for his age. Leader of 4th patrol. Can milk, ride, drive and swim. Rows a little.

John T., however, aged 11, was a little more problematic, despite his 'fair' ability and progress.

> HEALTH: good, no illness, but has fainted twice lately in Church during the hot weather.
> PHYSIQUE: Well-made, has grown considerably.
> CHARACTER: poor, lazy, but fairly truthful.
> APTITUDE FOR FARMING: no apparent calling so far. Can milk and swim.[4]

The file goes on to report on the general conditions of the accommodation and education, which was described as good. Clothing was also deemed to be in 'satisfactory' condition, though today it would be seen as quite inadequate, consisting of only two garments and underwear: no boots or stockings were worn. The health of the boys was held to be excellent, with no cases of recorded sickness since 1914. Food for growing boys appears simple, repetitive but relatively healthy —they had three meals each day and received satisfactory portions. A typical menu included:

> *Breakfast*: Porridge with milk and sugar, bread and dripping or jam, fruit (figs, peaches). Tea.
> *Luncheon*: Soup with vegetables (twice a week). Hot meat (five times a week). Vegetables, bread, fruit.
> *Supper*: Bread with dripping or jam. Tomatoes and cucumber or lettuce, and radish. Fruit. Tea.

Such menus reveal the limited but honest nature of the food, and it was shared by all. In keeping with the approachable ethos of the school, Fairbridge and his assistants would always dine with the boys. The principle continued many years after Fairbridge's death; a young

migrant of 1936, John Lane, describes his experience of mealtimes at
the school in its later, enlarged state:

> The main hall was a jungle of long wooded tables and forms… Each
> cottage had its own table in its own place, with a chair at one end for
> the Cottage Mother. In the centre of the hall, two tables lying end to
> end formed one long table. This was where the big boys from Welling-
> ton cottage ate and, because they were senior boys working on the
> farm, they were given boots to wear. When they entered or left the hall
> together, everyone knew about it.[5]

Over two decades after the first children arrived at Pinjarra, menus were
still regimented. Lane remembers their rigid adherence to days of the
week—'if you forgot what day it was, you had only to wait until dinner time, and you knew'. Despite the monotony, the wholesomeness of
the food remained—stews with farm-fresh meat, salad and vegetables,
soups packed with split peas and lentils, even a tasty form of curry,
and the ever-popular puddings. As with many aspects of institution
life, however, individual choice was not an option: 'You either ate what
was put in front of you or went hungry.' For growing children and
teenagers, working hard in the cottages and outdoors on the farm, this
needed little deliberation.

The primary aim and objective of the Fairbridge and similar schemes
was to train boys for farm work and girls (who first came to Pinjarra
after the First World War) for domestic service in rural areas overseas.
In 1912, when Kingsley Fairbridge commenced his work in Western
Australia, farming conditions could justify the hope that a properly
trained boy placed in employment as a farm worker would—if industrious, thrifty and able to gain sound practical experience—have a reasonable prospect in becoming a farmer in his own right.

Farm and garden work were therefore an important part of school
life. The boys undertook such work each day after school under the
supervision of Fairbridge and his assistants. They cropped oats and
hay and maintained a vegetable garden throughout the year; all the
vegetables eaten at Pinjarra were grown on the property. There was
also a fruit orchard, where the boys had practical lessons in pruning, as
well as assisting in picking and packing the fruit for sale.

Pigs, sheep, horses and turkeys were kept on the farm and all boys
helped with their upkeep, some more than others depending on their
skills and abilities. Senior boys rode and handled horses, but were also

taught to drive machinery and cars, reflecting new developments in agriculture. The boys also learnt domestic tasks: the washing of cutlery and crockery was done by a patrol of seven boys, while other teams washed down the dining tables and swept the dining room. The boys made their beds themselves, and another patrol took care of any sanitary work.

There was some time for relaxation as well, and sport was encouraged. The boys played football (Australian rules) and cricket. For the Christmas holidays, the boys from Pinjarra spent a month camping at the seaside resort of Mandurah. The spot was ideal for fishing, boating, bathing and other outdoor activities to help build up the boys' physical strength.

Even many years later, the Mandurah holiday continued. It had the status of an institution and was the focus of huge excitement among the Fairbridge children. In his account of farm school life, John Lane describes the place as 'an idyllic holiday spot on the coast' to which the children travelled by truck, singing songs handed down through the generations:

> There's a truck rattling back on the old Pinjarra track
> Along the road to Fairbridge Farm
> For the radiator's hissing—the sparking plugs are missing
> Beneath the summer sky,
> For there's kero in the petrol and sand in the gears
> And we haven't seen a garage for over forty years.
> There's a Reo rattling back on the old Pinjarra track
> Along the road to Fairbridge Farm.[6]

In fact, by Lane's time the Reo truck's engine had succumbed to old age and the chassis remained only as part of a horse-drawn cart; but its legendary status was clearly important to the children as part of the holiday and a sense of continuity in their often disrupted lives. Camping after Christmas was a familiar ritual, and the farm school children became an essential part of the summer by the lagoon: 'half the kids from Fairbridge Farm invaded Mandurah'. The 'sheer exuberance' described by Lane, a natural part of normal childhood, seldom appears in accounts of child migrants' experiences.

A report by Inspector R.W. Crouch of the Child Emigration Society was made to the State Children Department, in March 1916. Overall it is favourable, finding the farm school at Pinjarra to be generally 'well run' and recommending it to the State Department's close attention. Circulated to many Boards of Guardians who had supplied children to the school, the report also noted that Fairbridge himself had given every assistance in the inspection of the school.

Fairbridge's philosophy—evident in sharing the same food and physical work as his charges—was also shown in the fabric of the buildings. He was determined that the caring and training of his orphan children should not be associated with large, heavy buildings of brick and mortar reminiscent of the workhouses or reformatory schools from which the children might have come. Crouch commented that they were not of a heavy type but the reverse, although 'suitable for the purpose I think. This is in accordance with the original ideas of the Society'.[7]

The central building at Pinjarra was constructed of weatherboards and iron roofing and divided into three sections. The dining room was in the middle, with the kitchen, pantry, stores and laundry to the right, while the Fairbridges' private apartments were to the left. The old homestead building contained eight small rooms, one of which was used by Fairbridge as an office and study; there were also four servants' rooms and two rooms for visitors. At the front was a wide verandah where five of the boys slept; most of them were accommodated in two sleeping pavilions to the front of the main building. These were made of iron with three sides only, the fronts being entirely open. Both were lofty in construction, measuring 21 by 18 ft (6.4 by 4.8 m), and they each held 13 beds.

Inspector Crouch's report gave approval not only to the accommodation but also to the school's sanitation, health, food and standard of tuition. In terms of discipline, he reported that during 1915 there had been a number of occasions when corporal punishment had been required—unsurprising in a group of teenage boys. The causes had mostly been disobedience and stealing, notably for breaking into the orchard and lying. Fairbridge himself had administered the punishments.

After the First World War ended, Fairbridge returned to England with his four children and Ruby to secure further support. He emphasized the successful establishment at Pinjarra and the progress of the 33 young boys who had emigrated there in 1913—and who were now loyally running the farm in his absence for half the wages they might have received elsewhere.[8] Conscious that some of the Oxford Committee regarded his life's work as a mere 'hobby' (a notion angrily dismissed by Fairbridge as a 'cruel and bitter jest'), he urged his supporters to help him expand the school by funding a further 200 migrants, both boys and girls, including many war orphans. Certainly the need was urgent if the school was to survive. In June 1918 Fairbridge had taken half a dozen children from other institutions in Australia, at a drastically reduced capitation fee, in order to keep the teacher eventually allocated by the government at the school. Now the war was over, his farm school scheme had to regain momentum in the child migration field.

Within eight months he had raised £27,000 (over £500,000 in today's money), and on his return to Australia the old farm school was replaced by a new site of 3,200 acres. New cottages were built to house children emigrating from England in 1921 and were named after English icons such as Shakespeare, Raleigh, Livingstone and Rhodes. In 1923 two secretaries were appointed, one in London and one in Melbourne, to help with the administration, but Fairbridge himself was already succumbing to poor health. Recurring attacks of malaria, contracted years before in Africa, often sapped his strength. In the last eight months of his life he dedicated himself to his cause, overseeing the building of no fewer than eight cottages, three schoolrooms and a small hospital. In February 1924, a party of 100 children arrived from England from a variety of organizations, doubling the number under his care overnight. Sadly, Fairbridge's health was seriously failing, and he died on 19 July 1924 at the young age of 39.

The growth of Fairbridge Farm Schools

Fairbridge's work was to continue—and to expand further—after his death under the auspices of the Kingsley Fairbridge Society (formerly the Child Emigration Society). The farm school that he had established struck a chord with the prevailing social mood. It served two worthy purposes—child rescue and Commonwealth migration—which were seen to complement one another. Both supported the overall Fairbridge desire to promote settlement within the British Commonwealth of poor boys and girls who lacked ordinary family care and protection. Together with the training received at a Fairbridge Farm School, such children were expected to become good citizens of Australia, Canada and other Empire countries to secure its future prosperity.

The Fairbridge Farm School attracted many visitors to Pinjarra in the 1920s and 1930s, including the Duke and Duchess of York (later King George VI and Queen Elizabeth). Both were impressed by the calibre of children trained there and the potential offered by such schemes. The duke was keen publicly to endorse the Fairbridge philosophy, observing, 'I only wish that there were more farm schools all over Australia and other parts of the Empire—but they must all be run on the Fairbridge principle.'[9]

Royal support and the enthusiasm of the age brought rapid results. The farm school project received government grants from Britain and Australia in the 1920s and 30s, and there were private donations from trusts such as the Rhodes Trust, the Pilgrim Trust, the Gilchrist Educational Trust, the Thomas Wall Trust and the Coalfields Distress Fund. This allowed the Kingsley Fairbridge Farm School to develop into a fully fledged farm colony in the 1930s, providing 60 buildings for all of its activities. In the 1930s there was a need to expand further as Australian farmers demanded more trained farmhands, and over its life Pinjarra became home to hundreds of child migrants and inspired other groups such as the Catholic agencies (pp.209–15) to found their own institutions in Australia.

John Lane's book *Fairbridge Kid* paints a vivid picture of Fairbridge in the 1930s, when the school was at its busiest and the site extended over 3,000 acres. Over 300 children lived there at this time—Lane himself was allocated to Rhodes Cottage—and buildings included Fairbridge's original house for himself and his family (built with some controversy in 1921), the Principal's House, teachers' quarters, staff quarters, rectory, bakehouse, printing room, carpenter's store, engine room, laundry, office and houses for several other employees from headteacher and farm manager to gardener and dairyman. Farm outbuildings were also numerous, ranging from milking sheds and stables to pig-pens and machinery sheds. Lane was also impressed by the Church of the Holy Innocents on the site, especially the 'intricate internal pattern of beautifully sculptured beams and trusses carved from the rich red timbers of the bush'. A stained-glass window in the west wall, presented by the Old Fairbridgians' Association, commemorated Fairbridge himself.[10]

In June 1934 the Prince of Wales (later Edward VIII) launched an appeal for £100,000 (over £3.5 million in today's money) to establish more schools in the British Empire on the model of the Fairbridge Farm School in Western Australia. The prince himself donated £1,000 (£36,980 in today's money), stating his belief that 'this is not a charity, it is an Imperial investment, and it is as such that I commend the Society's appeal for £100,000 with all my heart for your generous consideration'. *The Times* reported his comments in its edition of 21 June 1934, along with extensive coverage of the appeal and the Farm Schools' work (plates 18 and 19). The prime minister, Stanley Baldwin, was also quoted, urging readers to contribute: 'Let us welcome this opportunity and accept this choice which is put before us today; we know that every penny we send will be spent wisely and in accordance with the experience gained by men and women who are giving their services and their lives of service to this great work. It is money that cannot be wasted and that cannot be ill-expended.'

The appeal focused on the success of the Fairbridge Farm School scheme, which according to supporters had by 1934 achieved three things. First, it claimed to give an opportunity of happiness and a career to the numerous orphans and destitute children in Britain. This remained a significant problem—Fairbridge had estimated in 1910 that there were some 60,000 destitute children in Britain, and the impact of the First World War and economic depression had exacerbated the situation. The optimistic assessment of the scheme's potential was backed up by some favourable statistics—only six of the thousand children involved in Fairbridge schemes across the Empire had been brought to Britain as 'failures'. The remainder were said to have successfully acquired skills and secured jobs abroad despite the difficult economic climate. Second, by emigrating children overseas the Fairbridge scheme was also addressing Britain's unemployment crisis, particularly acute in the 1930s. Third, a careful selection of children provided the Dominions with a steady flow of *good* citizens—an upright and productive population stock trained to work on the land.

The total amount of money raised by the appeal is unclear, but it certainly helped to establish further farm schools. Two were opened in Canada in 1935, one at Cowichan Station, Vancouver Island, and one at Okanagan Valley (both in British Columbia). Their establishment was a considerable achievement given Canada's resistance to taking any more child migrants only a decade earlier (p.192). The plans for the schools met with substantial support locally, in what was a conservative, English-oriented area of Canada. Wagner notes that the 1931 census shows almost two-thirds of the population of the Cowichan Valley to be still of English extraction.[11] And there were influential supporters—the prime minister of British Columbia, T.D. Patullo, was enthusiastic and keen to resume child migration, while the Provincial Secretary's Department asserted that even in the Depression cheap farm labour and female household servants were in short supply. A quarter of a century after his first attempt to found farm schools in Canada, Fairbridge's organization had arrived.

Links with the founder were strengthened in 1936 when Colonel Harry Logan was appointed principal of the Prince of Wales Fairbridge Farm School at Cowichan. He was, like Fairbridge, a Rhodes scholar, and he had heard the young student's first speech at Oxford in 1909 from which the Child Emigration Society was born. Logan was a valuable catch, raising the school's profile, attracting many visitors and enhancing its reputation in the wider world. Eminent and wealthy Canadians praised the school community and the organization behind it, and the ruling of no unaccompanied migrants under 14, passed in council in 1924, was quietly disregarded.

Over 330 children travelled from Britain to Vancouver, with Barnardo's and Middlemore Homes providing facilities en route. The Society was also active in Australia, however, and its second Fairbridge school was constructed in 1937 at Molong, New South Wales—the other side of the country from Pinjarra. Land was also considered for the development of farm schools in both New Zealand (at Tutira, an old sheep station not far from the city of Napier at Hawkes Bay) and at various locations in South Africa, but farm schools never actually opened at either place.

A farm school that did come to fruition was in Rhodesia, now Zimbabwe, where the Fairbridge Society also operated a scheme. Moves to establish a farm school started in the mid-1930s, but because of the war it was not until 1946 that the Rhodesian government supported the scheme with a grant of land and maintenance payments, and the Rhodesia Fairbridge Memorial College was set up at Induna, near Bulawayo, in Southern Rhodesia. It was run on similar lines to the farm schools in Canada and Australia, and accommodated children between the ages of 9 and 14, who were accompanied on the long journey from Britain by carefully chosen escorts. The first party of 18 boys to attend the Memorial College sailed from Southampton on 18 November 1946 on the SS *Carnarvon Castle*, arriving in Cape Town, South Africa, on 4 December. Some 276 children attended the college from 1946 to 1956, when it closed.

The children at Rhodesia were housed in families as small as possible under the supervision of a 'cottage mother'. Such arrangements were traditional in Fairbridge Farm Schools, although finding the right women for such a responsible but moderately paid role cannot have been easy. They were in charge of at least 14 children, responsible for allocating all household chores, getting the children to school and imposing discipline with few checks and balances. Some were feared: in Pinjarra, John Lane remembers his luck in being placed in Rhodes Cottage, run by a strict but fair grandmother 'with neat grey hair setting off a kind face'. He notes that in 1936 only seven of the 20 regular and receiving 'mothers' were themselves married; the vast majority did not have their own children nor necessarily much sympathy for the unsettled, uncertain migrants in their care.[12]

As with other institutions, a certain lawlessness—perhaps inevitably—existed at the farm schools. Older children and longer-established residents assumed authority over the younger ones and those newly arrived, often adding to the latter's distress. Such was the experience of a seven-year-old child who arrived at the Fairbridge school in Bulawayo just before Christmas: '... we hung up our stockings, and the next morning there was nothing in them because the seniors had come and robbed them while we were sleeping, and this was my first experience and you learned fast.'[13]

This blunt reality was at stark variance with the Fairbridge Society ethos, in which the child's happiness and well-being were set out as primary considerations. Children of all denominations were accepted by the Society, which offered to provide instruction in whatever faith a child belonged to, and in principle each child was to have the chance of training for whatever occupation best suited him or her. Yet most children still left the farms at 16 or 17 to take up farming jobs or domestic work, with the limited career prospects highlighted in later official reports. Some aftercare was provided for those who had left the schools, such as the Clubhouse at Pinjarra, built in 1933 by the Old

Fairbridgians' Association. This was designed to offer a welcoming base for anyone between jobs, or who had become unwell, or who simply wished to take a holiday in friendly and familiar surroundings. Although aftercare requirements began to dwindle after the 1950s, as the adults established themselves in Australia, the Association still exists today.

The Fairbridge Society also tried to ensure that the children sent abroad were those most likely to benefit from their experience. Sometimes this might be on health grounds, such as the asthmatic 10-year-old quoted by Bean and Melville whose mother, a single parent, was told by a doctor, 'You must get this child out of Glasgow.'[14] Along with three siblings he was sent to Bulawayo—'called "the desert" because it's high and dry and hot'. The suitability of the children chosen for emigration was carefully assessed, with experts from the Society itself, as well as from the respective governments, trying to pick only those best fitted for a life overseas. For some children it was an exciting, attractive prospect, like the 10-year-old boy who heard of Fairbridge schools through the Scout movement and was captivated with the idea—'I jumped at the chance and was most persistent. It was a great adventure—I was not too aware of the implications involved. I had never even ridden in a motor car!'[15]

At 10, time had not been on this young migrant's side—the most suitable age for children to go to farm schools was deemed to be between seven and nine. Those over 12 were accepted only in exceptional circumstances and, in contrast to Elinor Close's plans, there were no arrangements for enrolling infants and toddlers.

Responsibility for choosing children for emigration lay with the Fairbridge Society at its headquarters in London, assisted by officers well acquainted with life on the farm schools. The Society employed social workers to assist and advise in selecting children, and voluntary societies and local authorities also helped with collecting and assessing them. The emphasis on getting 'the right sort' shows how damaging and problematic—not to mention expensive—children who did not adapt could be.

The Society sought to minimize the distress, even trauma, of leaving Britain to go halfway round the world with what most older children, at least, appreciated was a limited prospect of return. Children allotted to a farm school were thus gathered together for a few weeks beforehand to get to know each other and their escorts, and to become used to the idea of emigrating. Members of the farm school's staff supervised the groups, encouraging communal tasks and introducing children to their new duties and responsibilities, as well as to the life and conditions overseas. It was particularly important for children from private homes to become accustomed to living in groups prior to going abroad. Every effort was made to enable children to fit in, but this was a period of probation. If they did not succeed, such children were usually returned to their former homes.

The Northcote Farm School

Over its life, the Kingsley Fairbridge Farm School at Pinjarra became home to hundreds of child migrants from Britain. Its perceived success encouraged others to emulate it, such as the Northcote Farm School, established in 1937 at Glenmore, Bacchus Marsh, Victoria, New South Wales. Founded by Lady Northcote, a keen follower and admirer of Kingsley Fairbridge and his farm school initiatives, the school formed a close relationship with the Fairbridge Society, although it always remained an independent concern.

The Northcote Children's Emigration Fund originally operated with the Fairbridge scheme, receiving (as Fairbridge did) many of its children from the Church of England Children's Society, as well as the National Children's Home and other childcare organizations. Thirty-seven Methodist children, for example, were sent from the National Children's Home to Northcote Farm between 1938 and 1939. The selection process again was conducted with care. Only when the Fund received full case histories, school and medical reports and intelligence assessments would they make a decision on individual cases. The Northcote Fund was also at pains to arrange suitable reception and assembly of children. Files at the National Archives reveal the initial success of Northcote through reports on individual children who were there. One of them, Sidney B., sailed to Australia in March 1939; after two years he was deemed ready for employment at the age of 15. In December 1941 his school report was Grade VIII and he had managed to obtain his school-leaving certificate with merit. The report thoroughly endorses Sidney's capabilities: 'The best type of boy in the School. Good in school and out. Sets a splendid example to others.

Would make a fine agricultural student if sent to a farm College.'[16]

Another report is for young Ernest G., aged 10 when he left Britain. Described after six months as very healthy though not strong, he was obviously an engaging little boy whose 'cottage mother', school-teacher and even principal, Colonel Heath, thoroughly approved of him. The colonel commended Ernest in June 1939 as an 'excellent type of boy. Has initiative and plenty of common sense. The G.'s [Ernest was accompanied by his brother] fit in uncommonly well and will make good settlers. Australia is fortunate to get such good material. This boy may be sent to his first employment on May 1st 1942.' Unfortunately in the following summer Ernest developed an 'acute rheumatic condition', although he apparently recovered fully with no lasting effects.

The Northcote Farm School ran on very similar lines to Fairbridge's schools, but it did not escape criticism. In the early 1940s Colonel Heath, the principal who commented so favourably on Ernest G., was forced to resign at the request of the trustees. A report was undertaken to investigate complaints made to the trustees concerning children entering employment from the Northcote school. It makes interesting reading.

In May 1943, there were 100 children at the Northcote Farm School and some 56 (43 boys and 13 girls) had been placed in employment. In addition, 13 boys had been called up for military service (the minimum age of conscripts was reduced from 21 years to 18 in mid-1942). Of the 56 in jobs, a high proportion had given trouble to their employees in one way or another. Mr Hancock, the secretary of the Northcote trustees in Melbourne, stated that he himself had had one girl working in his home, but had found her so unsuitable that in no circumstances would he ever take on another Northcote child. Such events (all of which occurred during Colonel Heath's tenure) convinced the trustees that the principal must be changed.

However, the report also notes that Colonel Heath had come from Pinjarra, where the results of the farm school were agreed to be excellent and where, according to Lane, he had been revered by children and staff. It was thus uncertain whether the children sent to Northcote had been badly selected or whether the Fairbridge scheme itself was no longer sound. The report also questioned the wisdom of emphasizing the training of boys to be rural workers, as agricultural conditions and prospects in Australia had changed significantly.[17] What might have been appropriate when Pinjarra was founded in the 1920s no longer seemed so clear-cut, and the prospects of a long-term career in agriculture were far less rosy.

Another factor to consider was an episode on Northcote's dairy farm in 1941. Several children fell sick due to insufficient care over cleanliness in general, and particularly with specific techniques for the cooling of cream. Shortly afterwards children fell ill again, this time through an illness contracted from pigs. The scale of farming at Northcote had obviously been too ambitious, maintained as it was by the labour of inexperienced boys with inadequate support from teachers. As a result, the children's overall health had suffered for over a year. Both the physical surroundings in which the children lived and the general administration of the farm left much to be desired.

The report concluded that no criticism was directed against the Fairbridge principle. However, it acknowledged that something had gone radically wrong with the internal management of Northcote Farm School.

Farm schools in a changing world

As the war approached its end, a gaze of new intensity was directed at the farm schools movement. Concerns about individual schools were complemented by awareness of changing economic conditions—the Depression of the 1930s had left a global mark, and Fairbridge's ambitions of training boys up to become farmers themselves were looking increasingly untenable. None of the farms in Australia designed to take children from Britain had received anyone between 1940 and 1945; all would thus be without child migrants in their care immediately after the war. It was time to take stock of the whole practice of migration.

By 1944, four farm schools in Australia had been established specifically to receive and train children from Britain. They were the Fairbridge Farm School at Pinjarra, Western Australia (Kingsley Fairbridge's pioneering institution, founded in 1912); the Fairbridge Farm School at Molong, New South Wales (established in 1937); the Northcote Farm School at Glenmore, Bacchus Marsh, Victoria (founded by the Northcote trustees in 1937); and the Barnardo Farm School at Mowbray,

Picton, New South Wales, established in 1929 (p. 203). All four farm schools were similar in type and planned as village settlements consisting of a number of cottages in which these varying numbers of boys and girls were housed (separately) under a cottage mother's care. Each also had a common dining hall (where all the meals except the evening meal were taken), a hospital, laundry, chapel, state school, an old boys' hostel, houses for the principal and other staff, and at some a domestic and manual training centre.

All four schools were situated in rural areas, and the farm land attached was worked under the supervision of a farm manager aided by one or two adult assistants. The bulk of the farm work was performed by trainee boys over 16, who at the same time learnt about farming methods (practical and theoretical) to fit them for employment on the land.

Although farm schools had sought from the first to have simple living conditions and to be self-sufficient in vegetables and fruit, the institutions inevitably came with a price tag. The capital cost of establishing farm schools was provided partly from public subscriptions, raised mainly in Britain in the case of Pinjarra, and partly by contributions from the British government. Contributions towards the children's maintenance again came from various sources—principally the British government, the Commonwealth government and the state governments of Western Australian and New South Wales.

The Fairbridge Society schools were all co-educational from after the First World War. The children received in all institutions were drawn mainly from orphanages or from public assistance committees in Britain, and initially organizations such as Barnardo's sent their children to Fairbridge schools (plates 20 and 21). However, a limited number also came from poor families who used the Fairbridge Society scheme to provide children with better opportunities than they could offer. In the main, the children could all be considered to come from underprivileged groups.

In 1944, towards the end of the Second World War, a report was commissioned by the British government on farm schools in Australia. Written by W. Garnett, Official Secretary to the High Commissioner for the United Kingdom in Australia, the report is now in the National Archives (DO 35/1138). It followed a series of alarming reports on various farm schools operating in Australia during the war years.

16 (*above*) A party of young migrants at a London railway station in 1928 prepare to set off on their journey to Australia. The Fairbridge school at Pinjarra, the destination of these children, had over 60 buildings by the 1930s, holding 300 children. **17** (*right*) This list in the National Archives features some of the first children to come to the Fairbridge Farm School at Pinjarra in 1913 (MH 102/1400). Aged between seven and thirteen and assisted by the Child Emigration Society, they came from several parishes including Droitwich, Islington, Kingston, Petworth, Rye and Taunton.

WHAT CHILD EMIGRATION MEANS

Shem Warrens.

"Good-bye to all that." A typical party for Fairbridge.

A new perspective. *New Companions.*

Fairbridge Weddings—Empire Settlement.

FAIRBRIDGE FARM SCHOOLS

AN IMPERIAL INVESTMENT

The Prince of Wales subscribes £1,000 and says:

"*This is not a charity, it is an Imperial investment, and it is as such that I commend the Society's appeal for £100,000 with all my heart for your generous consideration.*"

The Right Hon. Stanley Baldwin says:

"*Let us welcome this opportunity and accept this choice which is put before us to-day; we know that every penny we send will be spent wisely and in accordance with the experience gained by men and women who are giving their services and their lives of service to this great work. It is money that cannot be wasted and that cannot be ill-expended.*"

FAIRBRIDGE FARM SCHOOLS — SUMMARY

THE PAST: The first Fairbridge Farm School was founded in Western Australia by a young man of vision, Kingsley Fairbridge, one of the first Rhodes Scholars. He was striving after two ideals—to fill the empty spaces of the Empire with British stock and to give poorer children from the crowded cities of the British Isles a new life on the land in the Dominions.

The Fairbridge policy is as follows :—

The children, boys and girls, are taken overseas when they are young—at the average age of ten-and-a-half. They are housed on a country estate in cottages which become their homes. They receive the education of the Dominion or State up till the age of 14. During their last eighteen months at the school they are trained on the farm. When they go out to employment at fifteen-and-a-half an after-care and savings system helps them until they can acquire a sturdy independence.

Great obstacles were overcome in the early years, and the School is now working successfully on these lines.

THE PRESENT: Even during the recent years of great depression, when emigration from Great Britain has almost ceased, a constant flow of children has proceeded to and has been maintained at the Fairbridge Farm School. The Commonwealth and State Governments in Australia have continued their assistance towards the maintenance of the children. Amongst those who have passed through the

School, unemployment has been and is non-existent. In 1933 there were 1,000 applications for 100 children ready to leave the School.

The experience of the past and of the present suggests that this is the ideal form of Empire Settlement.

THE FUTURE: It was the aim of the Founder to establish Farm Schools throughout the Empire.

Because the first school has proved successful, the Society now seeks to pursue that aim and to extend to other parts of the Empire.

The Government of the United Kingdom is supporting the proposal to extend and the Governments of the Dominions will be asked to cooperate. To enable extension to be carried out, the Society will need £100,000. This sum will make it possible to establish three more Farm Schools on the Fairbridge model. Once they are established, there will be three more permanent centres overseas through which will flow from out of our overcrowded cities a continuous stream of British stock into the Dominions.

With the same care in selection and training and after-care supervision, it is reasonable to expect a result as successful as that of the first model—which has given employment to our children with acceptance to the Dominion. It is a piece of really constructive work; consequently the Society confidently invites men and women of good will to subscribe thereto.

18 (*above*) *The Times*' special feature on Fairbridge farm schools (21 June 1934) coincided with the launch of an appeal for funds by the Prince of Wales. The appeal sought £100,000 to establish more farm schools across the Empire. As a result two further schools were opened in Canada, a second in Australia and one in Rhodesia.

19 (*opposite*) Publicity for Fairbridge farm schools emphasized the wholesome rural settings in which children could train for farmwork, play sport and continue their education.

THE FAIRBRIDGE FARM SCHOOL STORY IN PICTURES

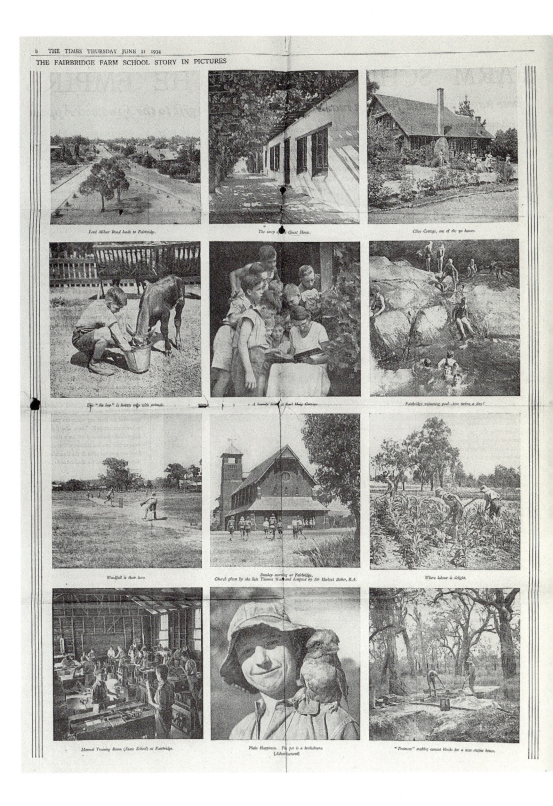

Lord Milner Road leads to Fairbridge.

The steps of the Guest House.

Clive Cottage, one of the 30 houses.

Eric "the imp" is happy only with animals.

A homely scene at Earl Haig Cottage.

Fairbridge swimming pool—two swims a day!

Woodfull is their hero.

Sunday morning at Fairbridge.
Church given by the late Thomas Wall and designed by Sir Herbert Baker, R.A.

Where labour is delight.

Manual Training Room (State School) at Fairbridge.

Plain Happiness. The pet is a kookaburra.
[Advertisement]

"Trainees" making cement blocks for a new engine house.

THE CHRISTIAN BROTHERS' ASSOCIATED SCHEMES FOR THE TRAINING OF POOR BOYS IN WESTERN AUSTRALIA

St. Mary's Agricultural School, Tardun

Christian Brothers Agricultural School, Mount Pleasant, Bindoon, W.A.

St. Peter's Intermediate Orphanage, Clontarf

St. Vincent's Junior Orphanage, Queen's Park

20 (*opposite, top*) A party of Barnardo's children embark on their voyage to Australia at Tilbury docks in the 1920s. Many went to Fairbridge farm schools until Barnardo's opened its own training farm at Picton, in 1929.

21 (*opposite, below*) A group of Fairbridge children and their escorts en route to Fremantle, Australia in 1931.

22 (*above*) A leaflet in the National Archives showing images of the Christian Brothers' orphanages and agricultural schools in Western Australia (DO 35/690/4).

23 (*right*) A list of children who arrived at Fremantle on the RMS *Otranto* in August 1938, under the Christian Brothers' migration scheme (DO 35/1138).

6.

"OTRANTO" LEFT ENGLAND 16. 7. 1938. ARRIVED FREMANTLE 16. 8. 1938.

Name of Migrant.	Present Age.	Chosen Occupation.	Present Address.
BARRY, John	18		
BATTY, Laurence	16	A.I.P.	On Active Service.
BYRNE, Ronald	14	Leaving Certificate.	Guildford
GOGGINS, John	16	Farmer	Tardun
CONNOLLY, Wm	15	Farmer	"
CLARKE, Denis	15	Farmhand	Bindoon
COLEMAN, James Francis	16	Farmer	Tardun
CLEMENTS, Roy Patrick	13	Electrician	"
COWELL, Patrick	13		
DONOVAN, Patrick	15		
FISHER, Wm. Robert	13	Farmer	"
GILBRIDE, Bernard	17	Undecided.	"
GOODWIN, Allen	15	Carpenter	"
GOODWIN, Patrick John	16	Farmer	Bindoon
GORDON, Andrew	14	Architect	Tardun
HANNAN, Reginald	17	Farmer	"
HURLEY, Henry James	16	Carpenter	Bindoon
KIRKLAND, Michael	15	Leaving Certificate.	Geraldton
MAIDEN, John	17		C.B.C.
McLAUGHLIN, Geo. Edward Henry.	18	Farmer	Tardun
		Truck Driver.	Bindoon.
MITCHELL, Thomas	15	R.A.A.F.	On Active Service.
NORMAN, Wm. Gerard	15	Teacher	Tardun
O'FARRELL, Robert	14	Stockman.	
O'BRIEN, Peter Vincent	16	Farmhand	Bindoon
ROSS, Peter	12	Carpenter	Tardun.
LYNCH, Derrick	13	Farmhand	Bindoon
ST. JOHN, Peter	15	Butcher	Tardun.
ST. JOHN, Paul	14	Teacher	"
SWERNEY, Terrence	12	Undecided.	"
WHALLEY, Joseph.	14	Farmer.	"
WOODS, Peter	14	Undecided.	Bindoon.
JOHNSON		Carpenter	Bindoon.
(transferred from Fairbridge).		Undecided	Tardun

24 (*above*) A party of child evacuees and two escorts bound for New Zealand in 1940 under the British government's CORB scheme (DO 131/15).

25 (*right*) A newspaper article describes the commemorative service for Michael Rennie, an escort who died, along with many children, in the *City of Benares* disaster. Louis Walden, who also attended the service, was one of the young survivors (DO 131/80).

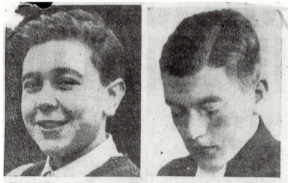

Special "Star" pictures of Louis Walden (left) and Michael Rennie, to whom he owes his life.

Torpedoed At 10

TWELVE-YEAR-OLD Louis Walden, of Kentish Town, N.W., sole survivor of one of the lifeboats of the liner City of Benares, the child evacuee ship torpedoed by the Germans two years ago, has had the adventure vividly recalled.

He stood with his father, mother and sister in the Church of St. Jude's, Hampstead Garden Suburb, while the Archbishop of Canterbury dedicated a painting of Michael Rennie, son of the vicar, the Rev. W. H. Maxwell Rennie, who gave his life trying to save some of the children.

I spoke to Louis Walden and his parents. They had been specially invited by Mr. and Mrs. Rennie, and few people in the packed church knew that this frail little fellow, who wore a blue raincoat with a black tie and sat in a reserved seat in the front row, was the lad who for nearly 14 days faced death in a boat lashed by mountainous seas.

Dived To Save Them

MICHAEL RENNIE was at Oxford studying for the Church. He gave up his vocation to become an escort for British children evacuated to Canada. There were 14 little ones in his lifeboat after the torpedoing, and day after day he nursed them, comforted them, sang and joked to them.

Some of the children were hurled into the sea by the force of the waves. He dived in time after time to save them. Then his own strength gave out, and in his exhaustion he fell overboard and was not seen again. Louis Walden was left, and he was rescued by a British destroyer.

Louis Walden has been in Scotland for more than 18 months, and when he came back to London, a couple of months ago, he called at St. Jude's vicarage and told Mr. and Mrs. Rennie of their son's last moments.

26 (*top*) A photograph from Barnardo's Australian Homes Album of 1929 shows the practical training in domestic skills that girl migrants received.

27 (*above*) A small group of boy migrants pose with escorts and trunks stamped 'Liverpool to Hamilton'. Liverpool was the main port of embarkation for Canada.

COPY.

1929 ARRIVALS: REPORTS DATED FEBRUARY 1936.   13

Name and Age.		Date of Arrival.	Remarks.
MUNDY, G.	23	4.3.29	Worked on South Coast for some years, at wage of 20/- to 25/- p.w., and keep. Saved about £150, and has just taken up a share farming proposition at Morisset.
VARNEY, T.J.	21	4.3.29	Has gone with Munday to take up a share farming proposition at Morisset.
MUNNOGH, J.S.	24	1.4.29	Was employed on farm work, with a Mr. Campbell at Terara, but saw a chance of improving his prospects by taking on carpentry work. Doing well - still living with the Campbells.
LANGFORD, F.E.	24	14.6.29	Has been in hospital in Sydney.
BELL, T.W.	23	7.9.29	Nominated his family 4½ years ago, and secured home and work on a dairy farm at Bega, with wages at the rate of £28 per month for the family. They are hoping to acquire a farm of their own. Bell is about to marry a local girl.

REPORTS DATED MARCH, 1936   ARRIVALS DURING 1929.

BEAL, John W.	23	4.3.29	Dairy work. Is with good employer. Receives bonuses for special work. Rather too fond of pleasure, but realises need to settle down. Hopes to marry soon.
MUNDAY, George	23	4.3.29	On shares - dairy work. Just returning to South Coast to start this proposition. His friend Tom Varney in job there.
VARNEY, Th.J.	21	4.3.29	Dairy work. Was in partnership with G. Munday growing vegetables, but returned to Sth.Coast where they feel they can do better in the district they know.
HILL, C.A.P.	24	23.9.29	Contract work. - brush falling. Has had constant work on same place for 3 years. Favourable prospects.
CRANE, Kenneth G.	23	21.11.29	Working on own account - milk run. Has good reputation and is doing well. Profits available when his lorry is paid off. Prospects good.

REPORTS DATED APRIL 1936

PARKINSON, Harry	23	11.4.29	Mixed farming. Been in same place since arrival. Thought well of and treated as one of the family.
WELLS, Stanley	24	11.4.29	Houseman. Been in same position 8 years. Wages £1 p.w. and keep.

28 (*left*) This official report of 1936 details the fortunes of former child migrants under the Big Brother scheme. Most seem to have established themselves successfully (DO 35/687/5).
29 (*above*) A leaflet advertising the Big Brother Movement which helped teenage migrants to settle in Australia (BT 298/410).
30 (*below*) A party of Little Brothers arriving in Australia in the 1950s. The scheme became popular after the war (DO 35/10274).

Garnett explores the results of the farm school system carefully, focusing on Pinjarra as the hub. Between 1912 and 1945, 1,168 children (70 per cent of whom were boys) boarded there, and it was here that the success or failure of Fairbridge schemes could best be judged. Allowing for 48 children who were repatriated to Britain and 49 who died, 1,071 former Fairbridgians still lived in Australia in 1945. Of those, 825 (77 per cent) had 'made good', while six were 'definite failures', 41 were 'doubtful failures' and 44 were 'still at school'. The whereabouts of almost a hundred (84) children were unknown—or contact had been lost for some reason. There was no record of the remaining 71, which meant in effect that these children had arrived when there was no complete record system in place.

Looking at these figures, Garnett concluded that the results did vindicate the farm school system, and that disturbed wartime conditions were probably responsible for the poor conduct of those recently entering employment. However, he did acknowledge that both the Northcote committee and the New South Wales committee had failed to appreciate the type of child they would be dealing with—those deprived of a normal home life, unsettled, lacking security and possibly resentful of authority. They thus did not possess the resources required to manage them.

Employment remained a concern, and the report admitted that the farm schools lacked facilities for children to gain qualifications for other careers. Fairbridge's dream of establishing a new generation—or rather, generations—of independent young farmers had not been realized by 1945, with only a handful of boys passing through Pinjarra (and a tiny proportion of those at the Barnardo farm in Picton) successfully setting up on their own account. This low take-up was not the fault of the training provided nor of character deficiencies among the boys—although the authorities recognized that even in ideal circumstances only a small number would have the personal qualities and qualifications to become successful farmers themselves. However, farming conditions in Australia between 1920 and 1940 were certainly-far from ideal, making hiring for wages unattractive and independent farming a risky business. As a result, only in exceptional circumstances could children trained at farm schools look to set themselves up alone.

The blunt reality of the situation was laid bare in Garnett's report.

Its substance was that the Fairbridge schools were designed to train
unwanted boys and girls from England to become labourers and servants—the two worst and most despised occupations in Australia—
on the country's farms. He noted that there was little or no potential
for a promising child in the schools to enter other forms of employment, and that there was virtually no prospect of Fairbridge boys running their own farms.

The report noted several other concerns: that the children's training, such as it was, was subordinated to making the farms contribute
to their upkeep by their labour; that the staffing of the schools—from
principal to cottage mothers—was poor; that Fairbridge students were
despised by Australians; and that the children were placed without
anyone first interviewing the employers or inspecting the place of
employment—in fact, according to the London Fairbridge Society
Office, merely on no more than a telephone call. Another anxiety
reflected the new social climate; much had changed during the war
years. Garnett perceived that, far from the children being brought up
in an Australian atmosphere, a farm school represented a British community on Australian soil. Until children left, they had few contacts
with Australians and little experience of the Australian way of life that
they would encounter as adults.

Garnett's report did propose some changes, particularly better
training. He recommended that hostels should be established with
links to farm schools to house children attending high schools or technical colleges. The children should have more employment options—
including provision of expert advice for those seeking to become independent farmers—and all farm schools should have domestic and
manual training centres. Garnett reiterated the Fairbridge policy of
sending younger rather than older children to farm schools, proposing
10 as the normal maximum age, but suggested that children should be
at least 16 before they were sent to employment. Nor should boys—or
girls—remain as trainees without pay once they had turned 16.

Although the report did not criticize the selection of individual children, Garnett did recommend changes among the staff, including
bringing child psychologists on to the Australian Fairbridge committees to assess difficult cases. He advised founding a Farm School Management Committee whose members (including women) could offer
both practical experience and special qualifications, and improving

the calibre of cottage mothers (dismissed as 'second-grade charwomen' by a visitor in 1950), in part by relieving them of domestic duties.

Many of Garnett's proposals were designed to improve conditions and increase life choices for the Fairbridge children. Others reflected a growing desire for more local management and greater Australian autonomy as the old order began to falter in the post-war world. Although recognizing that the Fairbridge Society in London needed to have confidence in how farm schools were run, Garnett's view was that appointments of staff and principals should no longer be made from there. He advised that the administration of Fairbridge schools should be placed in the hands of the Australian Fairbridge Society, more conversant with the real situation on the ground.

Garnett's report clearly emphasized the need for reform, such as a more efficient aftercare system that offered the children support without chaining them to their earlier lives. He recommended keeping complete records of the children but only releasing their past history to Australian authorities on special request, and stressed the value of travelling aftercare officers who would visit the children's prospective employers. In 1946 the Fairbridge Society asked the Home Office to appoint a welfare expert to advise on changes in its constitution, acknowledging the need to modernize if it were to survive. One proposal was to drop the word 'Farm' from its name and that of the schools, and another was to establish closer links between federal and state governments and the schools themselves. In this way, the children's education would be more in line with that of their Australian contemporaries, and some of the problems of segregated, isolated communities could be reduced. A programme of improvements took place over the next two years and emigration was resumed in 1948 for children in care, including those orphaned by the war.

The Fairbridge Society trustees adopted the recommendations of Garnett's report, reducing the number of children in each cottage from 15 to 12. They also lowered the age limit for applications to between five and eight years for an individual child and to 12 for a family unit—in the latter case at least one of the children had to be under eight. Younger children were thought to settle more successfully— they were also a longer drain on Britain's resources as the country struggled to revive economy and infrastructure after the war.

The first postwar migrant children destined for Northcote School arrived in Melbourne on 24 June 1948. The group of 20 children, including 16 boys and girls from the Church of England Children's Society, were met at the side of the SS *Ormonde* by a welcome party; the chaplain of the school was among them. All the children were reported to be in good health and had evidently been well cared for by the accompanying officers.

The National Archives holds original reports on children living at Northcote in the years after the Second World War (MH 102/1593). Not surprisingly, they emphasize educational progress, assessing all children over eight through a variety of tests on arithmetic, reading, spelling and other skills. The children often started from a low base, the result of institutional backgrounds providing limited education— and even that disrupted by evacuation during the war. Results varied, but spelling was acknowledged to be weak across the board and read- ing an issue for some. Diction also varied, presumably reflecting the children's regional backgrounds; the most common errors in speech reported were:

'H's dropped—e.g. 'I 'ope 'e comes.'
'H's added—e.g. 'The howl flies by night.'
'G's dropped—e.g. 'runnin'.'
'G's sounded—e.g. 'sing-ing', 'ring-ing'.

Arithmetic and reading also varied, reflecting the aptitude of individu- als. Differences were also interestingly quite marked between siblings relatively close in age. Peter Y., for example, aged eight years and seven months, was deemed to be progressing 'at a satisfactory rate', with an attitude considered 'good to very good', while his younger brother Victor, aged seven and two months, was obviously an attention-seeking little boy 'still quite a nuisance in class ... forces himself into the public eye ... improving but leaves much to be desired. Attitude is poor to fair.' Even twins could be viewed very differently; Alec and Leonard T., aged nearly seven, were noted as having 'good' and 'bad' attitudes respectively, with reading and spelling proving weaknesses in both. The reports clearly convey the personalities of each boy, and both emerge as engaging characters. Alec socializes well, is articulate ('speaks quite well and plainly') and has many appealing traits: 'Mixes and plays well with others... Truthful and very honest. Fond of affection and quite an intelligent little fellow.' Leonard is revealed as more of a loner ('Plays well with other children but fond of playing alone. Fond of staying around home and craves affection') but also possessing an attractive nature 'quite an intelligent little fellow though nervy... Inclined to be a little wayward at times. Very determined, truthful and honest.' The underlying tone is one of sympathy, recognizing the instability of the children's early lives and clearly hoping that beneficial influences and a new environment will help to overcome the legacy of this: 'Leonard is trying hard... He seems at times to be rather difficult but on the whole has settled down well and seems secure in his life here.'[18]

The authorities appear keen to credit progress in their charges and to give a generous if realistic assessment of their potential, even in the case of difficult boys. Cedric S., for example, aged seven, is described as 'an individualist who clashes at present with adult authority and the clannishness of other boys', but this is viewed as a passing phase and the report predicts that 'sympathetic handling should instil more social consciousness'. The reports often seem to appreciate that unsettling experiences have left their mark on children's confidence and conduct, balanced by an expectation that in such young children this can be reversed.

Dennis W., aged nine, is another example of a Northcote child to whom the authorities seem anxious to give the benefit of the doubt. Sent to Australia by the Church of England Children's Society (as were Alec and Leonard), the report notes that he:

> shows continued improvement in every way. Quieter and less quarrelsome and is harnessing his active mind to settled progress. Second visit to holiday foster parent in Melbourne very successful. Stanford Binet test in August 49 shows good average intelligence quotient... Dennis should develop into a fine type of boy if given the correct opportunities.[19]

Another Dennis W., three years younger and sent to Australia (like Cedric) by Middlemore Emigration Homes, is clearly lagging behind, unable to read and apparently undernourished at 3st 5lb ('No gain in weight despite special diet'). Yet the report recognizes the little boy's strengths and the improvements he has made: 'plays more easily and joins group games. Enjoys make-believe—has keen sense of humour ... Keen observation powers. Has improved in every aspect of activity and is more independent and secure.' Such observations are testimony to the resilience of young children uprooted in this way, and to the compassionate interest shown by many of those into whose charge they came.

Some of the more awkward children were given interviews with educational psychologists. Their behaviour is set out in a detail that reflects the concern authorities felt for children in their care. One boy of almost 10, Clive P., is acknowledged perceptively in a report from early 1949 to be 'a difficult but not really a naughty child' who, when not seeking the attention of others, was both 'friendly and good' with 'a sensitive nature'. Although he was seen as something of a bad penny who was likely to be found around any trouble, those compiling the report recognized his more sympathetic qualities: 'He is gentle with smaller boys and would give them rides on his back to and from school —he was rather afraid of boys his own size.' Sensibly, the psychologist's advice was to ignore attention-seeking ploys and bring the child to realize that he was no different from the others: 'I shall be very surprised if he does not improve out of all recognition if handled unobtrusively.' Typically, Clive's weaknesses were spelling, maths and handwriting, while his marks in English, reading, science, art, handwork and manual work were consistently much higher. This interest in the individual child—and in creating the best possible citizen for Australia—had been a key part of Fairbridge's vision, and remained a principle which his schools and Northcote sought to uphold.

Like Northcote, the Fairbridge Farm School in Pinjarra also began to receive children again in 1948. Despite efforts to address the problems highlighted in Garnett's report, however, the school continued to concern visitors. In 1950 Sir Percivale Liesching, Permanent Under-Secretary of State for Commonwealth Relations, spent 'an hour or two' at Pinjarra. According to his report, now in the National Archives (DO 35/3403), he was less than impressed by the headmaster who 'seemed to me a poor type who lacked any real interest in the children and looked to me to have some defect of character'; his wife was also deemed to be 'rather a lightweight'. He considered that lunch was 'a pretty poor meal' and that in general the children did not appear particularly healthy or well dressed, although he was favourably struck by their self-possession and confidence.

> I spoke to a dozen or more. Half said they were happy and did not
> want to go back (mostly the younger ones). Half said they would like
> to go to England—including the two oldest boys there, both of whom
> had been out a good time. They live in cottages of 10—a good idea,
> and the cottages are not bad, a bit spartan and lacking hot water. The

housemothers are a poor lot—second grade charwomen. The whole thing struck me as having the air of an orphanage. There seems to be no farm training at all, nor any workshops. I saw some football being played. The younger ones are taught on the spot and the older ones go to an Australian school nearby. They are planning a fairly big capital expenditure, about £50,000 or £60,000, I think.[20]

Overall Liesching was unsure about committing to a future investment of public funds in Pinjarra, although he noted that the Western Australians were 'very keen on it … it has become an accepted institution' —perhaps surprisingly, given the worries about the children's segregation outlined in Garnett's report. He recommended that the British government should have more involvement in selecting the head and in carrying out inspections, plus a greater degree of influence in how the school was run.

'Could do better' appeared to be the verdict on Pinjarra. As a result of such reports, the school's first task was to appoint a good principal and improve the calibre of its cottage mothers, which it duly did. Following the departure of the existing head in 1951, the school appointed one Alec Ball to take his place. Ball was a 43-year-old legal practitioner with no previous experience in organizations concerning young children—a surprising choice, but one whose personality had struck the selection committee at interview as quite outstanding.

The school was visited by the High Commissioner a few months after Ball's appointment as principal. He described the new incumbent in glowing terms:

> … it is, I think, very relevant that he gave up a very remunerative family Solicitors' business in Harvey in order to take a job on. At Harvey I heard how respected he was and the people there were full of admiration both for his public spiritedness and his work as Headmaster of the School.
>
> My own assessment of him would be that he is well suited to the job. He appeared to be on admirable terms with the children and I have no doubt at all about his personal qualifications or those of his staff whom I have met, but I was assured that children who received their primary education at Fairbridge took a high place in the local secondary school when it was time for them to go there. He had one boy whom he was hoping to send to the University on the mechanical side with the support of the Scottish Association who act as the child's Godparents.[21]

By 1951 the Kingsley Fairbridge Society was in its 42nd year. Its annual report still reflected an upbeat mood, confidently stating that 98 per cent of children sent to the Commonwealth had 'made good', although clouds were gathering—financial pressures, for example, had forced the Canadian farm school at Okanagen to close three years earlier. Three Fairbridge Farm Schools remained in operation, two in Australia (at Pinjarra and Molong, New South Wales) and one in Canada, the Prince of Wales School at Vancouver Island, British Columbia. The success of the CORB scheme (see chapter 6) in placing wartime evacuees with Dominion families provoked unfavourable comparison with the perceived isolation of Fairbridge children, particularly in Canada but also in Australia. The 1951 annual report for the Kingsley Fairbridge school at Pinjarra was nevertheless very positive; it described the children's general health as being very good, all having put on weight and grown. Visitors had remarked on the healthy, sturdy appearance of Fairbridge children, noting too their friendliness and polite behaviour; the appointment of a new principal that year had clearly improved the situation.

Supporters of Fairbridge schemes often pointed to their provision of holidays for the children—a long-standing tradition from Kingsley Fairbridge days. They still focused on simple outdoor activities; four or five weeks every year were spent at the seaside to develop physical strength and new skills such as swimming, and to encourage the children to build up independence and resourcefulness. Summer camps took place in January as they had for decades, and parties were organized there, while in winter picnics in the hills behind the school were popular. Friendships with children from urban areas were encouraged and visits were arranged by sporting teams, choirs and other parties to Perth and surrounding districts.

Educational standards at Fairbridge were also criticized in the light of the CORB scheme, which saw many evacuees gaining good academic qualifications and going on to university courses. Fairbridge's schools had not always had an easy relationship with the Western Australian government, particularly where the supply of teachers was concerned, although they were popular with some of the children. In the 1930s John Lane remembers how he enjoyed school as a respite from the drudgery and limitations of cottage life: 'On many mornings it was a relief to get to school ... I found every subject interesting, even to learning the ruling dates of many of the English kings. Now I was in Australia I was keen to learn all I could about my vast new country.'[22]

In post-war years the Education Department (formerly the State Children Department) worked closely with the school at Pinjarra. They sought to give children there the same opportunities as those enjoyed by Western Australian country children, and in 1951 the Pinjarra school was raised to the status of junior high school. As a result, courses were widened to include woodwork, mechanical drawing and domestic science, enabling children to develop a broader range of skills.

Yet despite these attempts at modernization and the calibre of individuals such as the new principal at Pinjarra, there was a sense in the 1950s that farm schools had become an anachronism. Both Canada and Australia were determined to give control and responsibility to local Fairbridge committees rather than have the fates of children growing up in their countries determined by organizations in Britain, and concerns over the limitations of Fairbridge training persisted. The Prince of Wales School in Vancouver finally closed in 1953, and fewer and fewer applications were received by the schools on behalf of children in care. Both the Middlemore Emigration Homes and the Church of England Children's Society, for example, had nominated a large number of children for sailings in 1948, 1949 and 1950, but the number suitable and available for emigration dropped significantly thereafter. In the early 1950s, applications for places at Northcote came mainly from a parent or parents making initial enquiries at Australia House in London. At the same time, the London Fairbridge office was itself questioning a policy of sending young migrants to institutions in Australia which held no Australian children—particularly when Britain was experiencing a shortage of agricultural labour at home. War-torn and weary, the world had moved on in many ways, and Fairbridge's passionate beliefs and grand imperial vision seemed already to belong to a distant age.

Chapter 6

Second World War
child evacuees

To say thank you seems very inadequate. Our great hope remains that in the future you will hear and maybe see in Bill something which will give you pleasure in knowing that you played a very important part in shaping.

Father of CORB evacuee, Library and Archives Canada

IN THE YEARS before and during the Second World War, around 14,000 children sailed from Britain to new lives overseas. Unlike those sent abroad by institutions, theirs was a temporary exile, at least in theory; they had homes and families to return to after the war. Yet many must have been lonely and homesick as the years dragged on and the separation began to seem endless. Adults and children grew, inevitably, less familiar to each other as young evacuees reached adulthood in a very different world from wartime Britain with its ration cards, gas masks and recurring dread of bombing raids.

The threat of air raids—and indeed of invasion—was a major factor in the British government's support of emigration, both within its borders and overseas. Conflicts in China, Spain and Abyssinia had revealed the tactics of modern war, with devastating aerial attacks on urban areas causing a high loss of life. The horrific consequences of large-scale air raids had haunted those in power, and so a massive scheme of evacuation from cities to more rural areas was planned in 1938, and implemented in September 1939. In only three days after war was declared, some one and a half million civilians—including children and non-essential workers—were moved out of densely populated cities to the relative safety of the countryside. Up to two million civilians had also evacuated through private arrangement.

Given the success of evacuation within Britain, the government's plans to send children overseas—thus exposing them to all the hazards of sea voyages in wartime—may seem strange. Yet the Children's Overseas Reception Board was conceived in 1940, in a climate of threatened invasion and large-scale air attack. As the war situation deteriorated, more affluent, middle-class parents began to dispatch their children overseas, sparking resentment at the lack of provision for ordinary families to do the same. More than 11,000 children had already been sent abroad in private schemes between 1939 and 1940. Their popularity was fuelled by stories of problematic evacuation in Britain—an unsurprising catalogue of complaints such as overcrowding, disorganized facilities, badly behaved children and aggressive carers in some reception areas. A clear precedent for overseas evacuation had been set.

International politics also played a role. As the volume of air attacks on Britain increased, the governments of the British Dominions and the United States of America were keen to show support and participate in an evacuation programme. On 31 May 1940 offers of hospitality for British children were made through the Canadian government's official channels as well as coming spontaneously from private homes. Similar offers arrived a few days later from Australia, New Zealand, South Africa and the USA.

The early days of CORB

On 7 June 1940, the Children's Overseas Reception Board (CORB) was set up to deal with these proposals. CORB's official terms of reference, now held in the National Archives, were 'To consider offers from overseas to house and care for children, whether accompanied or unaccompanied, from the European war zone, residing in Great Britain, including children orphaned by the war and to make recommendations thereon', and it took shape as an Inter-Departmental Committee (DO 131/43). The chairman, Geoffrey Shakespeare MP, was Parliamentary Under Secretary of State to the Dominions Office, and the committee included representatives of Britain's Home Office, Foreign Office, Ministry of Pensions, Scottish Office, Ministry of Health, Board of Education, Ministry of Shipping, Ministry of Labour, Treasury and the Dominions Office.

The chairman of the Board also set up an advisory council to assist on issues of selection, welfare and reception overseas. Representatives of societies with interest and experience in migration, such as Barnardo's Homes, Fairbridge Farm Schools, the Catholic Council for British Settlement Overseas, the Salvation Army and the Save the Children Fund, became involved in the council's work, as did youth organizations. There was also a special Board for Scotland with its own advisory council, although it had to follow the policy established by the Board in London. A Scottish liaison officer kept the Scottish Board aware of day-to-day decisions and overall progress.

Prior to the setting up of CORB, the schemes evacuating children privately had taken up invitations and generous offers from Canada, Australia, New Zealand and South Africa, as well as the USA. Other foreign nations also volunteered, notably in South America. Approximately 6,000 children were sent to Canada, for example, some accompanied by adults or in the care of designated passengers or stewardesses. Others were evacuated in parties or school groups organized through private sponsors. The establishment of CORB did not put an end to such arrangements, in part because CORB schemes were confined to the Dominions and to the USA, and catered only for schoolchildren aged between 5 and 16. Parents who applied were allowed—and encouraged—to name relatives or friends overseas to whom they would like their children sent.

It quickly became apparent that a considerable number of parents wanted to send their children to the USA. Within five weeks of announcing its foundation, CORB had received around 32,000 applications for evacuation to the USA; homes had been specified in 10,000 cases. CORB estimated that some 6,000 British children might be admitted to the USA each month, but the official scheme never materialized and —in striking contrast to Canada—no CORB children were in the end evacuated there. The problems were twofold: first, the US government, conscious of its precarious neutrality, decided to withdraw its ships from belligerent waters, compounding the transport problem; and second, complex immigration regulations meant that under US law no immigrant's passage could be paid by a non-profit-making organization, including CORB. Instead the American Committee for the Evacuation of Children lobbied for the rescinding of a law stopping unaccompanied children entering the USA (originally designed to prevent them being used as cheap foreign labour). The Committee went on to arrange for the private transport of some 838 children.

The British government decided that CORB would be funded on a contributory basis, as had been the case with the Home Evacuation Scheme. Parents of children at state schools were expected to pay a weekly contribution of nine shillings per child; poorer families paid six shillings or less, depending on their circumstances and assessment by the Assistance Board. Parents of children at private schools were expected to pay a weekly contribution of 20 shillings per child (later reduced to 10 shillings). In most cases the UK government paid the cost of all inland and sea transport and contributed to the child's maintenance. In exceptional cases some parents of children at private schools were asked to contribute up to £20 (£570 in today's terms) for the outward voyage only.

All money received from the parents helped to fund the cost of doctors, nurses, escorts, hostel accommodation at ports and general costs, including expenses incurred on the passage. However, the Board bore all travelling expenses for doctors, nurses and escorts.

Full steam ahead

From the very start of the operation between June and August 1940, the popularity of CORB was assured. Parents were prepared to endure indefinite separation to know that their children were living in safety, and the Board was inundated with over 200,000 applications before deciding to suspend further entries in early July. The applications were divided into three categories: category A, consisting of children at state schools; category B, which contained children at private schools; and category C, holding children whose parents were able and anxious to pay for all transport charges. Almost immediately it was decided that the Board should take no responsibility for children in category C, and their parents were simply advised to make what arrangements they thought best. Applications in A and B were dealt with by individual Local Education Authorities (LEAs). They included school reports and teachers' recommendations on the child's suitability for overseas evacuation, a medical examination form (certifying that the child was free from skin disease or tuberculosis) and a parent's consent form. Acceptance of any child was subject to a final medical examination at the port of embarkation.

Most of the chosen children lived in areas deemed more vulnerable to air attack; some also came from families already split up by evacuation within Britain. The authorities agreed to provide a proportion of accommodation for Scottish applicants, and each sailing party was selected with care to represent a cross-section of society. They included equal proportions of category A (state school) and category B (private school) children, and of boys and girls. There was a balance of English and Welsh, Roman Catholic and Protestant, and a further set percentage of Jewish children.[1]

Once the parties were composed to official satisfaction, the Board had to grapple with the problem of wartime transport. As ships were continually being sunk, damaged or diverted, and port facilities were frequently subject to change, securing space for a party of up to 500 children became increasingly difficult. In July 1940, three further factors delayed the timetable for the children's evacuation overseas. The French Fleet's defection removed a valuable number of escorting warships at a single stroke, even as the SS *Arandora Star* was torpedoed and sunk in the Atlantic en route to Canada. On board were 1,150 Italian and German internees as well as 374 British seaman and soldiers; over half of them lost their lives. This event, on 2 July 1940, swayed public sympathy towards the 'enemy aliens' and effectively served to end the policy of overseas internment.

Significantly for CORB and its evacuation plans, the SS *Arandora Star* had travelled without a convoy of ships in escort. The tragedy (only two months before the SS *City of Benares* disaster, pp.186–90) led to the decision that no CORB children would be carried by any ship unless in convoy.

The third development, the withdrawal of all US shipping from belligerent seas and ports, imposed an even greater strain upon the available British passenger-carrying ships. Many children were left in limbo with applications approved, preparing themselves for departure but unable to set sail.

Despite the difficulties, CORB saw the evacuation process as urgent and pressed ahead as fast as it could. It despatched 2,664 children, who became known as 'Seaevacuees', over a period of three months. As Wagner has noted, Canada received the bulk of them—1,532 in nine parties.[2] Three parties sailed for Australia, with a total of 577 children, while 353 went to South Africa in two parties and 202 to New Zealand, again in two parties (plate 24). A further 24,000 children had been approved for sailing in that time and over 1,000 escorts, including doctors and nurses, enrolled. At its height, CORB employed some 620 staff.

The CORB workload was considerable and its role complex. Aided by local authorities, the Boards, advisory councils and their staff were responsible for processing hundreds of thousands of applications. They sorted, selected and approved the children, contacted parents, arranged parties for sailing, provided escorts, collected children at the ports and saw them on their way. CORB also had to correspond with the authorities in destination countries about reception and care overseas, and to deal with the eventual return of children after the war. It was a challenging remit.

Organizing CORB overseas

The governments of host countries faced challenges too, as each country accepted full responsibility for the children once they arrived at the port of disembarkation. CORB also maintained a representative in each Dominion who would supervise the children's general welfare and deal with the inevitable problems that arose, including accidents and emergencies. Nonetheless, the care and reception of hundreds of evacuated children for an indefinite period of time was a huge responsibility, and individual governments set up their own systems to cope with it.

In Canada, the first Commonwealth country to offer to take in British children, the Immigration Branch of the Department of Mines and Resources was charged with the scheme's general administration. It was a complicated process. Legal barriers preventing unaccompanied migrants under 14 from entering Canada—established to deal with less palatable child migration in less palatable circumstances— had to be removed and a National Advisory Committee for Children from Overseas appointed, to advise about welfare and to collect and administer the necessary funds. The children's practical care was delegated to provincial governments, working through their existing Child Welfare and Children's Aid Societies. At the coalface, Canadians responded generously to the British 'guests', with at least 50,000 people expressing interest in offering the children shelter. Unsurprisingly given its enthusiasm and relative proximity, Canada was the destination of the first CORB voyage, which set sail on 21 July 1940.

The first batch of Australian evacuees left Britain on 5 August, after a stay in the Barnardo's Homes at Fazackerly in Liverpool.[3] Their official guardian in Australia was the Commonwealth Minister of the Interior, appointed by the National Security (Overseas Children) Regulations, although his guardianship was vested in the appropriate authority of each state. As in Canada, the Commonwealth government handled policy matters, but issues about the children's practical care devolved upon the state authorities, working through child welfare departments or local officers.

Both Australia and New Zealand hoped for possible future settlers from among the evacuee children, and many thousand offers of accommodation were received. The first party sailed for New Zealand on 16 August; it was in the end to be one of only two CORB voyages to the Dominion. On arrival, all entered the care of the Superintendent of Child Welfare, an officer in the Department of Education, under the British Children's Emergency Regulations. The New Zealand approach, in which children were allowed to settle for a few weeks after arrival before entering foster homes, revealed a new sensitivity to the stress of such a long voyage on children travelling without families.

Staff in the child welfare departments dealt with practical issues of children's welfare, while the Superintendent was concerned with policy matters. He also worked closely with the Department of the Interior, which was responsible for finding the evacuees suitable homes. Inevitably this took time and—as with Australia and South Africa—parents back in Britain had several anxious months to wait before receiving addresses to write to. Despite such teething problems, the CORB venture was considered to have been a notable success, sparking enthusiasm for a post-war Child Migration Scheme under the auspices of the Royal Overseas League. The Superintendent was again assigned guardianship over these later migrants, to be placed in foster homes before they reached working age. Over 250 children came to New Zealand via this scheme after the war, before its government brought the arrangement to an end in 1952.

Two parties of children sailed to the Union of South Africa in 1940, where the Minister of Social Welfare was appointed guardian (under the Control and Care of Overseas Children Regulations, 1940). The National Advisory Council of the Overseas Children's Reception

Administration (OCRA) was appointed to assist his department and to handle policy matters, and local committees were established to deal with issues on the ground. Some of the South African organization was less formal than in the other Dominions, and Wagner has pointed out that in more isolated areas magistrates may have provided assistance.[4]

Placing children appropriately was considered critical to the scheme's success, and reception committees were set up in each Dominion to collect, sort and approve the offers of private homes. A basic principle of CORB was that the children were to be absorbed into the homes of citizens and not placed in institutions—an important distinction from the child migration policies pursued before the war. The children could thus enjoy a normal home life, receive individual attention and identify far more easily with their surroundings. Their parents equally had the assurance that their children were being well cared for by people who wanted to help children from Britain; they were not faceless officialdom but individuals with whom personal relations could be established.

In all Dominions (with the exception of Canada), the children received an official welcome at the port of arrival. They were sent on as soon as possible to their final destinations, though a stay in central hostels for two or three days was often necessary and New Zealand deliberately gave the evacuees a breathing space after their long journey. In some Dominions, the escorts who had accompanied the children to their new country would also go with them to their new homes, which must have been a great comfort in a strange and distant land.

Foster homes were available in plenty, as sympathetic parents sought to assist youngsters so far from home. CORB received offers of 50,000 from Canada, 5,000 from South Africa and 10,000 from New Zealand and Australia combined. Foster parents in all Dominions had to undertake financial responsibility for the child—in Australia they were required to sign a contract preventing them asking the child's natural parents for financial help. However, foster parents were granted certain concessions; they were allowed $400 in Canada and a similar £50 in New Zealand, while in Australia they received the child allowance of five shillings per week. All Dominions also offered income tax concessions.

CORB used both 'nominated' and 'un-nominated' homes—the former chosen by the children's parents and the latter selected by the authorities abroad. Parents who approached CORB were encouraged to nominate their children to the homes of relatives or friends, as it was believed that this would uproot the children less and would help maintain links between parents and offspring. Un-nominated homes also proved very successful, however, sometimes avoiding long journeys inland when nominated homes were vast distances away. It also enabled the Dominions to place children in groups so that siblings, schoolfriends or children from similar parts of Britain could be reasonably close together.

There were no fixed conditions regarding foster parents, although preference was given to those with some British connection and children of their own who were being well brought up. Ideally they should not be too old but of good reputation, with reasonable financial security—foster parents needed to be able to look after and accommodate the children in comfortable circumstances, without incurring problems for themselves. Houses should be accessible to a school, as well as clean and large enough to take in an extra child or children without overcrowding—no child was expected to share a bed, and it was preferable that he or she should have a private room.

As a general rule, each home was inspected and foster parents interviewed. Every effort was made to place the children in the same class or type of home from which they had come—not an easy feat, given the scanty, inadequate information supplied by CORB on the small history card accompanying each child.

The voyage overseas

As for any child migrants, the voyage could itself be traumatic for evacuees. Unfamiliar sights, sounds and routines were compounded by the stresses of sailing in wartime, as well as the uncertainties of what awaited them on arrival. Children's experiences of the voyage depended largely on the skills of escorts recruited by CORB, who took charge of the evacuees from the accompanying teachers at the ports of embarkation. The Board also had to ensure that hostels were provided at the ports and that ships were inspected before children were sent on board—to confirm that sleeping, feeding, medical and security arrangements were up to standard.

Around 19,000 applications were initially received for the posts of escorts, and CORB organized interviews up and down Britain. Criteria for escorts were strict: it was essential, for example, to be an experienced sea traveller. They also had to be reasonably young, fit and immune from seasickness in order to look after their young companions. Each escort was in charge of 15 children and was responsible to a chief escort who dealt with shipboard routine and supervised all the escorts, children and medical staff. He or she also had to make reports on each escort and child on the passage, manage the formalities of disembarkation and resolve the many and varied problems that might emerge during the voyage.

In addition, escorts were given specific roles on board ship. Chaplain escorts, for example, supervised the 15 boys of their own faith allotted to them and also had spiritual responsibilities for the rest of the party. Another escort would be in charge of sport, requiring knowledge of team games and physical education. Others would look after games and competitions, or music, singing or choir practice. On longer voyages, such as those to Australia or New Zealand, lessons and talks were given about the countries where children were to begin their new lives. All in all, several thousand escorts were approved for duty, although only 237 were actually used by CORB, along with 18 doctors and 49 nurses.[5] (The selection of doctors and nurses was arranged in co-operation with the British Medical Association, the British Red Cross and the Ministry of Health.)

Sea voyages in wartime could be dangerous—the SS *Volendam* was struck by a torpedo on 28 August, although everyone survived and the 350 children on board did reach Canada safely. The recruited doctors, nurses and escorts recruited by CORB displayed great courage in these incidents, some of which were to prove fatal. Three escorts, two nurses and a doctor were killed, drowned or died of exposure when the *City of Benares* was torpedoed (p.187), and six escorts were killed or died of wounds when the RMS *Rangitane* was shelled and sunk on the return journey from New Zealand; another was taken as a prisoner of war and 15 others were held in captivity. Eight escorts were also captured after an attack sank the SS *Port Wellington* in November 1940. They were taken to a prisoner-of-war camp where one died; the others were released three years later.[6] Another ship returning to Britain, the SS *Port Brisbane*, was also torpedoed in November 1940; escorts on board were rescued after a terrifying period drifting in boats in the Atlantic.

Most voyages still passed off peacefully, however, punctuated by the normal routines of shipboard life. Unsurprisingly in a government scheme, many details were prescribed, such as the diets on board, drawn up by the Ministry of Health. Each child was allocated a daily ration of sandwiches, egg and cheese, packets of nuts and seedless raisins, dry biscuits and packets of cheese, barley sugar (not chocolate), apples, bananas and oranges.

In practice food could be more plentiful, as noted in the report of CORB's chief escort on the Polish liner *Batory*, now held in the National Archives (DO 131/19). The ship—carrying 477 children, 35 escorts (including two deputy chief escorts), 10 nurses (including a sister-in-charge), two doctors and a dentist—sailed from Liverpool to Sydney between August and October 1940. The chief escort, Charles Herbert Kilby, observes that despite extremely cramped conditions— created by the need to accommodate 600 troops at the last minute— the voyage, the first CORB sailing on the ship, passed off well.

> The whole of the crew, from the Captain downwards, took the children to their hearts. The Mess room stewards, in particular, worked tremendously hard, and did all they possibly could to make the voyage comfortable. The language problem did not present any great difficulties after the first day or two and Boat Drill appeared to be most satisfactory.
>
> Food was always plentiful. The ration of each child was exactly that of an adult, and at times I asked the Chief Steward to serve less, as so much was being wasted. Each child had unlimited helpings and the diet was balanced to give variety and nutrition. Both doctors and myself frequently sampled the meals and ate with the children. There was a shortage of fresh fruit at times, but this, owing to war conditions, was unobtainable and unavoidable. The escorts supervised the meals and ate in the same dining saloon. It was part of our programme to teach table manners, and with many of the poorer children, it was felt a most difficult task. By the end of the voyage, though, we all felt that these children would not disgrace us in any home to which they were sent.
>
> Water was the most difficult question. Early in the voyage, the fresh water was rationed, and taps turned on at infrequent intervals only, about three hours daily … [However] drinking water was available, day and night, and never once was this supply of icy cold water from the drinking fountains turned off.[7]

Other areas were easier to control, and CORB proposed an outfit for each child at sea which would fit into one suitcase. For boys it consisted of a gas mask, an overcoat and mackintosh if possible, a suit, pullover, hat or school cap, two coloured shirts, two pairs of stockings, two vests, two pairs of pants, two pairs of pyjamas, a pair of boots or shoes, a pair of plimsolls, six handkerchiefs, a comb, a toothbrush and toothpaste, a face flannel or sponge, a towel, paper and pencil, a ration card, an identity card, a birth certificate (if possible) and a Bible. A similar outfit was suggested for girls, with the addition of a pair of warm gloves and a sewing kit.

Because of the interruption of air raids, children would often spend up to three nights at hostels before setting sail. This interval could be put to practical use, such as last-minute medical checks and examinations to ensure that children had adequate food and clothing for the voyage ahead. The clothing was provided by UK businesses and overseas relief organizations and issued at the hostels by the Women's Volunteer Services (WVS). In addition to food and clothing, a consignment of sports equipment, games and toys was provided, together with adequate supplies of glucose, medicine and toiletries. Portable cinemas were also available on board each ship, with appropriate films, as were libraries and song sheets.

Any distractions were welcome on long voyages. In his report on the *Batory*'s 73-day journey (from 1 August to 16 October, stopping off at Freetown, Cape Town, Bombay, Colombo, Singapore, Fremantle and Melbourne), Kilby observes that 'early in the voyage, it became obvious that we were very short of material aids to occupy the children. With a very confined deck space, the children had perforce to sit for long periods, and when "school" proper had ended, there were many tedious hours to while away.'[8]

The lack of space clearly exacerbated the problem here, in contrast to the activities organized on the ill-fated *City of Benares* by escort Michael Rennie, who died in the tragedy. His CORB file, now in the National Archives, includes the following tribute paid to him and Rev. William H. King (who also died) by the chief escort, Miss Marjorie Day:

> I cannot speak too highly of Mr Rennie and Mr King. They worked really hard with their groups and in the best possible way. Mr King took prayers for us each morning on the aft deck immediately after breakfast and then I gave instructions for the day. Mr Rennie got games going and that day had been teaching the boys to lasso one another with a rope—and they also had wonderful tugs of war. He got deck tennis going too.[9]

The journeys were not without incidents on board, as could only be expected with many children crowded together. Accidents occurred running around the ship, with falls, bruising and scrapes not uncommon. All the children were given an individual identity disc with a registered CORB number to wear around their necks—the only way of efficiently identifying children in an emergency. Inevitably, some discs were lost, exchanged or defaced as the voyage progressed. Having said this, no major accidents were reported by the escorts, who seem to have controlled their assigned children reasonably well. The most serious incident on record was when a boy was scalped by a hawser— but he arrived at his journey's end well and recovering fast, though still somewhat bald.

The voyages also brought together an unusual mix of children who in Britain would have led different—and probably very separate—lives. Kilby, chief escort in the *Batory*, noted this with interest, emphasizing the children's eagerness to participate and to adapt to new routines.

> The party consisted of 249 boys and 228 girls, ranging from five years to sixteen years of age. These children were drawn from all types of home—some were the children of professional men—others were the product of the meanest slums. Some had been in attendance at Secondary, Grammar and good private Schools—others appeared to have been irregular in attendance at any school. The vast majority of children proved amenable to discipline, and eager to take part in the new routine and environment. By far, our most difficult cases were those drawn from the Scottish cities—Glasgow in particular.[10]

Settling into new lives

Such enthusiasm boded well for the children as they prepared for new lives abroad, and Kilby adds that the excitement of finally landing in an unknown country, full of unfamiliar sights and sounds, distracted the children temporarily from concerns about what lay ahead. Obviously this could not last, but in general CORB children settled down quickly and well, although most experienced homesickness in some degree. Younger children appeared to settle in more quickly than teenagers, who tended to feel a sense of superiority, partly because they had come from a country at war but also because they were British. As such, they tended to cling on to the habits of home and be sceptical about their new environment, although most did adjust and develop enthusiasm for the new country. From the Dominions' point of view, the children fitted well into the community. Their reserve and intelligence impressed their hosts, and added a measure of admiration and understanding to perceptions of the British overall.

Undoubtedly there were stark contrasts to home life, although overall parents and foster parents maintained good relationships. The most successful situations were those where foster parents sought, over many years, to keep parents very much in the children's minds. Photographs of parents were framed and children encouraged to write regular letters home—many of which, sadly, were never received as the vessels carrying them were torpedoed.

The dangers of returning children were one reason why the CORB authorities were generally reluctant to do so. Often they preferred to give the children time to settle, and sometimes to change an unsuccessful foster home for another, as in the case of nine-year-old Olive P., evacuated to Prince Edward Island in September 1940. Forms in the National Archives cite 'ill-adjustment' as the reason for the change and note the success of the transfer: 'since being with Mr M. has improved in every way' (DO 131/8). Her sister Audrey, three years older, also found the initial placement 'difficult', but records indicate things improved as she grew up and attended the Commercial College on Prince Edward Island. Shortly after leaving here, Audrey followed the pattern of many CORB evacuees and joined up, entering the Women's Division of the RCAF in 1943.[11]

Inevitably, some children did not behave well and the uncertainties of their situation—dispatched in wartime to an unknown country with no idea of when they might return (or what they would find if they did)—exacerbated the problem. Good foster homes could help, but in some instances it might have been better for children to return home—had they been able to. Take the case of 13-year-old William C. from Glasgow, for example, who arrived in Canada in September 1940 and was placed with relations in Welland. Described as a 'difficult boy', his history cards in the National Archives reveal that he was imprisoned for three months for being in possession of—and driving—a car without the owner's consent (DO 131/110). William did in fact return to Britain, but not until December 1943.

Officialdom continued to keep an eye on the evacuees, with organizations such as the Children's Aid Society reporting periodically on the health, school progress, adjustment, behaviour and recreations of the children under their charge. These were forwarded to the CORB representative abroad, who in turn sent a report to the London headquarters. Reports became less detailed and fewer in number as years went by and parents and foster parents built up their own strong relationships. Communications were assisted by other means, too. With letters unpredictable, Cable and Wireless Limited generously arranged a free monthly exchange of cables between all parents and children throughout the war. The BBC (in co-operation with the Dominions broadcasting companies) also organized a series of message programmes, including messages from children to parents and from parents to children, as well as some two-way conversations. These efforts were greatly appreciated by children, parents and foster parents; they did much to relieve anxieties and alleviate the physical distance and separation.

There were other practical issues to consider, too. The clothes the children arrived in, plus whatever they could carry in their limited luggage, soon proved to be inadequate. Most of the host countries refused the clothing grants offered by the British government, even though it was clear that foster parents could not be expected to pay for such things (despite many volunteering to do so). In Canada, the Children's Aid Societies became responsible for individual cases, whereas in Australia provision was made for up to £3 to be spent on each child's clothing. No central fund was raised in New Zealand and clothing was given either by a charity organization, such as the Smith Family Organization, or through the local relief committees. In South Africa, children were similarly clothed through special funds.

Generally speaking, the children enjoyed the same educational opportunities available to their foreign contemporaries. Broken school years and different school systems made it difficult to place children in their correct class at school, although such teething troubles were generally resolved after the first term or two. The majority settled well into their schools, although the change in education did not favour some. Brighter children placed in classes with older, more mature students sometimes struggled to compete, adding to the stress of recent arrival in a new country. Yet the educational systems could be advantageous, too, offering more opportunities than were available at home. Children who went to Canada from secondary schools in Britain, for example, were able to remain for a further year to their high school graduation. Had they stayed in Britain, they would in many cases have been expected to leave school at the age of 14. Many CORB children in Australia and South Africa proceeded to high school by winning scholarships, and between 1940 and 1944 some 40 CORB students went on to follow university courses.

Outside school, CORB children had various social activities on offer, including organized camps in their summer holidays. Older children often found summer employment on farms, in factories and shops and offices. Many had happy holidays and took the chance to see famous scenery—the Rockies in Canada, the Game Reserve in South Africa and the Rotorua Mountains in New Zealand. Such holidays broadened children's experiences and gave them opportunities to learn outdoor skills such as camping, fishing, hunting, canoeing and swimming.

On the whole, selected CORB children were healthy. Besides, it was agreed from the outset that no child would be refused participation in the scheme on the grounds of health (unless, of course, they were too ill to travel when the ship was due to leave, or were found to be carrying contagious diseases that put others at risk). All children were medically examined at the place of arrival and re-examined every six months; dental treatment was free, as was any surgery required. The mortality rate among the evacuees was extremely low—only three deaths were recorded in the first four years.

Many children became adults while living abroad and an increasing number left school for employment. Foster parents and child welfare departments sought to find children suitable employment, preferably with scope for training and development. A high proportion of CORB boys served apprenticeships to various skilled trades in all of the host countries, while others—in the tradition of child migrants—became interested in farming. The majority of girls took employment in offices or banks as typists, clerical workers or telephonists.

Of course, the war had an impact on those leaving school; several boys trained for the Dominions' merchant navies or joined their forces. Many evacuated boys became subject to the military regulations of their host country, although this varied from one Dominion to another. In Australia and Canada, for example, young men were called up for service at the age of 18, whereas in New Zealand it was 20, while in South Africa there was no compulsory military service. However, most CORB boys did not wait to be called up. In Canada, half of 18-year-old CORB boys returned to join British forces, the remainder joining the Canadian Services. Similarly, a number of CORB girls joined women's services in the Dominions, including the Australian Land Army.

The evacuation of children to the Dominions, hastily conceived in the pressures of wartime, was deemed by all governments involved to have been a great success. Despite the inevitable bureaucratic hiccups, such as children arriving without teachers' reports or much background documentation at all, the merits of a government-sponsored scheme, with scope for official intervention if required, were clearly portrayed. In Canada, the placing of children firmly in mainstream life compared favourably with the more segregated migration of, for example, Fairbridge Farm Schools; the Prince of Wales Fairbridge Farm School in British Columbia was a particular target, but those in Australia also caused concern (see chapter 5). The Prince of Wales School had hit financial problems when war broke out, and required support from both the Dominion and provincial governments to survive. Ishbel Harvey, superintendent of child welfare and a long-standing critic of the Fairbridge Farm School, met CORB's director Marjorie Maxse in 1944.[12] Harvey's indictment of the unequal systems and their impact upon the children involved is held among CORB papers at the National Archives: 'These children belong to both our countries and they have no chance at all. When I look at our lovely CORB girls and boys going back and then look at the Fairbridge ones I could sit down and weep.'[13] The school finally closed in 1953.

The City of Benares

Between 21 July and 20 September 1940, 18 voyages were made carrying 2,664 children to new lives in Canada, Australia, New Zealand and South Africa. Many more than 14,000 would have travelled overseas had it not been for the disastrous events on 17 September, when the SS *City of Benares*—packed with 197 passengers including 90 children—was torpedoed and sunk in the Atlantic. The ship, sailing from Liverpool to Canada, was struck down at 10 pm, when it was 600 miles from land—only two months after the destruction of the SS *Arandora*

Star. Many later claimed such an event was bound to happen, and that shipping children overseas had been an extremely perilous course.

The consequences of the attack were devastating, even by wartime standards, and it marked the effective end of all overseas evacuation from Britain, both public and private. Seventy CORB children were among 134 passengers killed, along with 131 of the 200-strong crew; loss of life was exacerbated by severe weather in the night, including gale-force winds, storms, rain and hail. The ship, built in 1936 and weighing 11,000 tons, had been fitted with up-to-date facilities for carrying passengers, with special provision for children. One of the last CORB vessels to sail, it had passed safety checks from Ministry of Shipping representatives prior to sailing. It left Liverpool in convoy on 13 September, with lifeboat accommodation for 494 people and additional buoyancy apparatus for another 452; regular boat drills were held on the voyage. Yet the combination of weather, darkness and isolation was to result in a death toll that shook Britain and its allies, and became one of the war's most notorious events.

From survivors' accounts, official reports into the tragedy could piece together the chain of events. The torpedo had struck the ship on the port side, below the cabins where many of the children were quartered; some of them may have been killed instantly by the explosion. The escorts immediately mustered the children at their drill stations in an orderly fashion and 12 lifeboats were launched. The process was difficult, due not only to the darkness but also to a heavy Atlantic swell and strong wind. The ship was sinking steadily by the stern and listing slightly, and it was hard to prevent water getting into the boats as they were launched. The four surviving escorts stated that repeated searches were made for any surviving CORB children before the lifeboats finally drew away from the ship; none seem to have been left behind alive.

Following a night of bad weather, only 113 survivors were picked up by a warship the next day. Among them were 13 children and 18 women, of whom seven children and two adults were part of the CORB scheme. A further 46 survivors were rescued from a lifeboat eight days later, of whom six children and two escorts were travelling under CORB.

Reports from survivors made harrowing reading for those who had lost friends or family, and of course for the parents of children involved. The National Archives holds the testimony of a passenger,

Dr Martin Bum, who describes the chaotic scenes in launching the lifeboats. His own boat:

> came down with one side tilted and was filled with water immediately. I found a partly destroyed rope ladder and managed to jump down into the boat, landing between many children… We drifted away in heavy sea and the boat was filled entirely with water… The heavy seas swept many of the children from their seats into the middle of the boat and partly out of the boat. The children, who were very brave, suffered very heavily … they were mostly only dressed in pyjamas and lifebelts.[14]

The *Montreal Gazette*, 23 September 1940, describes how children were thrown into the sea from their lifeboats and quotes a nurse, Doris Walker, who saw them floating in the water from on board the listing ship: '"I couldn't look twice," she said.'

Bum describes the difficulty of keeping children in the boat and above water, particularly as the night wore on and they fell prey to exhaustion and exposure. Despite his best efforts, and those of CORB escort Michael Rennie, even children within the boat slipped below the water level and drowned in the darkness, as the doctor vividly recalled:

> Each time when we had just managed to get a child to his seat or to a projected space then the next wave carried him away again. The children began to become weak. Many of them became quiet and in the darkness I suddenly discovered that the heads of some of them were already underwater. It was difficult to help them all. Some of the children were clinging together in the hope of finding a hold, but some of them might have been dead.[15]

Rennie, a 22-year-old escort and student at Keble College, Oxford, displayed exceptional courage, not only by comforting and singing to the remaining children but also by diving repeatedly into the heavy sea to rescue those swept overboard. Drenched and exhausted, he eventually collapsed in the waterlogged boat and drowned before the others could pull him out. As the chairman of CORB, Sir Geoffrey Shakespeare MP, noted when he recommended Rennie for a posthumous George Medal, his courageous actions undoubtedly caused his death. Rennie's parents supported the recommendation, but ultimately the request was not granted.

As time wore on, Bum and the Third Officer struggled to keep passengers and the remaining children alive, and to remain conscious themselves. Desperately thirsty, they rescued tins of condensed milk from the bottom of the boat and sucked the liquid through holes in the tins. He notes that by this time, the second day, the children were mostly semi-conscious, and that he and some of the other adults were battling to keep them above water in the flooded boat. More were to die in quick succession before the destroyer that rescued them finally arrived, as Bum and a passenger frantically waved handkerchiefs tied to an oar. On board the survivors were plied with warm drinks and food and given clothing by the crew, but an exhausted 14-year-old boy nevertheless died on the ship.

In the end, only one child out of 13 in the lifeboat survived the ordeal: 10-year-old Louis Walden, of Kentish Town, London. Interviewed by CORB, he spoke of the heroism of escort Michael Rennie, and two years later attended a commemorative service at St Jude's Church, Hampstead Garden Suburb, where Rennie's father was vicar (Michael himself had been preparing to enter the Church). The Archbishop of Canterbury dedicated a memorial painting of the young escort who, as his father wrote, had at least been spared 'to do his job of work to the end' (DO 131/80). Local newspapers noted the event (plate 25); the shock waves of the *City of Benares* disaster were still news, even after two further years of war.

The tragic loss experienced by Rennie's parents was shared in homes across Britain. They came from Cardiff and Sunderland, Liverpool and the suburbs of London—Wembley, Southall, Twickenham and Hillingdon. Many were siblings, and as the *Montreal Gazette* noted, 'whole families of children were lost. Three sons of Cyril Pugh of Liverpool were victims. Three daughters of William Beasley of London went down. Five of Jim Grimmond's children, who survived a recent bombing of their London home, are gone.' Also recorded as missing were the Short brothers, William (nine) and Peter (five), from Sunderland, although the older boy was later rescued after eight and a half days at sea. Their case file at the National Archives includes a letter enclosing a donation of £5 (over £140 in today's terms) forwarded by CORB to the family: 'I know that money brings no compensation to grieved parents whose children have been lost in the frightful tragedy at sea but there may be those whose circumstances are such that some financial help may be welcome... I have been one of the lucky ones—my wife and three children crossed safely a week ago.'[16]

The boys' father, John Short, replied to the generous gesture with dignity, acknowledging its practical help at a traumatic time: 'It will get some of the clothes for my boy who was saved from this tragedy. It would have been grand if I could have had both of my boys saved but I thank God for sending one. The homes that have not got any back must be terrible, because I know what it is like to miss one.'

Returning home

For those already evacuated, return became even less feasible in wartime, although some parents did request their children's return in 1941. As the threat of invasion receded and the air bombardment of Britain lessened, there seemed less immediate need to endure the misery of separation. Yet under the terms of CORB, children were due to return only 'as soon as practicable' after the end of the war, and many were away for four or five years. In that time they forged new family ties and were shaped by a country outside their parents' experience. Relationships disrupted by evacuation inevitably took time to re-establish when the evacuees came home.

Some children did return before the war ended, but they were in a minority. A handful of cases came back where they had broken the law, and from 1942 it was agreed that any boy approaching military age could return provided he had his parents' consent and that a form of authority and release from responsibility had been signed. In 1943, the age for Canadian returns was lowered to 16 for boys and 17 for girls, and for the other host countries to 16 for boys and 18 for girls. Up to January 1944, those returning under CORB numbered 56 from Canada, 4 from South Africa and none from either Australia or New Zealand. By the end of the year, however, figures had increased to 222 (Canada), 25 (South Africa), 16 (Australia) and 3 (New Zealand).

Return arrangements were made by CORB representatives in the Dominions, and some adult passengers were asked to supervise the evacuees on their voyage home. They were met on arrival by Ministry of Health port officials, who gave them travel tickets and any necessary money and assistance. Younger children were escorted to their homes. Some parents were dissatisfied with the length of time required to get their children back, and their reasons for requesting the return varied. In some cases it was to allow them to undertake apprenticeships or special training. Other circumstances could be the serious illness of a parent, or the child's inability to settle down to a new life abroad. CORB carefully considered such requests but would not agree to all, particularly if the children were very young. In these cases, in order to get their children back, parents needed to withdraw them from the scheme and make their own arrangements for a return voyage, provided the authorities in host countries agreed and a passage could be found. As CORB came to an end, the number of children withdrawn from its scheme was relatively low. In Canada 25 had left, in Australia 10, in South Africa 4 and in New Zealand none. These figures were deceptive, however, as they included three girls who had married, one boy who had been adopted by his foster parents and 18 children who had been joined by their parents overseas.

In total, the CORB scheme sent 2,664 children to Australia, Canada, New Zealand and South Africa between July and September 1940. Although evacuation ceased when the SS *City of Benares* was torpedoed, the Board remained active. It was only disbanded, along with the advisory councils, four years later, at which point the perceived German military threat had diminished. And, unlike many other child migrants in this story, the evacuees did, in the main, return. The war was over and they could move into a new stage of their lives, bringing the benefit of their experiences to a weary Britain and ravaged Europe. It had been a strange—for some an extraordinary—time, but by the end of January 1946 most of the CORB children had come home.

Chapter 7

The final phase

How different this from the popular conception of the arrival
of the emigrant in a strange land. Here actually were members
of a government joining with the Archbishop of a great
diocese to welcome 37 boys come to make their future in
the vast territories of Western Australia. Not even the most
distinguished visitor could expect a finer welcome ... these
boys were ... heartily and civically welcomed.

The Record, official organ of the Archdiocese of Perth,
Western Australia, 1938

The exigencies of wartime had driven the CORB programme, but
most other child emigration came to a halt in the Second World War.
Even before that its patterns were changing, and political pressures
had made an impact much earlier in the 20th century. Before 1914
Canada remained the destination of most children, as in the previous
century, but the mood was changing in the 1920s, with opposition to
young, unaccompanied migrants significantly increased. In 1924 the
Director of the Canadian Council on Child Welfare, Charlotte Whitton, denounced the practice at a convention of the magnificently titled
Imperial Order of the Daughters of the Empire, demanding, 'Why are
so many children being brought to Canada? ... The only fair inference
is that juvenile immigrants are being sought for placements in homes
and on conditions which the Canadian authorities will not accept for
our children.'[1] She went on to describe the use of children in farm work
as 'a cheap labour that approaches perilously near a form of slavery'.
Many of the overworked, poorly paid children would probably have
agreed with her.

A British parliamentary delegation was dispatched to Canada to
explore the whole process of sending young children to live and work
there in 1924. It found that provincial child welfare associations
opposed the practice almost without exception as professional child-

care became more sophisticated. That same year the federal Canadian government passed an order in council that effectively barred unaccompanied children under 14 from entering Canada legally. Following criticism of child migration agencies—particularly Barnardo's Homes —for allegedly failing to give children placed in Canada adequate care or supervision, the ban was made permanent in 1925. The following year as many as 4,000 children still sailed to Canada, but numbers had declined hugely by the end of the decade.

Only six girls and fewer than 500 boys travelled to Canada in 1931, the consequences of the Depression as well as internal resistance. The nation was suffering economically and 'Home Children' destined for work on farms, in factories or in domestic service were expendable. Barnardo's sent very few children there after 1932, and some of its migrants—as well as those of other institutions—returned to Britain when they could, faced with limited prospects of making a living. Canadian child migration, at least for the time being, had reached the end of the line.

Britain thus needed alternative countries to receive child migrants, and Australia presented the obvious choice. Schemes had already been established there after the First World War, as heavy wartime losses had created a shortage of manpower. Agencies were swift to take advantage of this—in 1920, for example, the Church of England sponsored the passage of 174 people to Australia, including a large number of children. Kingsley Fairbridge (see chapter 5) was another early example of someone who recognized Australia's potential, inspired by a vision of simultaneously offering children new opportunities and harnessing the Empire's vast agricultural resources:

> I saw great Colleges of Agriculture (not workhouses) springing up in every man-hungry corner of the Empire. I saw little children shedding the bondage of bitter circumstances, and stretching their legs and minds amid the thousand interests of the Farm. I saw waste turn into providence, the waste of unneeded humanity converted to the husbandry of unpeopled acres.[2]

Over 900 children were dispatched to Fairbridge Farm Schools in Western Australia during the 1920s, and both the man and the society he founded were highly influential. Yet his was by no means the only— or even the first—organization to send children to Australia. Barnardo's Homes, for example, had sent its first few children to

Australia as early as 1871, although the first official party of Barnardo boys, sponsored by the Sydney Millions Club, did not arrive in New South Wales until 1923. Barnardo's was to go on to handle nearly 1,000 cases in the years up to 1930—many of whom went to Fairbridge Farm Schools—and to maintain its profile in Australia in the post-war world.

Other schemes concentrated primarily upon older boys—desirable, as they would soon be available to work. An early example was the Dreadnought Scheme. In 1911 the trustees of the Dreadnought Fund (originally established in 1903 to purchase a Dreadnought battleship for presentation to Britain) entered into an agreement with the New South Wales government to bring out British boys between the ages of 16 and 19 'of good character and physique at a rate of about twenty every fortnight and to pay the Government £5 for each of the lads sent to the training farm'. The first 12 'Dreadnought boys' arrived on 21 April 1911, to be followed by 27 more on 15 June. In total, over 5,500 Dreadnought boys emigrated to Australia under its auspices between 1911 and 1939. A slightly later development, the Big Brother Movement, was responsible for the migration of a further 12,500 boys aged 16 and 17 between 1925 and 1983, with numbers significantly lower after 1967. Founded by Sir Richard Linton, a New Zealand-born businessman, philanthropist and politician, the Movement arose through discussions between Australian and British business leaders at the 1923 Wembley exhibition.

A Catholic organization, the Christian Brothers, also became a major player, this time dealing with children of all ages (plates 22 and 23). The Christian Brothers began the migration of Catholic children in the 1920s in response to the numbers of Protestant children arriving through schemes managed by Barnardo's, the Big Brother Movement and Fairbridge Farm Schools, all of which drew largely if not exclusively on Protestant organizations. Overall it is estimated that between 6,000 and 7,500 children were dispatched to Australia during the 20th century, with roughly 3,500 arriving before the Second World War and a similar number between 1946 and 1967, when child migration effectively ceased. The war proved a turning point in attitudes towards migration and expectations of the children that Britain supplied. They were no longer viewed purely as Empire-fodder, destined for a future in agriculture or service, and officials and organizations sought to modernize and improve conditions for post-war arrivals. The process was patchy and not an entire success, but it did ultimately lead to the end of migration in this form.

In the 1920s and 1930s, children were considered an attractive category of migrant to Australia. Young and adaptable, they could assimilate more easily, and they had a long—and hopefully productive—working life ahead. They were easy to house cheaply and the Commonwealth of Australia approved over 40 homes for the housing of child migrants. Most of these were run by voluntary and religious organizations, as we will see. The Australian government did not provide homes specifically for migrant children, but it did contribute towards the capital expenditure of organizations setting up suitable homes. Financing was a complex process, as both the Commonwealth and state governments in Australia contributed towards running costs. The British government also paid maintenance for children who had emigrated to approved institutions in Australia.

A new attitude was emerging in this later phase of emigration, in which Australia was becoming the key destination. Philanthropic and religious motives remained, but were complemented by an overt political desire to populate the Empire with reliable stock. This was clearly and consciously articulated at the highest levels of government, and found legal expression in the Empire Settlement Acts of 1922, 1937, 1952 and 1957. The Acts empowered the Secretary of State for Commonwealth Relations to make contributions to 'Empire Settlement' schemes up to a maximum of £1,500,000 a year 'in association with the government of any part of His Majesty's Dominions, or with public authorities or public or private organisations either in the United Kingdom or in any part of such Dominions'. They helped to set up agreements between the Secretary of State and various child migration authorities. These established procedures regarding the admission of migrant children to up to 50 farm schools, homes and other institutions in Canada, Australia and Southern Rhodesia. Child migration now reached across the Empire and was openly acknowledged as 'a truly Imperial work'. The Acts were far-reaching, and unaccompanied children were not the only beneficiaries. Another was the Australian Assisted Passage Scheme, which began in March 1947 and over the following decade assisted some 200,000 families in migrating to Australia.

For children arriving alone, however, the official body responsible for their fate was the Overseas Settlement Board. From 1922 it conducted migration, consulting closely with the local authorities, voluntary homes and individual households concerned. Voluntary homes contributed by far the largest number of children as registered child migration societies. Those involved—to a greater or lesser degree—formed an impressive range of philanthropic and religious organizations with concerns in Canada, Australia or both: Dr Barnardo's, the Salvation Army, the Catholic Emigration Association, the Church of England Waifs and Strays Society, the Child's Emigration Homes, the Children's Aid Society, the Liverpool Sheltering Homes, the National Children's Homes and Orphanage, Dr Fegan's Homes, Annie Macpherson Homes Ltd, the Orphan Homes of Scotland, the John Kirk House, the Dakeyne St Lads' Club and the Craigielinn Farm. They forwarded details of children committed by the courts to their care to Homes and bodies sponsored by the Imperial and Dominion governments, such as the Fairbridge Society. When an application was made, local police were brought in to ask parents their views of the proposed emigration, and also to assess their character and environment. If the parents agreed, the organizations considered whether the child was likely to suffer from 'adverse influence' if he or she remained at home, and what the alternative prospects would be within the emigration scheme abroad.

Pressure could be—and often was—brought to bear on parents, not least by the organizations themselves. Ann Howard and Eric Leonard cite a correspondence between a mother, reluctant to have her son sent such a distance, and the forceful Chief Migration Officer: 'I'm sorry to note that you do not like the idea of us sending Oswald to Australia. We can offer him better prospects under our own supervision in Australia than anything we can offer him in this country, and I therefore urgently ask you to give this matter your most serious consideration.'

In 1933, in the midst of the Depression, such arguments carried weight, and the mother's poignant reply accepts the inevitable separation: 'I think you know best what to do for Oswald and I would like to come and see him before he goes to Australia... Could you please tell me where to stay for the night? I have not very much money and I don't know my way around London at all.'[3] At least she got to say goodbye to her son—the matron kindly put her up for the night.

The Empire Settlement Acts were strict about how much information voluntary organizations had to supply to the Home Office. They had to brief them fully about their methods of choosing children to be sent abroad, and the criteria used to select them. Details were required about the care and preparation of chosen children until they left Britain, as well as travel arrangements and the level of information sent to Australia about individual children and their background. Any proposal to emigrate children from Approved Schools, or those placed in care under the Children and Young Persons Act 1933, needed the consent of the child and of the Secretary of State, and consultation with the parents where these were deemed to be 'fit persons'. Such bureaucracy was designed to protect the young and vulnerable from hasty or inappropriate decisions, and to look objectively at a process that totally transformed the children's lives. The intention was to manage migration in a more up-to-date and efficient way, but as the century progressed the limitations of the system were to be graphically exposed.

Barnardo's Homes in Australia

One of the highest profile—and most influential—of organizations involved in emigrating children, Barnardo's emerged swiftly as a major player in Australia. Barnardo himself had initially targeted Canadian destinations, following the lead of Maria Rye, Annie Macpherson, Father Nugent and William Quarrier, and his first official party of 51 boys, bound for Quebec, left Britain in August 1882 (see chapter 3). The boys, aged between 14 and 17 with many years' training in Barnardo's Homes behind them, sailed from Liverpool in the SS *Parisian*; many others would follow in its wake. By 1939 Barnardo's had sponsored the emigration of approximately 30,000 children to Canada alone.

Barnardo did not ignore the potential of other parts of the Empire, however, and began to experiment with small-scale, unofficial schemes. Three pauper children from London's East End—Timothy, John and Bessie Regan—were befriended by an Australian, Horace Stevens, and his wife, and emigrated to Australia under Barnardo's auspices as early as 1871. Despite the difficulties of the long voyage, other small parties of Barnardo's children were also dispatched before 1881 to Australia, South Africa, and Auckland and Christchurch in New Zealand.

In 1883 another unofficial group of eight boys left Barnardo's Stepney Causeway Home, the first of his Homes, to start a new life in Australia.

Barnardo's talent for publicity and fund-raising for his initiatives was a major factor in their success, and in October 1891 he embarked on this in Australia. A party of 'musical boys' gave performances through the eastern states of Australia to help promote Barnardo's work overseas. The tour proved a success, raising awareness of Barnardo's in many potentially useful areas—it covered Queensland, New South Wales, Victoria and South Australia, as well as Auckland and Christchurch in New Zealand. Valuable contacts began to emerge in Australia, coinciding with the appointment of Lord Brassey as the new Governor-General of Western Australia. Brassey had been president of Barnardo's in Britain and had promised to provide land from his holdings for a Barnardo farm in Australia. Now a 'friend at court' for the organization, he began to lobby the Western Australian government on its behalf, and several parties of Barnardo's children emigrated to Western Australia between 1896 and 1914. Despite such efforts, organized emigration of Barnardo's children did not really take off until after the First World War.

Another fund-raising musical tour did take place, however, again on an ambitious schedule. Ten children, aged between 13 and 14, and two accompanying adults arrived at Fremantle in 1908 and toured for a year in Australia. They performed almost every night, when not travelling, on bagpipes, hand bells and ocarina (a type of flute), proving a very popular part of the entertainments (they also included religious talks and an explanation of the Homes' works). The party then moved on to repeat their success in New Zealand, where the boys all decided to remain—unlike the earlier band of children who had all returned to Britain. As farewells were said in Christchurch, the children, all of whom had been offered work on nearby farms, were each given a watch, £10 and a Bible signed by William Baker, chairman of the Barnardo council. The boys were also allowed to keep their bagpipes, an appropriate gesture, as in Australia alone the tour had raised over £10,000 (£570,000 in today's money) for the Homes.[4]

Although knowledge of Barnardo's Homes was increasing in Australia, the first official immigration scheme—to New South Wales—did not start until 1921 (many years after Barnardo's own death in 1905). It was sponsored by an Australian organization, the Sydney

Millions Club, formed in 1916 with the ambitious aim of establishing a million British farmers on a million farms in New South Wales and Victoria. The Millions Club was approached by Mabel Cameron, who had been sent to Australia by William Baker, the successor to Dr Barnardo. Her remit was to raise funds for, and awareness of, Barnardo's migration work.

It was not always an easy task, as concerns about child migration persisted. The issue of hereditary delinquency was frequently raised, often by the medical profession, anxieties which Barnardo himself had addressed in his lifetime: 'I have myself proved over and over again that a new and healthy environment is more powerful to transform and renovate than even heredity has been in placing and evoking taint.'[5] The organization reiterated his convictions, confident in the ability of a new start to overcome the deprivation of early years and any un-happy genetic 'legacy' that might exist.

Successful negotiations with the president of the Millions Club, Sir Arthur Rickard, resulted in the arrival of 47 boys on the SS *Berrima* in 1921. Rickard had his own agenda and was keen to support child migration schemes as a tool in his government's White Australia policy —a regular influx of productive white settlers was seen as an aid in keeping out the Japanese and Chinese and other Asian settlers. The first party of boys, all aged over 14, had more immediate concerns. Their reception hostel was in New South Wales, at a former Red Cross hospital at Scarborough at Botany Bay—a name long associated with the misery of transportation. It was run by a Matron Weigall who later established the Police Boys' Clubs in New South Wales. However, this was to prove inadequate as the numbers of children increased. They arrived on ships such as the SS *Demosthenes* (1924), the SS *Euripides* (1923 and 1924), the SS *Berrima* (1926), the SS *Ballarat* (1926), the SS *Barrabool* (1928) and RMS *Otranto*, which made voyages in 1933, 1937 and—in a final post-war journey—in 1956.

The voyage out was an exciting experience for most of the children —a brief interval of relaxation before confronting their uncertain futures in an unknown land. Allan Moore quotes the vivid account of Arthur Turrell, who sailed with the other 'excited, inexperienced young hopefuls' from Barnardo's on the SS *Demosthenes* in 1924. The party left Tilbury on the day of the FA cup final—one can only hope that somehow he got to hear the result!

I do recall the romantic hours we used to spend on deck on still
evenings under starlit southern skies, with our first view of the Southern Cross blazing above us and the muffled throb of the ship's engines
in our ears ... someone would be strumming a banjo or mandolin,
with some of us sitting on deck chairs, hatchway or taffrails, balanced
precariously above the waters, listening with rapt attention to old well-
loved tunes or singing along with them.[6]

The children enjoyed playing in waves breaking over the fore part of
the ship, and Turrell remembers the 'magnificent spectacle' of Table
Mountain at sunrise 'with the mountain wearing its cloudy "table-
cloth" and that mysterious dark continent brooding behind it'. On
arrival at Albany, Western Australia—the southern tip of another
'mysterious continent'—the boat dropped off some boys en route for
the Fairbridge Farm School before sailing across the choppy Great
Australian Bight to Melbourne. The party was entertained at Melbourne by the Society of Friends (Quakers) before progressing to a
reception by the Lord Mayor at Sydney. The official welcome made less
impression on the young boy than recognizing Charlie Chaplin on a film
poster for *The Gold Rush*—a reassuring link with memories of home.

A new home was established in Ashfield, the purchase of land and
property there coinciding with the arrival of the first party of Barnardo
girls in 1923. The girls, 32 in number and all older children, sailed on
the SS *Euripides* in March 1923, accompanied by three watchful
guardians who must have had their work cut out. They were permitted
to arrive by the New South Wales government on condition that they
were to be placed out in positions as domestic servants for two years.

The Barnardo's committee in Australia was particularly keen on
girls; to maintain momentum and enthusiasm, it ideally wanted regular supplies of 100 girls a month and 50 boys every two months.[7] More
boys were available through other projects such as the Dreadnought
Scheme, while girls were a relatively rare commodity. Moore cites the
experience of Kathleen Rourke, a Barnardo's girl who on finishing her
schooling requested to join her two sisters in Australia; permission
was granted, and she sailed on the SS *Berrima* on 11 February 1926.
Delighted to be going, she notes drily that, while the lady doctor and
nurse were seldom required professionally, 'they had to take a somewhat more demanding role of handling a pack of girls suddenly let
loose on the world for the first time. Some of us had the very devil in

us, causing many headaches for our minders'.[8] She, too, was captivated by the beauty of Cape Town's Table Mountain 'looming over us
as we entered the harbour, a thing of exquisite beauty'. The girls were
escorted on a trip up the mountain in a charabanc by local Girl
Guides, and given a tour of the city. Another troop entertained the
party at Fremantle with a 'marvellous' meal, although poignantly
what the young girl recalled most strongly was 'the lattice fence with
wisteria hanging all over it, bringing a longing for a home of my own'.

Her first experience of Australia, however, was to be domestic service, which swiftly replaced any opportunities for a career. Rourke
observes how, like most of the other girl migrants, she was destined for
'domestic service at a very low wage ... your life was ordered by the
people for whom you worked, and it did not include deserting your
duties to better yourself. Needless to say, I was not a success and as I
grew older grew more and more discontented ... there was no hope
without experience.'[9] Only at the age of 23, independent of the
Homes, was she able to develop the career she sought, beginning with
a book-keeping and typing course.

Rourke typically came from Barkingside in Essex, where the
Barnardo Girls' Village Home was founded in the 1870s. Designed to
house around 1,500 girls, the Village consisted of a collection of cottages around a green, plus its own church and school; the structure
influenced Fairbridge Farm Schools and Barnardo's own farm school
at Picton. The training that the girls received at Barkingside sought to
equip them with the domestic skills required to find a place in service,
and so make their way in the world (plate 26). Boys were taught a craft
or trade in their own Homes, for example at Stepney Causeway, the
first Barnardo's Home, which opened in 1870. Barkingside today holds
the Barnardo's archives, with material dating back to 1874 and including 500,000 images and films of the organization's work in Canada
and Australia. It also features accounts submitted by former Barnardo's
children, as well as records of the individuals who passed through its
doors. More material from Barnardo's is held at the University of Liverpool's Department of Special Collections and Archives (p.241). It
includes documents ranging from Barnardo's own sermons and publications to children's records and fund-raising appeals—and papers of
the organizations that Barnardo's took over, such as the Macpherson
Homes and the Liverpool Sheltering Homes. Access to details of

children is restricted, but much remains to give a flavour of Barnardo's aspirations and achievements, and of how the organization changed lives so radically in Britain and abroad.

A poignant account of travelling from Barkingside to the Fairbridge Farm School in Pinjarra, Western Australia, has been provided by Joan Halls (née Roles) in her book *Miracle of Fairbridge*. It describes how, together with her younger sister Kath, she was selected in 1933 to be part of the *Otranto* party after their parents had given permission for them to be sent to the Fairbridge school. The governor of the Barkingside Village Home vividly portrayed the lovely boat trip in store for them, and the freedom of open spaces they would enjoy once in Australia. The girls had six weeks to make up their own minds, but it did not take them long—the excitement of moving outside the Village setting was almost overwhelming for an 11-year-old girl and her younger sister.

It was not unrelieved pleasure, however. Excitement turned into apprehension and doubt when both children had to have smallpox injections and to say goodbye to their parents and friends. They travelled to Australia House, where they met others in their party, and then proceeded to Tilbury Docks, where they received money for the first time. On board ship, the sisters shared a two-berth cabin and relished the novelty of mealtimes with shiny glasses, silver cutlery, delicious smells and stewards, obliging throughout in smart white coats. Standards on board seem to have been good. Berths had personal washbasins, fluffy towels and fresh drinking water—fortunately for hygiene, everyone had their own drinking glass. Normally restricted to the third-class areas, the girls occasionally explored beyond them, and were once invited to morning tea by a first-class passenger who presumably felt sorry for two small girls en route to an unknown land.

Halls notes that new foods, for example fricasséed rabbit, were sampled on board, a pleasure tempered by unpleasant new experiences such as seasickness.[10] The stifling heat in the Suez Canal brought with it hordes of flies, and became even more intense in the Red Sea. New sights crowded in upon the girls, from the rock of Gibraltar looming in the distance, to their first encounters with non-white people, to the crossing of the Equator—followed by a full day outing at Colombo, where they saw large cats, tigers, lions, elephants and chimps at a tea party! Arrival jitters crept in on leaving Colombo and discipline became more strict. At last the voyage was over and Pinjarra became a reality. On arrival Joan and Kath were allowed to stay together, assigned with 12 other girls to Livingstone Cottage. A Colonel Heath, later obliged to resign from Northcote Farm School in the 1940s, was the governor (p.158).

The Roles sisters' destination, a Fairbridge Farm School, was not unusual for Barnardo's children. Over 400 British migrants (some 232 British boys and 176 girls) were dispatched to Fairbridge schools in Australia before Barnardo's opened its own farm training school for boys at Mowbray Park, Picton, in 1929. Located 50 miles south of Sydney and adopting many Fairbridge features, it was designed to accommodate 100 boys aged from 8 or 9 to 14 or 15. Like the Fairbridge schemes, the farm school at Picton contained a number of cottages in a village-like settlement. A large house already existed when the Mowbray Park site was acquired in 1928; it was assigned as a cottage for the senior boys, and a further four cottage homes were built, each accommodating up to 20 boys. Cottage mothers cared for the children in each 'house', and—in a pattern very similar to Fairbridge Farm Schools—there was a common dining hall, hospital, laundry, chapel and houses for the staff. At Mowbray Park the staff consisted of a superintendent and lady superintendent, cottage mothers, a senior matron, an assistant to the superintendent and a games master—sport was always considered important in developing the children's physique. The children attended the Central School and Elementary School at Picton, where they were encouraged to mix with the local children and their parents.

Picton was set in a rural environment, and for some former migrants —such as the 'old boy' cited by Howard and Leonard—recollections of their youth there were almost idyllic. 'Those five years at Picton were among the happiest in my life ... it took me a while to get used to the dryness of the landscape ... but I soon revelled in the wide open spaces and long summers. My memories of childhood are filled with running barefoot, swimming nude in the creek, catching turtles, stealing birds' eggs and chasing rabbits with our motley collection of dogs.'[11] Another boy who came to Picton in 1930, George B., also offers a positive assessment: 'Mostly I have very happy memories of that time. We swam, fished for eels and the market gardener and his wife made a bit of a pet of me... We were well-dressed and well-shod and well-fed, better than many kids in the thirties.'[12]

In total, Barnardo's emigrated 2,361 children to Australia and most of them passed through Picton. Many were employed and forged a career on farms; there was not much option, as schooling ended at the age of 14. Dennis U. was one who suffered from the educational disruption, having to repeat three years of elementary school in Australia despite having started at high school before leaving England.[13] Although critical of the school's limited aspirations for its children — 'The farm school was a place where they trained cheap labour for the Aussie farmer' — Dennis came to enjoy both the farm work and sport, playing cricket and rugby against nearby town teams. The shock he felt on first arriving at Picton was shared by many young migrants, unprepared for the Australian landscape or climate. 'All one could see was a hot brown land, no green grass but plenty of dead trees. It reminded me of country I had seen in cowboy films… I thought about the boys who had gone to Canada and I didn't want to be where I was.'

There were some compensations at Picton. Dennis was happy with his cottage mother who 'was very nice to us and did a lot to make our stay a happy one', and the boys themselves had a strong code of loyalty, shielding one another against authority. The growing boys had mixed little with girls, however; even though there were girls at their school, contact was strictly limited. Barnardo's established a girls' house nearby in Burwood in the 1920s, with individual cottages on the Barkingside model accommodating up to 12 girls. Burwood was run by a matron assisted by staff, and girls there attended Burwood Central Domestic School.

A report by Barnardos Australia in the National Archives describes how, between the ages of 12 and 14, boys were given instruction in poultry farming, gardening and light farm duties as part of their regular curriculum (MH 102/2328). Older boys, aged 14 to 16, were given 'full technical farm training', while those not opting for farming as a career had — in theory at least — the option of higher education. This did not always seem to happen in practice, however. Henry G., for example, who came to Picton in 1929, recounts that 'I should never have gone on the farm. Mr Davy, schoolmaster at Mowbray Park, wanted me to go on to higher education, but there was no way.' Instead he was dispatched after training to a farm in Maitland for seven years, from 14 to 21, where conditions were typically harsh. 'I think I got two days off in seven years, cows having to be milked, not knowing what a holiday was. I slept on a straw mattress in a shed … with rats scurrying overhead.'[14]

Another Barnardo's migrant of 1921, James I., also had a very tough experience on a Maitland dairy farm. He arrived in Australia on the SS *Berrima* in 1929, aged 10, and was sent to work straight away. 'There were 60 cows to be milked morning and night, and only James, the boss and the boss's son, a young lad, to do all the work. James said he went to school each day and got a hiding each night.'[15] He ran away to learn carpentry two years later.

Another Barnardo's boy, Eric D., was sent to Australia in 1932 after two years in the organization's care. Also aged 10, he first thought Picton 'dreadful', arriving in a freezing cold winter which seemed even more hostile than the blazing summer heat that daunted Dennis U. Eric, who had chosen Australia as a destination because he loved the sea and it was the longest voyage available, found himself on an Estonian-owned farm where he slept 'in a hut made of packing cases on a concrete base', working long hours for 10 shillings (£15 in today's money) a week. He was removed by Barnardo's official Mr Ladd, because conditions were too severe (an example of aftercare working in practice), to be replaced by five adult men who came and left in quick succession.[16]

Barnardo's Homes received British government assistance towards the maintenance of children resident at Mowbray Park until 1939. The rate, unsurprisingly, was prescribed and unvarying—four shillings per week per boy, with a further grant of £3.15s per boy per year towards the aftercare cost of those who had left Mowbray Park. The financial equation was always tight, and the migration of Barnardo's children, like those of other schemes, was brought to a standstill by the Second World War. However, Barnardo's was established as a major player in Australia by this time, and its experience was keenly sought by the British government when they came to implement the CORB child migration scheme (see chapter 6).

The Big Brother Movement

The Big Brother Movement also played an important role in arranging the emigration of British children—this time only boys—to Australia.

Founded in 1924 by Sir Richard Linton, it aimed to promote the emigration of selected boys, providing each arrival with a designated 'Big Brother' to replace absent parents and friends (plate 29). The Big Brother was to offer moral and practical support, and 'endeavour to ensure that each new arrival will become an effective Australian citizen'. In many ways the scheme proved a success. Most of the original 'Little Brothers' who went out in the 1920s and 30s, for example, served with the Australian forces during the war, and many of them gained commissions or went on to work in established businesses.

The Movement's aims were worthy, but financing was always problematic. It received a grant in aid from public funds from 1925 to 1931, during which period it placed over 2,000 boys aged from 15 to 19 on farms in New South Wales and Victoria. The Great Depression (and the suspension of assisted migration from Britain) saw the scheme itself suspended in 1931, but it resumed again in 1937. Contributions from the British government towards the cost of the Movement's London office started again, lasting until 1940 when the Second World War made the expense prohibitive. A grant was also made in 1938 to the Victoria and New South Wales branches, through whom the aftercare work in Australia was carried out. The Victoria branch was wound up, however, in 1941.

The original plan—to select Little Brothers who wished to obtain employment on farms (and thus gain valuable experience of sheep and cattle)—was extended in later years to include youths who wished to enter urban business or other employment. Little Brothers looking for rural employment were enrolled at the Big Brother Movement Memorial Training Farm, 'Karmsley Hills', which was based at Cecil Park, Fairfield, and reached via Liverpool, New South Wales. The boys received about a month's training at the site. Youths at the training farm were given the opportunity to decide whether they really wished to work on the land before being placed on rural properties far removed from the Movement's headquarters—a sensible precaution, designed to benefit all concerned. Those who remained committed to farming were then placed in positions on farms and stations with the help of the Movement's District Big Brothers in the areas concerned. The boys' decisions changed over time, reflecting the changes in Australia itself.

All British applications to the scheme were dealt with by the Big

Brother Movement office at their headquarters in Australia House, Strand, in London. The London office also acted as a go-between for Little Brothers and their parents and family, the latter applying to the office for news of their sons. Reports on the status of boys were received from time to time, the greater flexibility in providing information reflecting the differences between the Big Brother scheme and those run by other migration organizations. Critically, the Big Brother Movement did not involve school-age, underprivileged children from institutions; its recruits were intentionally drawn from a higher social class than that of other child migrants. Of the first 1,515 Little Brothers brought to Australia between 1926 and 1929, 121 had attended a public school and 914 of the remainder had some secondary education, mainly in grammar schools. Essentially applicants needed to be male, aged between 15 ½ and 18 and of European parentage. To be selected, youths needed not only to show a strong desire to settle and make a career for themselves in Australia, but also to have no friends and relatives there able to sponsor them individually and provide the guidance and support essential for their first few years settling into a new life. Such was the role that the Big Brother Movement offered to fulfil.

Responsibilities were present on both sides, of course. Before sailing, each Little Brother had to sign a statement agreeing to follow his Big Brother's advice, not to drink spirits or gamble, and to consult his Big Brothers—or failing that the Movement's headquarters—if he got into trouble. Little Brothers were required to open an account at a savings bank and to save at least half their wages, and to maintain regular contact with their parents and Big Brothers (writing at least once a month was proposed). They were not to leave the employer allocated by the Movement without their Big Brother's permission, and they had to be prepared to be flexible, taking up a position in any state of the Commonwealth if need be. A sense of responsibility to the Movement as a whole was also requested, and Little Brothers were asked to subscribe 12 shillings per year to a welfare fund.

The procedure, from date of application to date of sailing, took up to six months—possibly more, as boys would not be included in a party for sailing until they had reached the age of 15 ¾. Boys selected for the Movement were formed into parties. Every two months a party sailed, with its contingent of boys in the charge of escorting welfare officers. On arrival in Australia, officers delivered the boys over to the organization.

Each boy selected and sponsored by the Movement received an assisted passage, and so would have to pay only £5 (£167 in today's terms) himself. The remaining fare (including a free railway ticket between home and the port of embarkation in Britain) was borne by the Australian government. However, participation did involve other costs. Each Little Brother had to pay at least £8 capital expenditure, together with £6 for incidental expenses (£270 and £200 today). These covered pocket money for the voyage and a £1 fee (£33 today) for an obligatory Commonwealth medical examination.

The level of support that Big Brothers could offer their Little Brothers varied, as did the level of interest they brought to their responsibilities. Logistics were sometimes a problem, with the Big Brother being someone from a provincial city while the Little Brother was often stationed on a remote rural property. In such circumstances their chances of meeting face to face were extremely low, and maintaining written contact became consequently more difficult. As the Depression started to bite, many Big Brothers experienced financial difficulties or even faced ruin, and in such straits their Little Brothers were often ignored. As a result some 350 Little Brothers returned to Britain during the 1930s.

Many stayed, however, and the National Archives contains fascinating reports dated May 1936 which relate to Little Brothers who had arrived in 1922 (DO 35/687/5). The youngest had now reached the age of 29 and the eldest 31. Similar reports were completed in 1936 for arrivals in 1929, whose ages now varied between 21 and 25. The reports, put together as part of a case to decide on further government subsidies, reveal an interesting variety of fortunes (plate 28). Many boys' activities since leaving the Movement simply could not be traced; but some had indeed found work on farms and others had taken different employment in rural areas. Occupations ranged from working on the railways to managing a picture theatre (cinema) and working in bar or as a taxi driver. Some former Little Brothers were now working as insurance agents or fruit agents; others had become dairy or mixed farmers. One had tragically died at the age of 25 through a burst blood vessel near the heart, possibly caused by over-exertion.[17]

Some Little Brothers, such as the friends George M. and Thomas V., chose to take up share farming—in their case dairy work at Morisset on the south coast, an area both were familiar with. An earlier enterprise growing vegetables had proved less successful, and the boys had decided to try their fortunes in the area they knew. Another Little Brother 'saw a chance of improving his prospects by taking on carpentry work'; he was doing well, still living with the family at Terara who had employed him for farm work. The boys' personal situations were noted as well as their careers—whether they were engaged, married with children or had brought their family to Australia too. All of these were viewed with approval as evidence of stability and long-term commitment.

Actual brothers are shown to have gone into business together, such as T.G. and Benjamin A., who were renting an orchard of 75 acres with complete plant; their prospects were deemed to be good, as were those who stayed in their placements for several years and became integrated into family life. Harry P., for example, had been in the same place, working in mixed farming, since arriving seven years earlier; he was 'thought well of and treated as one of the family'.

Criticisms were also made, however, of Little Brothers whose conduct left something to be desired. Reports of laziness and insubordination were duly noted; Norris S., a railway labourer, was 'inclined to argue' and not the most dedicated of workers, while Robert W. was described as 'a great talker of the malcontent type'. Sometimes the faults were seen as those of youth, which could be ironed out as the boy matured. One such, John B., was allegedly 'rather too fond of pleasure', but he did at least seem to be aware of the fact, recognizing that he needed soon to settle down. The report notes with approval that a potential engagement was in the air. Passivity was also a failing in official eyes, and William A. was castigated for appearing 'to have no ambition or much initiative'. Of course, the reports are one-sided, and the real feelings of the Little Brothers as they struggled to develop careers in the aftermath of the Depression are seldom recorded.

The Christian Brothers farm schools

The Christian Brothers were another major player in child emigration to Australia. A Catholic teaching order founded in Ireland in 1802, they had managed orphanages in Western Australia since 1897, when they took over the boys' orphanage at Subiaco from the Sisters of Mercy. Further orphanages were built and managed at Clontarf (1903), Castledare (1929) and Tardun (1926) as the Christian Brothers in Australia sought to emulate the success of the Fairbridge Society. The order responded to the growth of the Fairbridge Farm School at Pinjarra, south of Perth (pp.145–51), which had attracted large numbers of British children, by developing their own farm school at Mullewa-Tardun. This remote site—65 miles east of Geraldton—was an extension of the Clontarf orphanage near Perth. Its intention was to train older British boys in farming and farm management, and to place the most successful ones in their own farm properties.

This was not all it could offer, however. The Christian Brothers were all trained as teachers, though they were not ordained and did not receive pay. Those recruited in Australia were trained at the Strathfield Christian Brothers College in Sydney, and their normal work was to staff Catholic schools at the request of the church authorities. One of the advantages of the migration scheme that they were proposing was an opportunity to train boys for employment in fields outside agriculture, depending on their individual aptitude. Training centres could cater for different requirements, and there was scope for higher education through the Christian Brothers' residential colleges. Coupled with the Brothers' extensive training in teaching, it sounded an attractive option to a British Catholic organization, the Crusade of Rescue and Homes for Destitute Catholic Children. The seed was sown at the Crusade of Rescue's annual general meeting in 1937, when Canon Craven hinted at a scheme for sending British boys to the Christian Brothers' Agricultural School at Tardun. They also considered sending girls to a convent in Perth for training in domestic service.

Joseph Lyons, the prime minister of Australia, as well as the premier of Western Australia, Mr Wilcox, and Mr Casey, the Australian treasurer, emerged as warmly in favour of such a scheme when they visited Britain in 1937. They had a high regard for the Clontarf School and were anxious to have 'suitable' boy and girl migrants. In co-operation with the Crusade of Rescue, they approached the Overseas Settlement Committee, offering to provide children with a Catholic version of a Fairbridge Farm School. The Christian Brothers adapted their scheme to include some Catholic boys from Britain shortly before the outbreak of the Second World War. Proposals became reality when, in July 1938, 37 Catholic boys left Britain for Western Australia after being selected and approved by the Christian Brothers and Australian authorities. *The Times* (18 April 1939) reported the migration under the headline 'The Fairbridge Ideal':

> At Tardun, in the northeast wheat belt of Western Australia, the Christian Brothers of the Roman Catholic Church have pioneered just such a venture as Fairbridge must have dreamed of. Boys from Western Australian orphanages who are adjudged to have a bent towards farming are taken at 14, to the Christian Brothers' Agricultural School at Tardun. There, the Brothers have acquired 20,000 acres of mixed farming country; 6,000 acres of it cleared, and a staff of 12 men, nine of them Brothers, to undertake the training of the boys. Those who prove reliable and capable are sent, when their training ends, to be managers of farming properties. Each who emerges successfully from this further test receives a farm and a four bed roomed cottage at Mount Pleasant, in the Midland district where the Brothers have established a community settlement on 17,000 acres of land. This is a kind of undertaking which the Fairbridge Movement might well emulate. A fitting tribute to Fairbridge himself.

The boys were accorded plenty of attention on their arrival in Perth. *St Peter's Net*, the fascinating official newsletter of the Crusade of Rescue and Homes for Destitute Catholic Children, gives insights into the hopes and expectations of those seeking to emigrate children, and the difficult social conditions in Britain with which they had to contend. It includes in its edition of 1938 a report from Reverend Brother Conlon of the Christian Brothers in Tardun. This in turn is taken from *The Record*, the official organ of the archdiocese of Perth, Western Australia, and it describes the official welcome given to the 37 boys in glowing terms:

> The party of 37 British boys was accorded a civic reception in the Fremantle Town Hall, and later was received at the Clontarf Orphanage by an official party... How different this from the popular conception of the arrival of the emigrant in a strange land. Here actually were members of a government joining with the Archbishop of a great diocese to welcome 37 boys come to make their future in the vast territories of Western Australia. Not even the most distinguished visitor could expect a finer welcome, and we doubt whether any may ever receive a finer. Let us hope the boys will not get swelled heads over it

all. If anyone were to address to us one half the compliments that
were showered upon them by the responsible members of the Western
Australian legislature, we are certain that we should feel vastly more
important than we do at present. But the thing to note is that these
boys were welcomed, and not merely welcomed but heartily and
civically welcomed.

The Leader of the Opposition, C.G. Latham, observed that he himself
had come to Western Australia as a boy in similar circumstances 47
years previously in 1891, and that he was proud to be there to welcome
them. He hoped they would have as good a time as he had. And he
hoped that girls would come out also.

The Crusade of Rescue echoed that wish as it prepared to send out
the second batch of boys in 1938. It was hoped that girls would follow
in due course, and enthusiastic tributes were paid to Reverend Brother
Conlon, father of the scheme. By 1939 the first three groups of British
child migrants—114 boys in total—had arrived at the Christian
Brothers' orphanages in Western Australia. Initially the St Mary's
Agricultural Schools in Clontarf and Tardun were used for British
child migrants, and the movement is often referred to as the 'Tardun'
or 'Clontarf' schemes. Lists of these boys, whose ages range from 7 to
14 years, can be found in the National Archives (DO 35/690/5 and
DO 35/1138).

One of these boys was nine-year-old Michael Hannigan, who
describes his experiences on the website of the Blaisdon Hall (Old
Boys) Salesian School.[18] He and three other boys had been living in
St Joseph's Home, Enfield, Middlesex, run by the Sisters of Charity.
Along with 37 boys from other Catholic orphanages in England, a
Christian Brother and two Sisters of Nazareth from Hammersmith in
West London, they boarded the RMS *Strathaird* and sailed from Lon-
don on 8 July 1938.

Hannigan enjoyed the 'fun-filled' voyage, enlivened by many
'strange sights', and was excited to arrive at Fremantle on 9 August.
The party was given a civic reception complete with band, an event
reported with enthusiasm in the local press, and then waited a few more
days for the arrival of RMS *Otranto*, which brought another 31 boys
and two accompanying Sisters of Nazareth. The group then set off on
the final leg of the journey, to Tardun itself, and Hannigan graphically
portrays the boys' nervousness as the trip neared its end:

The contingent of 68 boys, mainly 7–11 years old, the four Nuns and several Brothers embarked on a steam train for a 300-mile journey north of Perth to the Agricultural School run by the Christian Brothers … On leaving Perth we were soon into the vast and sparsely populated bush land which got ever more desolate with every mile. Eventually we arrived at a small railway station called Tardun … to be met by three trucks. We clambered aboard and travelled a further 10 miles into the bush, to suddenly come upon what was to be our home for the next six to ten years!

Since departing England in July we were on a high—so much had happened. New sights and experiences, new friends made among the boys, we had been feted and fussed over on arrival at Fremantle and had a 300-mile train trip! Reality wasn't long in coming, however.

An agreement was made on 24 April 1939 between the British government and the Christian Brothers of Western Australia for financial support for no more than 110 British child migrants and the extension of the training school at Tardun. This was agreed under the Empire Settlement Acts of 1922 and 1937. They allowed the government to co-operate with private organizations (including religious orders) in preparing and carrying out schemes for affording joint assistance to those who intended to settle in any part of His Majesty's Overseas Dominions. Children were a key part of such schemes.

On this initial wave of enthusiasm, it was hoped that large numbers of Crusade boys and girls would emigrate to Australia in similar schemes. The Christian Brothers established four destinations for young migrants: Clontarf Boys' Home and St Vincent's Orphanage at Castledare, both near Perth; the remote Agricultural School at Tardun, where boys chosen to receive agricultural training were sent directly they arrived; and St Joseph's Farm School at Bindoon, about 60 miles from Perth, where boys were taught elementary agricultural science, care of stock, milking, personal laundry, cooking and techniques for growing fruit and vegetables. At Clontarf, migrant boys received a full course of primary education including training in wood and metal-work. They were also taught trades such as carpentry, plumbing, brick-laying, plastering, moulding, tailoring and shoemaking.

For many of the children, the sudden separation from friends made on the voyage compounded the trauma of arrival—an experience vividly recounted by this 12-year-old girl: 'We came off the boat like we were sheep. When we got to the bottom of the gangplanks we were all separated, some of my friends went off in different directions and I didn't ever see them again … we were taken out to the bush to Bindoon; that was the most frightening part, right out in the bush. We thought it was the Black Hole of Calcutta.'[19]

Another boy, Laurie Humphreys, came to Bindoon aged 13 in 1947. He sailed on the SS *Asturias*, the first ship to bring children from British orphanages to Fremantle after the Second World War. Humphreys' powerful account of his experiences contains fascinating detail about Boys' Town Bindoon, including his dramatic first impression of the site: 'as we turned the final corner into Boys' Town Bindoon, the harsh reality of the difference from what we'd left behind in England and what we'd come to was very apparent. There were no trees, only bleak, rather spectacular looking buildings. It was very quiet at night. The night sky, with so many bright stars, was strange.'[20]

The Christian Brothers set a target of bringing some 50,000 orphaned or abandoned children to Australia, but such figures were never achieved. It was evident even by 1942, five years before Laurie Humphreys' arrival, that this was no longer tenable—the War Orphans Act, passed in the aftermath of the *City of Benares* disaster (pp.186–90) forbade all children to leave Britain in wartime and forced all organizations to suspend their emigration programmes. After 1945, as both countries struggled to implement economic recovery, a mood for change began to influence the social policies of both, and child emigration never resumed on the scale of the pre-war years.

The immediate post-war years in Australia saw rapid expansion, rising wages and a shortage of labour. The last in particular helped to develop a government-sponsored immigration scheme, starting in 1948, initially targeting an intake of 70,000 a year. This figure, together with natural increase, would, the authorities calculated, result in an annual population increase of two per cent—the maximum increase thought possible without economic strain. Crucially for the child migration organizations, however, pre-war immigration policies of solely developing the land were abandoned and immigration was no longer encouraged exclusively from the mother country. The large number of displaced persons from Central Europe offered an immediate source of trained immigrant labour, and many were eager to come; in the first three decades following the war, over two million new immigrants settled in Australia. They included about one-third from Britain, both child migrants, as organizations got their activities going again, and also over one million families benefiting from the Assisted Passage Scheme. Colloquially known as the £10 Poms, British migrants paid this nominal fee for their passage to Australia in return for agreeing to settle there for a minimum of two years.

The Garnett Report

The need for change in child migration had been signalled in a series of reports on farm schools undertaken during the Second World War. They prompted the British government to commission W. Garnett, Official Secretary to the High Commissioner for the United Kingdom in Australia, to prepare a report in response. Garnett was to explore conditions not only at Fairbridge Farm Schools (see chapter 5), but also at the Barnardo Farm School at Picton and in schools run by the Christian Brothers.

The original intention of Kingsley Fairbridge had been to train boys to take on and run their own farms, but economic conditions in Australia through the 1920s and 1930s made this a virtually impossible goal for any of the schools. Only 50 of the 940 migrant boys who passed through Picton by 1945 managed to establish themselves in their own businesses. Garnett realized that only a tiny proportion of the boys could become independent farmers, and recommended changes in the schemes to allow children to follow aptitudes in other areas. To assist this, he proposed setting up hostels in connection with farm schools, to house children studying at high schools or technical colleges, and recommended that Domestic and Manual Training Centres should be provided at all schools.

Garnett also advised on staff changes at the farm schools, including creating Farm School Management Committees with more women and others with special training in handling children. He identified the segregation and isolation of the communities as inherent problems, and proposed more efficient aftercare arrangements, including travelling aftercare officers who would also visit prospective employers.

Garnett's report stressed that change was essential if farm schools were to continue receiving support in the post-war world, and the organizations were swift to take note. In 1945 Barnardo's opened a new group of homes at Normanhurst in Sydney, which sought to bring the children into closer contact with Australian society. Three cottages cared for children aged 10 and over who attended local schools; they later gained apprenticeships in the area or took up positions in shops or offices. After the war, there was a noticeable shift from the rural economy to the city. Australia had become more industrialized and opportunities other than farming were opening up for child migrants. As a result, Barnardo's approached the Overseas Settlement Department to seek grants for aftercare for boys and girls placed in occupations other than farming.

The story of Michael H., who sailed to Sydney on the *New Australia* with a Barnardo's party of child migrants in 1953, is a striking rags-to-riches tale. Recounted by Ann Howard in her book *C'mon Over!*, it shows what could be achieved by a lucky—and enterprising—few. Michael worked on several farms in difficult conditions before finding a more successful placement with a family of Plymouth Brethren, where he became interested in farm mechanization. He studied engineering at night school and came to Sydney to work on the installation of swimming pools, as well as acting as an impromptu door-to-door salesman for barbecue sets. By the age of 27 he had purchased his first boat, *Islander III*, and set out with friends to travel the world.

A fortunate encounter at Papua New Guinea prompted Michael to hire his yacht to miners from the local copper mines, and to learn diving and salvaging techniques. He became a freelance salvage expert, learned to operate sonar and radar, and successfully located a German cargo boat, loaded with tin, at the bottom of the South China Seas. Michael became a millionaire as the result of this find; another one, a 17th-century Chinese junk full of beautiful Ming dynasty china, contributed to his burgeoning art collection.[21] It was a long way from his early days in the cowsheds.

Meanwhile, reports on child migration continued. The first after the Second World War was made in 1950 by the catchily named Interdepartmental Committee on Migration Policy (also known as the Syers Committee). It recommended pursuing schemes of child migration whether or not the Empire Settlement Acts were renewed (a thorny political issue at the time, as Britain's empire began to fragment in the new world order). However, there was a proviso to continuing the scheme: that British authorities should be satisfied with the conditions awaiting children overseas. In practice their satisfaction (from half a world away) depended on the views of the government of the Commonwealth of Australia. Another report, entitled 'Child Migration to Australia', was commissioned by the British Home Office in 1953 from one John Moss, a retiring County Welfare Officer from Kent who had served on the Curtis Committee on Child Welfare in 1944. Officials were preparing Regulations for the control of voluntary migration agencies, and Moss's report was designed to provide information on institutions where the Home Office had relatively few details. It concluded in favour of the practice, commenting that the societies maintained a high standard in their homes and institutions in Australia and produced 'remarkably successful results'. Yet another report, by the Garner Committee in 1954, also recommended continuing existing schemes, but with a movement towards placing children in family homes in Australia rather than institutions.

Changes were happening on the ground, too. More and more former farm boys relocated to the urban areas in the post-war years, and in 1959 Barnardo's large farm school at Picton was closed. A smaller school opened at Scone, New South Wales, reflecting the declining interest in farming shown by the children. In 1960 the Burwood Girls' School was closed, and the Normanhurst complex of three cottages was converted to family group homes. The changes illustrated Barnardo's new emphasis on smaller children's homes which more closely resembled the average family home.

The migration of Barnardo's children from Britain to Australia finally ceased in 1967, by which time most schools had started to admit Australian children. By the late 1960s, Barnardos Australia was firmly established, and it was no longer viewed as an inherently British institution. Instead, the organization had become more of a service for Australian children in need through the provision of fostering and counselling.

The Christian Brothers' schools

The Christian Brothers' schools were also assessed in the reports of Garnett and others. A series of unfavourable reports on the schools appeared in 1942 and 1943, placing the prospect of future migration in jeopardy. One Ronald Cross, for example, High Commissioner for the

United Kingdom in Canberra, visited the St Mary's Agricultural College at Tardun in October 1942. In his report to Clement Attlee (then Secretary of State for Dominion Affairs), Cross states that he met Brother Sandes, principal of the college. On approaching the main establishment he was taken aback to see a number of boys looking like ragamuffins—barefoot and dressed in extremely old, untidy and dirty-looking shirts and shorts. The whole place was reported to be suffering from serious overcrowding, with 248 children accommodated in an area designed for half the number. The explanation was that boys from other Christian Brothers' schools and boys from Geraldton High School had been evacuated to Tardun as the army had requisitioned their premises.

Michael Hannigan, who had arrived at Tardun in 1938, had first-hand experience of the overcrowded conditions. Describing 1942 as 'a year of some upheaval', he remembers how the sudden arrival of the 'refugees' brought the war home to those in the remote bush:

> Although we had experienced little evidence of the war, being so isolated, the first week of March an influx of 150 boys, five Brothers and six nuns arrived. Forty-six Australian boys, boarders from St Patrick's College Geraldton and 104 orphans from Clontarf, Perth, were evacuated to join us. So suddenly we had more than double the number of people to accommodate. It was a logistical nightmare, chaotic at times, but somehow we managed![22]

All of the British migrants were based at Tardun, and Cross described their accommodation as 'rough'. Boys slept in dormitories and on covered balconies crammed to—and beyond—capacity, with beds covered by old rugs in dilapidated condition. Bed linen was torn and not very clean, and kitchens were rough and unappetizing. Classrooms were also overcrowded and untidy.

Cross's report was particularly damaging to the Christian Brothers in comparison with the Fairbridge Farm School at Pinjarra, which he visited subsequently. This he described as fresh, clean and homely, commending the amenities it had developed in flowers and shrubs. The negative comments on Tardun were starkly reinforced.

Garnett's report in 1944 was also in the main unfavourable to the schools run by the Christian Brothers. St Vincent's Orphanage at Castle-dare, which primarily housed children under 10, was described as being poorly equipped, with a very low standard of accommodation.

Other factors counted against the orphanage, such as its lack of Sisters to assist young migrants. The greater involvement of female staff —and an improvement of the calibre of those currently in place—was to become a key recommendation of Garnett's report.

St Joseph's Farm School in Bindoon, however, made a more satisfactory impression, and the 23 boys in residence were said to be in excellent health and spirits. This was an agricultural and trades school, to which boys wishing to enter trades were sent from Tardun and Clontarf once they reached school-leaving age; older children came directly from the ship, as did Laurie Humphreys, aged 13. Each boy, in addition to farm training, was taught a trade, and almost all intended to be carpenters, plumbers, painters or masons. Many boys were learning construction and were at the time of the report responsible for building an extension to the site. Time spent at the school was recognized by Australian trade unions as an apprenticeship, and consequently was valuable to the boys in their future careers.

Laurie Humphreys, who arrived at Bindoon in 1947, describes his experience of life there as 'work, eat and sleep with occasional play' such as cricket matches with local clubs. He acquired a range of skills, from milking cows to felling trees with an axe, horse-riding and building haystacks to working on an impromptu building site—a two-storey technical school, constructed by the boys themselves. Although the agricultural work was 'hard' for 'fourteen year olds who had not worked on the land before', the building site was somewhat alarming for untrained boys operating by trial and error: 'it seemed to take ages to dig the foundation and was a bit scary standing in a 3 foot trench with a pick swinging inches from your face. When a concrete pour was pending, it was all hands to the shovels, taking it in turn to mix the concrete which was done by hand.'[23] Fortunately Laurie's talent for driving established him as a truck driver for the enterprise, responsible for getting sand, gravel and metal dust safely to the site.

Even at Tardun, agricultural work was mixed with some introduction to expedient building techniques—Michael Hannigan recalls how the boys were put to 'quarrying for granite stones that were used to build the outer walls of a beautiful, two-storied Convent built during the first year. At times we had to use gelignite for blasting. The larger suitable stones were loaded onto horse-drawn drays... The rest was put through a mechanical crusher.'[24] At the time of Garnett's report in

1944, 50 children from Britain had come to Tardun, including Hannigan. They had arrived under the auspices of the Catholic Emigration Association, from orphanages across England, Wales, Scotland and Northern Ireland: those run by the Sisters of Nazareth and the Sisters of Charity were particularly popular sources. Garnett noted that the boys at Tardun appeared to be happy and healthy, despite the living conditions which he described as 'primitive', with a general lack of comfort and no protection from flies. Bathing facilities were also reported to be limited and the dormitories spartan. There were also no libraries.

The general standard of comfort provided by the Christian Brothers' institutions was deemed to be low. Clontarf was recognized as superior to the others, which were no doubt suffering from dwindling funding in the privations of war, exacerbated by their isolation. The boys at Clontarf received a full course of primary education, including elementary training in wood and metalwork. They were also taught trades such as carpentry and tailoring. Over 200 miles from Perth, Tardun was perceived to be very remote and the 31,0000 acres of land were suitable only for wheat and sheep farming, not offering an opportunity to learn about mixed farming. Tardun's isolated setting was noted with concern in the report, and Garnett suggested that boys should remain at Clontarf for their primary education, transferring to Tardun or Bindoon only when older, according to individual training needs.

A list of migrant boys at Tardun in June 1946 in the National Archives shows the limited options of 'occupation' available (DO 35/ 1138). Many of the younger teenagers were 'students' still involved in education; others were full-time 'farm trainees' and older boys of 17 and 18 (plus one enterprising youth of 16) had been engaged as farmhands outside Tardun. Michael Hannigan recounts the arbitrary nature of the selection process:

> The Brothers had finally decided what to do with we six. Four went to work full time on farm duties and the other two of us were chosen to undertake further education ... as boarders [at] St Patrick's College, Geraldton... To this day I do not know why that decision was made, nor why we two were the lucky ones... For each of the next three years I spent ten months away from Tardun being exposed to a totally new world and social structure.[25]

The facilities for higher education offered by the Christian Brothers' scheme—albeit to only a very few of the boys—were among the 'valuable features' that impressed Garnett. His report also commended the training provided in crafts and trades that gave a solid foundation for boys entering the world of work. He recommended that the migration scheme should continue, subject to improved conditions at St Vincent's Orphanage, Castledare, and a general improvement in the institutions' living conditions. Garnett further proposed that no boys over 16 years and 9 months should be housed at Tardun, as at this age they should be trained and ready to take up employment. He also recommended that Nazareth House at East Camberwell in Melbourne should be encouraged to receive girls once migration resumed after the war.

Catholic institutions in Britain did begin to send children to Australia again after the interruption of the war years, although numbers remained low. The Crusade of Rescue sent out children via the Australian Catholic Immigration Committee until as late as 1963, but adoption in Britain was increasingly viewed as a preferable option. The Catholic Church also sent boys to the St John Bosco Boys' Town, a large institutional building dating from 1951 in Glenorchy, Hobart, Tasmania. Dormitories were sizeable, containing up to 30 beds, and 24 migrant boys (out of a total of 75, the other boys being Australian) were in residence there in March 1956. Another destination was St Joseph's in Neerkol, near Rockhampton in Queensland, which unusually accepted both sexes and thus was good for siblings migrating together; 32 boy and girl migrants (out of a total of 200 children) were living there at the same date. And Nazareth House in Melbourne did start to receive girl migrants from Britain as Garnett had advised; 51 were accommodated there in 1956.

Little encouragement was given to girls who wanted to pursue a career, even when they displayed the aptitude for one. Bean and Melville quote the experience of a child who came to Australia at the age of eight and, like others in her group, was destined to enter domestic service. As she observes, it was a question of pragmatics:

> You see, we had nowhere to go. We needed live-in jobs. I went to the Dominicans to be a nun. I'd expressed a wish to join, but I was hoping I could be a teacher first. I would have liked a bit more time, but they put it over me that I had to join at 16. I thought, well, if I could learn to be a teacher in the Order, it wouldn't be so bad. But then they wanted me to do all the lay sister work, which was the cooking, the cleaning.[26]

Leaving the institutions was never easy for the child migrants faced with a largely unfamiliar adult world. Laurie Humphreys was abruptly told he was leaving Bindoon in 1950, within a week of his seventeenth birthday. 'Brother Kearney called me in and told me I was leaving to work in a small country town called Toodyay, for the Road Board. I can't remember any farewells.' He had lived in an institution for 13 years and now confronted 'a new world to me and a complete change of lifestyle'.[27] Michael Hannigan won a scholarship to the University of Western Australia in Perth, but as 'a totally unsophisticated lad of sixteen' he found the bustling city overwhelming:

> For seven and one half years I had lived a monastic life style in a male community of some 100 persons. The only female contact of any note was with the Nuns. Suddenly I was in a city of several hundred thousand — 50% of them female. There were other wonders too from trams to cinema theatres ... I had not been prepared for this. I had left a strict ordered discipline and now found myself completely on my own with no one to turn to for advice or guidance. I'm not sure I would have taken any notice anyhow! I was out of my depth and had no idea how to adapt to a study regime at University level. By the middle of the year it was obvious I was in trouble.[28]

Fortunately, Michael's pass in Grade 12 in 1945 was high enough to allow him to be selected as a public servant. He took advantage of a job offer in the Taxation Department in September 1946 and embarked upon a secure career in public service — a lucky outcome and an example of how some child migrants found their way to success against all odds.

Another young migrant who benefited from education via the Christian Brothers' scheme was Dennis M. who arrived at St Vincent's Orphanage, Castledare, in 1955. He was later sent to Clontarf, where he recalled 'a harsh disciplinary regime', but selection for schooling at Aquinas College helped him to a good job as a clerk at the Commonwealth Bank. Dennis eventually became a manager at the bank. In later years he was able to track down many of his long-lost family with the help of organizations for former child migrants (pp. 240–49).

New name, new age

As attitudes to migration changed after the war, the 'Big Brother Movement', with its emphasis on involving Australians to provide practical and moral support, seemed in many ways more attractive than the traditional approach. The Movement sought to capitalize on this, launching an appeal after the war for £50,000 to revive the scheme and develop its plans for settling more British children in Australia—under the care and guidance of prominent citizens. It changed its name to the Big Brother Youth Migration Movement and stressed that the 'Little Brother' would go to an individual home; he would be looked after by a 'Big Brother' and not by any form of institutional control.

Interest was raised and by 1947 New South Wales had vacancies for 500 Little Brothers. The first post-war party sailed for New South Wales in June 1947 under the Australian Assisted Passage Scheme; each boy had to find £5 for the voyage (£130 in today's money) and the Movement had first priority for shipping passengers. In 1949 the Big Brother organizers extended their activities to Tasmania. They could now recruit boys to settle and work in both rural and urban employment. The Movement gathered momentum in the post-war years, sending over 3,100 children from Britain to Australia under approved child migration schemes (plate 30). The British government awarded a grant towards the cost of the London office in 1948–9, but for reasons of economy no further funding was forthcoming.

The number of Little Brothers leaving Britain and entering Australia increased from 59 in 1947 to over 100 in 1948 and 1949 and 224 in 1950. It peaked at 316 in 1951, after which the intake remained relatively constant, about 200 each year, until the late 1950s. Attempts to expand the operation were made, including asking other European countries if they would like to participate in the Big Brother scheme, but only Britain and Malta ever accepted. It endured, nonetheless, and from its beginnings in the very different world of 1921 brought over 6,500 Little Brothers to Australia. Even as late as 1957, the scheme sponsored the voyages of 212 Little Brothers, of whom 188 came from England, 19 from Scotland, 3 from Northern Ireland and 2 from Wales. The majority (154) of the boys still sought work in farming, but 58 (almost 25 per cent) were now interested in town employment, reflecting the shift away from farming experienced by other child migration movements. In 1964, for the first time in the history of the Movement, the number of Little Brothers deciding to follow non-farming careers was greater than those intending to work in rural occupations.

Gunning Lodge, a hostel at Burwood near Sydney in New South Wales, provided accommodation for boys who decided on urban employment. It was named after Mr Tom Gunning of Mosman, Sydney, whose bequest enabled the Movement to purchase the Lodge in 1951, assisted by an interest-free loan from the Commonwealth and state government. The hostel offered a much-needed temporary solution for these Little Brothers until other suitable accommodation and employment could be arranged. By 1954 its use had soared and over 325 boys had been accommodated for varying periods during the year.

The Big Brother Movement maintained thorough records on its participants, and the results reveal its overall success. They were impressive, although unlike other organizations the scheme had never drawn upon young, underprivileged children from institutions. A report from the Sydney Office of 1951, now in the National Archives, notes that over 1,000 of the post-war migrants were now over 21 years old and had reached the stage of encouraging families, relatives and friends to migrate to Australia (DO 35/10274). Of the 2,000 boys nominated since 1945, more than one-fifth had been followed by their families, who had now also settled in Australia. Most boys had gone on to build or buy their own home to receive their families and—perhaps the greatest achievement of all—many former Little Brothers had offered to become Big Brothers for future arrivals.

In terms of farming, 168 Little Brothers had passed through the Movement's training farm near Sydney. They had been placed in farming positions across Australia, ranging from New South Wales to Victoria and Tasmania. Gunning Lodge at Burwood had taken 44 boys to train for urban work of various kinds, including craft trades, banking, insurance, industrial chemistry and retailing. The Movement was impressed with the high qualifications achieved by many of the boys, who were now making excellent progress in their chosen careers.

Positive testimony is also provided by Little Brothers themselves—who had, of course, chosen to enter the scheme. Extracts from the first reports of boys who left the training farm in 1957 included encouraging comments such as:

> I am very satisfied with the employment. Meals and accommodation are very good.

> It is a very interesting job, and I am not overworked. We are getting on well together. They are a very nice family and are treating me as one of the family.

My bed has adequate blankets and food is not spared at mealtimes.

Good food. Nice room of my own. Very nice people.
Am earning £6.10.9 a week clear, and banking £6.0.0 per week.

Nor was this simply the first flush of enthusiasm from inexperienced boys. Significantly, the report also featured extracts from those who had entered farming after the Big Brother scheme and now had several years under their belts. One pre-war Little Brother now possessed a property of 50,000 acres, while another 'is enthusiastically happy in his present job, where he is in some share farming basis in addition to wages. He gets on extremely well with the family.' A third, now aged 23, had also made good progress, staying at the same place for nearly seven years and accumulating savings of around £3,000 (£45,000 in today's terms). With luck he would have achieved his ambition of buying 'a small grazing property of his own' in the next few years.

The final chapter

Other agencies were, of course, also involved in bringing children to Australia after the Second World War. Religious denominations were heavily involved. In 1947 the Church of England sponsored the building of the Swan Homes near Perth, designed to accommodate Protestant youths. By 1953 some 211 children were living at the Homes, and 350 in total were sent there between 1947 and 1960. The Church of England also sent children to the Clarendon Church of England Home, Kingston Park, Tasmania.

The Methodists and Presbyterians played a smaller role; around 90 Methodist boys came to Australia in small parties between 1950 and 1954, and were accommodated in Methodist Homes containing Australian children in care. One of these, at Victoria Park in Perth, held three young migrants aged under eight from Britain in 1956, while eight migrant children (out of a total of 98) were living at another Home in Burwood, Victoria. In turn, the Presbyterian Church established a Home at Dhurringile at Tatura, Victoria, which received 80 boys between 1950 and 1964.

The total number of children sent to Australia by the Salvation Army is difficult to confirm, but it was certainly active in the schemes. The Salvation Army in New South Wales brought 60 children there from Britain in 1947 alone. It applied to the British government for recognition as an approved organization, and sought to establish its four Homes—at Canowindra, Arncliffe, Bexley and Goulburn in New South Wales—as approved institutions for child migration. A special youth training camp was also founded at Riverview, near Brisbane, with the familiar aim of giving boys special training in farming.

Although the numbers of children coming to Australia had declined in the 1950s, concern about the process and the conditions they experienced remained. In 1956 the Secretary of State for Commonwealth Relations charged a British fact-finding mission to 'collect information as to the arrangements for the reception and upbringing in Australia of migrant children by the various voluntary societies concerned with the migration of children by the various unaccompanied by their parents'. The National Archives contains reports on each of the 26 institutions visited, from across all Australian states (BN 29/1325). They explored institutions in cities as far apart as Perth and Hobart, Sydney and Adelaide, organized by religious authorities from Catholic to Presbyterian, Methodist to Church of England. The mission reported back on factors such as premises provided, position/locality, furnishing and equipment, staff, education, children's activities, recruitment and selection and placement of school leavers, as well as other general comments.

As a result of their findings, the report divided institutions into three categories. Those in the first group, A, were deemed unfit to receive any more children, in a stark realization that some of the problems were endemic and could not be resolved. Those in group C were considered satisfactory, while institutions in group B were held to have supplied insufficient information to make a judgement—a limbo position that was hardly a ringing endorsement.

For many Homes and the organizations behind them, the results were revealing. Among those with a satisfactory rating were the Barnardo's Homes at Burwood (which closed anyway in 1960) and Normanshurst, both near Sydney, as well as Northcote Farm School, the Clarendon Church of England Home in Tasmania and the Methodist Homes at Victoria. Another Methodist Home at Victoria Park had not given enough information and was consigned to group B, as were the Church of England Swan Homes and the Catholic-run Nazareth House in Melbourne and Clontarf Boys' Town in Perth.

Those in group A were understandably the greatest concern, and they included the Fairbridge Farm Schools at Pinjarra, Western Australia, and Molong, New South Wales, plus St Joseph's at Neerkol near Rockhampton, Queensland. The report was highly critical of five places in group A, spread across Australia and run by a variety of organizations. They were Dhurringile Rural Training Farm at Victoria (Presbyterian); the Salvation Army Training Farm at Riverview, Queensland; the Methodist Home at Magill, Adelaide, South Australia; St Vincent's Orphanage, Castledare, Western Australia; and St John Bosco Boys' Town, Glenorchy, Tasmania (both Catholic).

The mission's report, published in August 1956, was influential in bringing child migration schemes from Britain to an end. It highlighted the institutional nature of the care in most places visited, compounded by the poor quality of many staff (with little or no specialist training), the harsh separation of brothers and sisters sent to Australia and the children's continuing isolation and lack of contact with ordinary community life. The report emphasized the desirability of placing children in foster homes where a more normal type of family life could be enjoyed.

The mission also expressed concern over decisions behind the migration of individual children, and recommended that the Home Secretary's consent should be required to send any child to Australia under the voluntary societies' auspices. The societies themselves agreed to modernize their arrangements in Australia, but resisted the principle of requiring the Home Secretary's consent for future schemes.

Despite the fact-finding mission's concerns about migration, some institutions had been found satisfactory, and the Empire Settlement Act of 1952 was renewed on 31 May 1957. This meant that the British government still contributed towards the maintenance of child migration in both Australia and Southern Rhodesia. Agreements were made with eight voluntary organizations in 1957 regarding the admission of migrant children to 38 farm schools, Homes and other institutions in Australia. All these agreements committed the British government to paying 10 shillings per week (£7 in today's money) towards the maintenance of each child under 16. Six of the agreements also provided for the cost of an outfit for each child. The financial burden was split between the countries, with the Commonwealth government of Australia also contributing £A5 as outfit allowance and A10s a week as maintenance allowance for each child. The state governments involved also made weekly maintenance payments varying from A5s to £2. Passages to Australia were provided under the Australian Assisted Passage Agreement.

Yet time was running out for child migration, even in a modified form. No longer inspired by individual philanthropy or an imperial vision, held up to critical scrutiny through official reports, it could not endure in the brave new world of the late 1950s and 1960s. The British Catholic Rescue Societies stopped all their plans to emigrate children to Australia shortly after the publication of the fact-finding mission's report in 1957, and while other organizations continued to emigrate children, they were in much smaller numbers. The decrease led gradually to the last party of British child migrants—a group of nine Barnardo children—who arrived by air in Australia in 1967.

Social conditions and attitudes changed markedly in 1950s and 1960s Britain. The austere years of rationing largely came to an end in the 1950s as the social services of the welfare state were gradually improving the country's health and economy. In 1957, Prime Minister Harold Macmillan defined the new mood in his optimistic declaration that 'most of the British people have never had it so good'—the consequence of increased productivity in major industries such as steel, coal and motor cars leading to a rise in wages, export earnings and investment.

The social stigma of illegitimacy and one-parent families was gradually beginning to reduce. Hard-hitting television documentaries and plays such as *Cathy Come Home* (1966), which dealt with homelessness and its effect upon families, also made audiences more aware of social problems. Britain in the 1960s was therefore a significantly different place from Britain in the immediate post-war years. The longstanding policy of child migration sat uncomfortably with the new social realities and opportunities the country now offered.

Attitudes were changing, too, at a child welfare level. The provision of counselling of families and fostering to families became more acceptable than institutional care, whether in Britain or overseas. This was not ubiquitous, and some child migration schemes involving older teenagers survived beyond 1967, such as the Big Brother Movement. It continued to emigrate 19-year-old youths—old enough to make their own decisions—to Australia until 1983, but by and large the migration of children came to an end in the 1960s.

In the 1980s and 1990s much controversy about the policy of child migration emerged, fuelled in part by new books and the impact of a BBC/ABC television mini-series, *The Leaving of Liverpool*, in 1992. Greater awareness and understanding of child migration issues developed in Britain and Australia, and the British, Canadian and Australian governments undertook to carry out their own enquiries. Organizations and institutions, as well as former child migrants, co-operated.

Following these, the authorities concerned with migration began to make an official response. In 1997 it was accepted by the British House of Commons Health Committee that responsibility for matters relating to the welfare of former child migrants rested with the Department of Health. A report by the House of Commons Health Committee, chaired by David Hinchcliffe MP and entitled *The Welfare of Former British Child Migrants*, was published in 1998.[29] Following its publication, the serving health secretary Frank Dobson promised assistance to former child migrants by establishing a central database of information in the UK. He also announced a support fund of £1,000,000 over three years to assist those without means who had found their family to reunite. The British government also made extra funding available for the Child Migrant Trust.

In 2001, the Australian Senate Community Affairs References Committee published *Lost Innocents: Righting the Record, Report on Child Migration*. The report was critical of child emigration policy in general and of the treatment many former child migrants experienced in Australia, especially in certain Catholic Homes in Western Australia and Queensland. The Western Australian Legislative Assembly passed a motion on 13 August in which it apologized to former child migrants for any abuses they suffered in the state's institutions during their childhood. The Congregation of Christian Brothers of Western Australia, the Queensland government and churches, the government of South Australia and the Catholic Church's Joint Liaison Group on Child Migration followed suit. At the same time, Barnardos Australia stated that in hindsight child emigration schemes were barbaric and a shameful practice, and that it was completely against any practice that they would currently uphold.[30] The various reports, findings and recommendations may prove to be the last act in assessing a controversial policy which commenced nearly 400 years ago—and changed thousands of children's lives for ever.

Afterword

CHILD MIGRANTS left a legacy in the minds and attitudes of those who came after them, whether or not the latter were aware of their past. In Canada today, according to the Home Children Canada website, these descendants make up 11.5 per cent of the Canadian population, and have developed a significant voice. Andrew Morrison, whose PhD thesis *Thy Children Own Their Birth* deals with the impact of child migration on their descendants, discovered through interviews with those involved that they were proud of what their parents, grandparents or great-grandparents had achieved, despite the odds:

> It just adds an additional element of poignancy when you know that my great grandfather came here ten years old — not a soul in the world, not a lick of family here to support him — on his own hook, and wound up ... a master carpenter. At least while he was living, reasonably affluent, successful, very likely respected. I don't see how anybody could see that as anything other than a triumph.[1]

They admired their relatives' fortitude, discipline and ability to put the past behind them. Interestingly they felt, like the philanthropists so many years before, that Canada did in fact give their ancestors opportunities in life that they would not have had in Britain, and for this they were grateful, as were the few surviving Home Children.

However, this is not to overlook some of the negative effects. Emotional and psychological scars sometimes lasted into adulthood, impacting on descendants and family life. A common observation was that their relatives could not show affection: 'She had a hard time, I think, showing her love, because she had never had it shown to her. So maybe she didn't know how.'[2] Relations with their own children could be difficult for those who had not grown up with close family bonds. Morrison quotes a woman who struggled for years with her Home Child mother before she came to understand and forgive her:

> Everybody's affected by ... what's happened before... And so, that's why I think at some level, I needed to start exploring a little bit, so I could come to peace with who mum is... But that took a long, long time to be able to do that, until I started to understand.[3]

Other descendants were astonished to learn that their ancestors had been Home Children—usually after they had died, since they never mentioned it while they were alive. For some of those brought from Britain, the fact was better forgotten and they went out of their way to lose contact with the families they had lived with or people who had come over with them. They colluded with a deep-seated belief that child migrants were slum children with a bad past—or, worse, that they were illegitimate, a huge source of shame. As a result, many Home Children did not talk about their childhood or their past—some even preferring to lie about it—so their background was a source of mystery to their descendants, a missing piece of their personal history. Now, thanks to the raising of awareness about Home Children and the research tools available today, all the descendants who feel the need to trace their ancestry can do so.

In Australia, child migration is still very much part of living memory, and its profile has also been raised significantly in recent years. The subject gained attention in Britain in 1986 when a social worker, Margaret Humphreys, investigated the case of a woman who claimed that she was put on a boat to Australia by the British government at the age of four. Humphreys discovered that thousands of children had been shipped from children's homes in Britain to 'new lives' across the Empire. She went on to form the Child Migrant Trust, and started to publicize evidence of the darker side of child emigration, including instances where children had been told that their living parents were dead. The Trust she formed sought actively to reunite former child migrants with their surviving parents and other relatives, and records of Humphreys' work were published in *Empty Cradles* (Corgi, Transworld, 1994).

The organizations that were responsible for sending child migrants overseas have now set up their own services to help trace relatives and provide counselling to those emigrated by their institutions. One such is CBERS Consultancy (*www.cbers.org*), established by the Christian Brothers. CBERS helped Dennis M. to find his mother, five brothers and six sisters after 40 years apart. He had been born out of wedlock and placed as a three-week-old baby in an orphanage in England, to be looked after by the Sisters of Charity of St Paul of the Apostles. In 1954 he was selected to go to Australia, and was sent first to Castledare and then to Clontarf. Attempts to trace his family while in the care of the Christian Brothers proved fruitless, but in the late 1970s he renewed his efforts. With the help of Father Hudson's Homes, where he had spent some of his early years, he was reunited with his mother in England. After a strange initial encounter ('It was like meeting a stranger ... my mother was apologetic about giving me up. I just said it was water under the bridge.'), they were able to maintain contact over 25 years. Through the careful and sensitive work of CBERS and the Australian Child Migrant Project, Dennis also eventually got to meet his siblings and discover a flourishing extended family. His story is one of many reunions featured on the CBERS website and in their monthly newsletters. During the 1990s CBERS, together with the Australian and British governments, helped to fund reunification trips for over 250 clients to meet family in the UK and Malta. The government travel assistance ended in 2005, and today CBERS provides counselling and remains a source of news and information.

As well as helping former child migrants to trace their families, the organizations have taken on a new role in Australia. Barnardos Australia has a range of integrated welfare programmes and services to help Australian children who have suffered neglect, abuse and the humiliation of poverty. The Big Brother Movement — which continued to emigrate British teenagers to Australia until the 1980s — now helps young Australians by conducting research into homelessness, education and career development. The Movement also runs an awards programme that reverses its former role by enabling young Australians to visit Britain in a number of vocational categories, ranging from ballet to football. It maintains contact with hundreds of former Little Brothers through newsletters, reunions and its website *www.bbm.asn.au*.

The Old Fairbridgians' Association also helps former 'Fairbridge

Kids' to stay in touch and enjoy the camaraderie of their earlier lives. Originally formed in 1930, the Association sought to provide aftercare and support for Fairbridge boys and girls who had left to take up jobs in the outside world. It is still active today, encouraging communication between Old Fairbridgians through a regular newsletter for members, and organizing get-togethers, for example on ANZAC Day and at Christmas. An important event every year is the celebration of Founder's Day—on the Sunday closest to Kingsley's death (19 July 1924), many Old Fairbridgians visit the farm at Pinjarra and meet up with old friends over lunch in the Clubhouse. The Association also assists Old Fairbridgians who are interested in obtaining historical records and information in their search for family connections.

Both in Canada and Australia, organizations have developed in different ways to reflect the needs of former child migrants and their families. The internet has transformed communication and made networks of support and assistance much easier to maintain; it has also encouraged a new generation to discover more about their family's past. As the organizations and societies evolve, they continue to assist child migrants and their descendants to trace, come to terms with and understand the importance of their own personal history.

Notes on the text

INTRODUCTION

1 Joy Parr, *Labouring Children: British Immigrant Apprentices to Canada, 1869–1924* (Croom Helm, 1980).
2 *Autobiography of Kingsley Fairbridge* (Oxford University Press, 1927), quoted in Philip Bean and Joy Melville, *Lost Children of the Empire* (Unwin Hyman, 1989), p.80.
3 Ann Howard and Eric Leonard, *After Barnardo: Voluntary Child Migration from Tilbury to Sydney, 1921 to 1965* (TARKA Publishing, Australia, 1999), p.91.
4 Howard and Leonard, ibid, p.111.
5 ibid, p.91.
6 ibid, p.148.
7 Allan Moore, *Growing Up with Barnardo's*, (Hale & Iremonger, Australia, 1990), p.113.
8 Howard and Leonard, ibid, p.44.
9 Laurie Humphreys, *A Chip off What Block? A child migrant's tale*, (Laurie Humphreys, Australia, 2007), p.20.
10 Alison Benjamin, 'Criminal Circles', The *Guardian*, 19 July 2006.
11 Bean and Melville, *Lost Children of the Empire*.
12 Report from the Governor of the Cape of Good Hope to the Secretary of the Colonies, relative to the conditions and treatment of the children sent out by the Children's Friend Society, 1840, p.11, quoted in Gillian Wagner, *Children of the Empire* (Weidenfeld & Nicolson, 1982), p.17.

13 Wagner, *Children of the Empire*, p.17.
14 Wagner, ibid, p.32.
15 Wagner, ibid, p.32.

1 | Two women pioneers

1 Gillian Wagner, *Children of the Empire* (Weidenfeld & Nicolson, 1982), p.40.
2 Marjorie Kohli, *The Golden Bridge* (Natural Heritage Books, 2003).
3 *http://list.uwaterloo.ca/~marj/genealogy/children/Organizations/rye*
4 *http://list.uwaterloo.ca/~marj/genealogy/children/Organizations/ryeiln1877*
5 ibid.
6 Wagner, *Children of the Empire*, p.47.
7 ibid, pp.48–50.
8 Library and Archives Canada, RG 17, vo.25, file 252, quoted in Wagner, *Children of the Empire*, p.51.
9 Wagner, *Children of the Empire*, p.52.
10 Kohli, *The Golden Bridge*, p.87.
11 ibid.
12 Kenneth Bagnell, *The Little Immigrants*, new edn (Dundurn Press, 2001).
13 Kohli, *The Golden Bridge*, p.91.
14 Philip Bean and Joy Melville, *Lost Children of the Empire* (Unwin Hyman, 1989), p.141.
15 Kohli, *The Golden Bridge*, p.25.
16 'Report as to Children Sent by the Bristol Incorporation of the Poor to Canada under the protection of Miss Macpherson, June 1874'. The National Archives: MH 32/20.
17 ibid.
18 Bagnell, *The Little Immigrants*, p.32.

19 'Report to the President of the Local Government Board by Andrew Doyle, Local Government Inspector, as to the emigration of pauper children to Canada 1875'.

20 The National Archives, HO 45/9991.

21 ibid.

22 'Report to the President..., 1875'.

23 WAGNER, p.84.

24 'Report to the President..., 1875'.

25 'The Report of the Proceedings of the Committee of the House of Commons on Immigration and Colonisation (1875)'. The National Archives, MH 32/20.

26 ibid.

27 ibid.

28 KENNETH BAGNELL, *The Little Immigrants*.

29 LILLIAN M. BIRT, *The Children's Home-Finder* (James Nesbit, 1913).

30 BEAN and Melville, p.145.

31 ibid, p.144.

32 Letter to Sclater Booth, The National Archives, MH 32/20.

33 ibid.

34 *http//:ist.uwaterloo.ca/~marj/genealogy/children/Organizations/ryeiln1877*

35 ibid.

36 KOHLI, *The Golden Bridge*.

37 JOSEPH JOHN KELSO, *Special Report*, 1897, p.35, quoted in Wagner pp.156–7.

38 KOHLI, *The Golden Bridge*.

2 | Journey to a new life

1 *Our Waifs and Strays*, May 1885.

2 *Our Waifs and Strays*, July 1887.

3 ibid.

4 *Our Waifs and Strays*, August 1887.

5 ibid.

6 PHILIP BEAN and Joy Melville, *Lost Children of the Empire* (Unwin Hyman, 1989), p.142.

7 ibid, p.143.

8 GILLIAN WAGNER, *Children of the Empire* (Weidenfeld & Nicolson, 1982), pp.65–6.

9 *Our Waifs and Strays*, November 1906.

10 Quoted in JOHN STROUD, *Thirteen Penny Stamps* (Hodder & Stoughton, 1971).

11 ibid.

12 ibid.

13 The Church Army's Annual Report, 1906.

14 MARJORIE KOHLI, *The Golden Bridge* (Natural Heritage Books, 2003).

15 Quarrier Homes, online at *www.thereformation.info/quarrierhomes.htm*

16 REVEREND JOHN URQUHART, *The Life Story of William Quarrier* (S.W. Partridge,1904).

17 ibid.

18 MARJORIE KOHLI, *The Golden Bridge* (Natural Heritage Books, 2003), p.172.

19 URQUHART, *William Quarrier*.

20 ibid.

21 WAGNER, *Children of the Empire*, pp.157–8.

22 KENNETH BAGNELL, *The Little Immigrants*, new edn (Dundurn Press, 2001), p.156.

23 KOHLI, *The Golden Bridge*.

24 *The Children's Advocate*, vol.22, p.151, quoted in WAGNER, *Children of the Empire*, p.139.

25 WAGNER, p.98.

26 *The Spectator*, Hamilton, Ontario, 29 May 1873.

27 ibid.

28 WAGNER, p.153.

29 CHRIS UPTON, *From the Gutter to Canada*, online at *http://icbirmingham.icnetwork.co.uk*

30 BEAN and Melville, p.137.

31 KOHLI, *The Golden Bridge*.

32 *One Hundred Years of Child Care, the Story of the Middlemore Homes, 1872–1972*, quoted in Wagner, p.72.

33 PATRICIA ROBERTS-PICHETTE, *John Throgmorton Middlemore and the Children's Emigration Homes*, online at *www.bifhsgo.ca/pdf/jtmiddlemore.pdf*

34 ibid.

35 BEAN and Melville, *Lost Children of the Empire*, p.141.

36 ROBERTS-PICHETTE, *John Throgmorton Middlemore and the Children's Emigration Homes.*

37 PHYLLIS HARRISON (ed.), *The Home Children* (J. Gordon Shillingford, 1979/2003).

38 ibid.

39 KOHLI, *The Golden Bridge.*

40 N.R.P. BONSOR, *North Atlantic Seaway* (David & Charles, 1975).

41 Letters from the *Isle of Man Times* reprinted in the Isle of Man Industrial Home's Annual Report for 1892, online at *www.isle-of-man.com/manxnotebook/famhist/genealogy/emig.htm*

42 BONSOR, *North Atlantic Seaway.*

43 HARRISON, *The Home Children.*

44 *Our Waifs and Strays,* November 1906.

45 BEAN and Melville, *Lost Children of the Empire*, p.139.

46 ibid, p.137.

47 HARRISON, *The Home Children.*

48 *Our Waifs and Strays,* July 1887.

49 WILLIAM BOWMAN TUCKER, *Gold Quartz: An Autobiography 1859–1934*, online at *http://epe.lac-bac.gc.ca/100/200/300/glenn_nelson_adams/gold_quartz/wbtfwd.htm*

50 BEAN and Melville, *Lost Children of the Empire*, p.131.

51 WILLIAM BOWMAN TUCKER, *Gold Quartz.*

52 *Our Waifs and Strays*, November 1905.

53 HARRISON, *The Home Children*, p.34.

3 | Barnardo, the biggest player

1 S.L. BARNARDO and James Marchant, *Memoirs of the Late Dr Barnardo* (Hodder & Stoughton, 1907).

2 JOY PARR, *Labouring Children: British Immigrant Apprentices to Canada, 1869–1924* (Croom Helm, 1980), p.108, quoted by WAGNER, *Children of the Empire* (Weidenfeld and Nicolson, 1982), p.102.

3 NORMAN WYMER, *Father of Nobody's Children* (Hutchinson, 1954), p.13.

4 ibid.

5 ibid p.34.

6 ibid p.41.

7 ibid.

8 JUNE ROSE, *For the Sake of the Children* (Hodder & Stoughton, 1987), p.43.

9 GAIL H. CORBETT, *Nation Builders: Barnardo Children in Canada*, new edn (Dundurn Press, 2002).

10 *Night and Day*, June 1884.

11 Quoted in CORBETT, *Nation Builders.*

12 T.J. BARNARDO, *Something Attempted, Something Done* (John F. Shaw, 1889).

13 CORBETT, *Nation Builders.*

14 T.J. BARNARDO, *Something Attempted, Something Done.*

15 WAGNER, *Children of the Empire*, p.118.

16 BARNARDO and Marchant, *Memoirs of the Late Dr Barnardo.*

17 WAGNER, *Children of the Empire*, p.122.

18 ibid, p.135.
19 BARNARDO and Marchant, *Memoirs of the Late Dr Barnardo*.
20 T.J. BARNARDO, *Something Attempted, Something Done.*
21 CORBETT, *Nation Builders.*
22 25th Annual Report of Dr Barnardo's Homes. The National Archives: HO 144/310/B6159.
23 ibid.
24 MARJORIE KOHLI, *The Golden Bridge* (Natural Heritage Books, 2003).
25 JOY PARR, *Labouring Children.*
26 *Night and Day*, vol. XX, October 1896.
27 *Night and Day*, vol. XXI, May 1897.
28 25th Annual Report of Dr Barnardo's Homes. The National Archives: HO 144/310/B6159.
29 PARR, *Labouring Children.*
30 ibid.
31 T.J. BARNARDO, *Something Attempted, Something Done.*
32 WAGNER, *Children of the Empire*, p.234.
33 CORBETT, *Nation Builders.*
34 PHILIP BEAN and Joy Melville, *Lost Children of the Empire* (Unwin Hyman, 1989), pp.144–5.
35 ibid, p.148.
36 JUNE ROSE, *For the Sake of the Children* (Hodder & Stoughton, 1987).
37 CORBETT, *Nation Builders.*
38 WAGNER, *Children of the Empire*, p.232.

4 | The Catholic emigration movement

1 FATHER ANTONY F.M. CONLON, *The Flaminian Gate Revisited*, a talk given at the Faith of our Fathers 2000 Conference in London, online at *www.latin-mass-society.org/flaminian.htm*
2 SHAWN DAY, *Where's Poor Paddy? The Contrasting Results of Irish Migration to Glasgow and Liverpool, 1790–1850*, April 2002, online at *www.uoguelph.ca/~sday/pdfs/Irish.pdf*
3 CONLON, *The Flaminian Gate Revisited.*
4 FREDERICK J. McEVOY, '"These treasures of the Church of God": Catholic child immigration to Canada', Canadian Catholic Historical Association, *Historical Studies* 65 (January 1999), online at *www.umanitoba.ca/colleges/st_pauls/ccha/Back%20Issues/CCHA1999/McEvoy.htm*
5 *Boys and Girls*, July 1896.
6 *The Olive Tree Genealogy*, online at *www.rootsweb.com/~ote/orphans/father-nugent-orphans1881.htm*
7 CANON J.O. BENNETT, *Father Nugent of Liverpool* (The Nugent Care Society, 1949).
8 MARJORIE KOHLI, *The Golden Bridge* (Natural Heritage Books, 20037), p.249.
9 *The Catholic Encyclopedia: Herbert Vaughan*, online at *www.newadvent.org/cathen/15311b.htm*
10 GILLIAN WAGNER, *Children of the Empire* (Weidenfeld & Nicolson, 1982), p.144.
11 25th Annual Report of Dr Barnardo's Homes. The National Archives: HO 144/310/B6159.
12 ibid.
13 ibid.
14 Dispute as to the custody of boy discharged from Roman Catholic School to care of Aunt, and eventual emigration to Canada. The National Archives: HO 144/524/X76100.
15 *Boys and Girls*, January 1898.

16 House of Commons Select Committee on Health, Minutes of Evidence 11 June 1998, online at *www.publications.parliament.uk /pa/cm199798/cmselect/cmhealth /755/8061101.htm*

17 ibid.

18 McEvoy, '"These treasures of the Church of God"'.

19 William Francis Conabree, 'Believe me, my friends, it's the truth', *Home Children Canada*, online at *www.orphantrainriders.com /HomeChild/HomeArticles.html*

20 *British Home Child George James Robbins and the Robbins Family*, online at http://*community-2 .webtv.net/cupidsattic/British HomeChild*

21 Phyllis Harrison (ed.), *The Home Children* (J. Gordon Shillingford, 1979/2003).

22 McEvoy, '"These treasures of the Church of God"'.

23 Harrison (ed.), *The Home Children*.

24 McEvoy, '"These treasures of the Church of God"'.

25 ibid.

26 Wagner, *Children of the Empire*, p.220.

27 McEvoy, '"These treasures of the Church of God"'.

5 | Farm Schools and Kingsley Fairbridge

1 Marjorie Kohli, *The Golden Bridge* (Natural Heritage Books 2003).

2 Gillian Wagner, *Children of the Empire* (Weidenfeld & Nicolson 1982), p.196.

3 The National Archives, MH 102/1400.

4 The National Archives, MH 102/1400.

5 John Lane, *Fairbridge Kid* (Fremantle Arts Centre Press, Australia, 1990), p.108.

6 Lane, *Fairbridge Kid*, p.142.

7 The National Archives, MH 102/1400.

8 Wagner, *Children of the Empire*, p.202.

9 The National Archives, MH 102/1400.

10 Lane, *Fairbridge Kid*, p.104.

11 Wagner, *Children of the Empire*, p.243.

12 Lane, *Fairbridge Kid*, p.106.

13 Philip Bean and Joy Melville, *Lost Children of the Empire* (Unwin Hyman, 1989), p.145.

14 ibid, p.139.

15 ibid, p.139.

16 The National Archives, DO 35/1138.

17 The National Archives, DO 35/1138.

18 The National Archives, MH 102/1593.

19 The National Archives, MH 102/1593.

20 The National Archives, DO 35/3403.

21 The National Archives, MH 102/1406.

22 Lane, *Fairbridge Kid*, p.110.

6 | Second World War child evacuees

1 The National Archives, DO 131/43.

2 Gillian Wagner, *Children of the Empire* (Weidenfeld & Nicolson, 1982), p.196.

3 Wagner, *Children of the Empire*, p.249.

4 ibid, p.252.

5 The National Archives, DO 131/43.

6 Wagner, *Children of the Empire*, p.251.

7 The National Archives, DO 131/19.

8 The National Archives, DO 131/19.

9 The National Archives, DO 131/80.

10 The National Archives, DO 131/80.

11 The National Archives, DO 131/8.

12 WAGNER, *Children of the Empire*, p.255.

13 The National Archives, DO 131/33.

14 The National Archives, MT 9/3461.

15 The National Archives, MT 9/3461.

16 The National Archives, DO 131/8.

7 | The final
   | phase

1 GILLIAN WAGNER, *Children of the Empire* (Weidenfeld & Nicolson, 1982), p.224.

2 *http:/en.wikipedia.org.wiki/ Kingsley_Fairbridge*

3 ANN HOWARD and Eric Leonard, *After Barnardo: Voluntary Child Migration from Tilbury to Sydney, 1921 to 1965* (TARKA Publishing, 1999), p.138.

4 WAGNER, *Children of the Empire*, p.198.

5 ibid, p.206.

6 ALLAN MOORE, *Growing up with Barnardo's* (Hale and Iremonger, 1990), pp.48–50.

7 WAGNER, *Children of the Empire*, p.207.

8 MOORE, *Growing up with Barnardo's*, pp.51–3.

9 HOWARD and Leonard, *After Barnardo*, p.41.

10 JOAN HALLS, *Miracle of Fairbridge* (Hesperian Press, 1999).

11 HOWARD and Leonard, *After Barnardo*, p.119.

12 HOWARD and Leonard, *After Barnardo*, p.51.

13 MOORE, *Growing up with Barnardo's*, p.72.

14 HOWARD and Leonard, *After Barnardo*, p.47.

15 ibid, p.30.

16 ibid, p.52.

17 The National Archives, DO 35/687/5.

18 *www.blaisdonbrotherhood.info*

19 PHILIP BEAN and Joy Melville, *Lost Children of the Empire* (Unwin Hyman, 1989), p.140.

20 LAURIE HUMPHREYS, *A Chip Off What Block? A Child Migrant's Tale* (Laurie Humphreys, 2007), p.19.

21 ANN HOWARD, *C'mon Over!* (TARKA Publishing, 2002), pp.168–9.

22 *www.blaisdonbrotherhood.info*

23 HUMPHREYS, *A Chip Off What Block?*, pp.19–22.

24 *www.blaisdonbrotherhood.info*

25 ibid.

26 BEAN and Melville, *Lost Children of the Empire*, p.150.

27 HUMPHREYS, *A Chip Off What Block?*, p.25.

28 *www.blaisdonbrotherhood.info*

29 *The Welfare of Former British Child Migrants* (The Stationery Office, 1998).

30 Committee Hansard, 22.3.01, p.467, Barnardo's Australia.

CONCLUSION

1 ANDREW N. MORRISON, *Thy Children Own Their Birth: Diasporic genealogies and the descendants of Canada's Home Children*, Ph.D thesis, University of Nottingham, June 2006.

2 ibid.

3 ibid.

Tracing records of child migrants

Records of child migrants are dispersed among private and public archives across the globe.

THE NATIONAL ARCHIVES (TNA)

The National Archives (TNA) is the UK government's official archive. Increasingly its records are being put online, making them accessible via its website *www.nationalarchives .gov.uk*. Its collection includes records relating to government dealings with and administration of child emigration schemes, including some personal papers. Descriptions of records can be found on the online Catalogue at *www.nationalarchives.gov.uk /catalogue*.

• HOME OFFICE AND POOR LAW UNION RECORDS
Before 1972, responsibility for the application of various Acts relating to children lay with the Home Office. The series of records MH 102 consists of policy files in the Home Office six-figure registered file series. Related policy files in the CHN (Children) series, which originated in the Home Office in 1949, can be found in BN 29 and BN 62, with representative case files in BN 28. The vast majority of these files are closed for 75 years, though it is possible, following the Catalogue prompts, to request a review of the information from closed material under the Freedom of Information Act 2000. Earlier files can be found in general series of Home Office registered papers in HO 45 and HO 144,

under the subject cuts *Children* and *Emigration*. The records are mainly policy and correspondence files relating to the emigration of children under the Children Act, 1908, ch. 67; they include schemes for the emigration of children to Canada and Australia.

The documents concerning child emigration in MH 102 are also primarily policy and correspondence files. They relate to schemes between 1910 and 1960 set up by the UK, South Africa, Canada, New Zealand and Australia. Records include movements set up by Dr Barnardo's and Barnardo's Homes, the Fairbridge Society, the Overseas Migration Board and the Big Brother emigration scheme. Some personal files are closed for 75 or 100 years. Again, following the Catalogue prompts, you can request a review of information from closed material under the Freedom of Information Act 2000.

Few series of TNA documents provide individual details of child emigrants. Local Government Board Poor Law records in the series of MH 12, for example, tend to record only statistical information on the numbers of children sent overseas from individual Poor Law Unions, though they sometimes include Poor Law Union posters giving notice of the names and ages of children being sent abroad.

The document MH 19/9 contains Local Government Board copies of enclosures and reports regarding the emigration of pauper children to Canada between 1887 and 1892. Within this document are detailed reports on pauper child emigrants resident in Canada from 1887 to 1892. The reports, compiled by the Secretary, Department of Agriculture, on instruction from the Dominion of Canada Immigration Officer, give comments about children's condition, health, character, schooling and frequency of church attendance, and on each child's view of their new homes. The reports cite the Union or parish from which they were sent, as well as each child's name and age and the host's name and address. Further Canadian government inspectors' reports and statistical information regarding child migrants are in Parliamentary Papers; copies are available on microfiche at the National Archives.

• CHILDREN'S OVERSEAS
RECEPTION BOARD RECORDS
Probably the richest source of material on child migrants at TNA consists of records concerning the Children's Overseas Reception Board (CORB), set up in 1940 to deal with the overseas evacuation of children. Records in DO 131 consist of administrative files, a selection of case files relating to children (DO 131/94–105) and their escorts (DO 131/71–87) and register of child applicants (DO 131/106–13). The vast majority of files can be searched in the Catalogue by name of child. Most of these files were destroyed under statute in 1959. Dominions Office policy files relating to the activities of the Board are in DO 35.

• OUTGOING PASSENGER LISTS
Finally, through its website, the National Archives in partnership with *FindMyPast.com* has digitized the details of some 30 million people who left ports in the United Kingdom and Ireland for final destinations outside Europe and the Mediterranean between 1890 and 1960. The site *http://www. ancestorsonboard.com/* contains details of child migrants bound for Canada, Australia, New Zealand and South Africa, such as their full name, age and UK address (from 1922), and you can carry out a person search

using the first and last name. You can also refine your search by departure port, destination country, destination port and name of ship. The records are being released by decade from 1890, and all should be available online by early 2008. Until a record has been digitized, access to the original manifests in the series BT 27 is still permitted.

OTHER ARCHIVES IN THE UK

• LOCAL RECORD OFFICES
Local record offices throughout England and Wales hold Poor Law Union papers and Board of Guardian records which provide detailed information relating to child migrants. For example, within the Greenwich Board of Guardians papers at the London Metropolitan Archives are papers relating to child emigration to Canada covering *c.* 1907 to 1920 (LMA ref: GBG 218/1–238). These contain details of orphans and pauper children sent to Canada through agencies such as the Salvation Army, the Catholic Church and various children's homes. For further information on records held in local archives in England and Wales, go to *www.a2a.org.uk*. For contact details of other repositories, go to *www .nationalarchives.gov.uk/archon*.

• UNIVERSITY OF LIVERPOOL
The Department of Special Collections and Archives at the University of Liverpool *http://sca.lib.liv.ac.uk/collections/* holds the archives of the Fairbridge Society as well as the National Children's Homes (now NCH Action for Children) and Barnardo's. The archives are subject to access restrictions, and records of individuals are normally closed for 100 years.

The Fairbridge Society archive material at the University of Liverpool includes papers on the establishment and foundation of the society 1908–20, council and executive committee papers 1910–87 and policy, planning and finance papers *c.* 1921–78. It also contains Fairbridge Society publications 1908–98, children's records 1912–83, publicity and fund-raising papers 1909–82, papers re property 1932–78, emigration policy papers 1914–82, information about activities in Australia 1909–83, in other overseas areas 1931–79 and those of the Old Fairbridgians *c.* 1918–80s.

The Barnardo's Archives material at the University of Liverpool includes papers of Dr Barnardo, such as his sermon notes 1861–1905, correspondence 1880–1905 and publications written by Thomas Barnardo and others 1867–1996. It contains council papers and minutes 1877–1980, child care papers 1905–*c.*1970, papers relating to fundraising and appeals, press cuttings and childcare, and papers post 1970, including children's records, aftercare records and administrative records. There are also papers of organizations taken over by Barnardo's such as Johnson and Curtis Charities, Liverpool Sheltering Homes, Macpherson Homes, Reformatory and Refuge Union, Children's Aid Society, St Matthew's Orphanage and Miss Sharman's Homes.

• BARNARDO'S ARCHIVES
The Barnardo's Archives in Ilford— online at *www.barnardos.org.uk*— holds many case histories of former children and admission and discharge registers, although access restrictions exist for records relating to individuals. The child migrant index at *http://www .barnardos.org.uk/what_we_do/work* *_with_former_barnardos_children.htm* holds files of some 30,000 Barnardo children who were emigrated to Canada. It also has records of the Macpherson Homes and Marchmont Homes between the years 1882 and 1939, which acted as clearing houses for children sent overseas for adoption. Normally, access to the index and Barnardo's records is limited to proven descendants only.

• CATHOLIC CHILDREN'S SOCIETY ARCHIVES
The Catholic Children's Society Archives at 73 St Charles Square London, W10 6EJ holds records relating to its homes and emigration schemes, to both Canada and Australia. Records of individuals are normally closed for 100 years, though there is a database of children who went overseas from 1938 to 1963. The Archives also has a complete collection of registers of Catholic workhouse children 1870–1920, plus admission and discharge registers for its homes at St Charles School, Brentwood, 1872–1950, St Nicholas' Industrial School and North Hyde School. It also contains copies of *St Peter's Net* 1898–1973, the official newsletter of the Crusade of Rescue and Homes for Destitute Catholic Children.

• THE CHILD MIGRANTS TRUST
The Child Migrants Trust was established in 1987 to assist former child migrants in finding relatives. After research has located relatives, social workers perform the delicate task of counselling and making the first contacts between the client and family members. The Trust in the UK operates from 28 Musters Road, West Bridgford, Nottingham NG2 7PL, tel (0115) 982 2811, fax (0115) 981 7168, *www.childmigrantstrust.com*

It also operates from two addresses in Australia: 5 Thomas Street, Nedlands WA 6009 (PO Box 674, Nedlands WA 6009), tel: (08) 9386 3605, fax: (08) 9386 3695; and 228 Canning Street, North Carlton Vic. 3054, tel: (03) 9347 7403, fax: (03) 9347 1791.

• THE CHILD MIGRANT
CENTRAL INFORMATION INDEX
The Index contains basic information about individual child emigrants; it is taken from the available UK records of known sending agencies and acts as a signpost to those agencies holding personal records. The Index is available to former child migrants, parents and siblings, and to any nominated representative but, as access is restricted, it is not available over the internet. Initially the index relates to child migrants sent to Australia, Canada and New Zealand on government-assisted schemes between 1920 and the late 1960s, but it is not a complete listing of all former child migrants. The Index was moved from the National Council of Voluntary Child Care Organisations (NCVCCO) to the Department of Health in 2002, and any enquiries should be directed towards their website *www.doh.gov.uk/childinf.*

LIBRARY AND ARCHIVES, CANADA (LAC)

Between 1869 and the early 1930s, Canada's National Archives hold much relevant material, an increasing amount becoming available via its website at *www.archives.ca.*

• INCOMING PASSENGER LISTS
Incoming passenger lists in the series RG 76 from 1865 to 1935 contain information such as the passenger's full name, age, country of origin, occupation and intended final destination. They are arranged by port and date of arrival, with the exception of some years between 1919 and 1924 when manifests were replaced by an individual form (Form 30A) for each migrant. Information on these forms includes name of ship, date of sailing, port and date of arrival, name, age, occupation, birthplace, race, citizenship, religion, destination and name of the nearest relative in the country from which the immigrant came.

Passenger lists from before 1925 are not indexed by name. Unless you know the month, year and port of arrival, your search is likely to be long and uncertain of success. It may be useful to search using the National Archives (UK) online outgoing passenger lists first. For the years 1925 to 1935, the Immigration Records Database is available online at *http://www.collectionscanada .ca/archivianet/020118_e.html.* This site provides information relating to passenger names, and volume, page and microfilm reel numbers of the Canadian incoming passenger lists.

Records of immigrants arriving at Canadian land and sea ports from 1 January 1936 onwards remain in the custody of Citizenship and Immigration Canada. To request a copy of another person's immigration record, write to Citizenship and Immigration Canada, Public Rights Administration, 360 Laurier Avenue West, 10th Floor, Ottawa, ON, K1A 1L1; include the full name at time of entry into Canada, date of birth and year of entry. Additional information is helpful, such as country of birth, port of entry and names of accompanying family members. It must be accompanied by a signed consent from the person concerned or proof that he/she has been dead for 20 years.

• THE HOME CHILDREN
DATABASE
Compiled from data within the incoming passenger lists, members of the
British Isles Family History Society of
Greater Ottawa are indexing the names
of British child migrants. The database
can be searched online at *www.collec
tionscanada.ca/archivianet/020110_e
.html*. It covers the period 1869 to 1930.

• IMMIGRATION BRANCH
RECORDS AND JUVENILE
INSPECTION REPORTS
There are also records of the Immigration Branch Central Registry which
corresponded closely with the various
sending agencies such as Barnardo's.
These are in the series RG 76 B1A; they
cover the years from 1892 to *c.*1946 and
include annual reports, information
booklets and some lists of children's
names. The files cover the years from
1892 to *c.* 1946. Similarly, Juvenile
Inspection Reports are available in RG
76 C4C. These are essentially inspection
reports, carried out by immigration
officials, on children brought to Canada
by organizations in the 1920s, although
a few records are dated as early as 1914
and some as late as the 1930s.

• MIDDLEMORE HOMES
LAC also holds microfilm copies of
the records of the Middlemore Homes
organization. Between 1873 and 1936
over 5,000 young child migrants aged
between 2 and 18, originating mainly
from Birmingham, arrived in Canada
under John Throgmorton Middlemore's emigration scheme. Volunteers
with the British Isles Family History
Society of Greater Ottawa (BIFHSGO)
are compiling an index for those
records. If you locate an entry,
BIFHSGO will provide you with the
specific archival references so that you

can borrow the relevant microfilm reels
from Library and Archives Canada or
order copies of pages. The index can be
accessed at *www.bifhsgo.ca/home_
children_emigration_scheme.htm*.

THE NATIONAL ARCHIVES OF AUSTRALIA (NAA)

The National Archives of Australia
collection holds records relating to the
policy of child migration, together with
those relating to the service organizations and churches who sponsored the
children, provided for their education
and placement, and arranged their aftercare, as well as individual case histories.

• MIGRANT SELECTION DOCUMENTS
The range of papers usually found in
migrant selection documents includes
application forms, medical reports and
other papers completed by applicants
for assisted migration to Australia from
the UK. Applications for child migrants
were usually completed by a guardian,
and the associated forms normally
feature a wide range of personal details
such as birth certificates, school reports,
maintenance guarantees and even police
character reports. These documents
may also have the name of the organization sponsoring the migration (for
example, Barnardo's, the Christian
Brothers or the Fairbridge Society). The
majority of these records are arranged
chronologically by date of ship arrival
in Australia, so it is important to have
the ship's name, the approximate date
of arrival and the state in which the
person arrived.

• INCOMING PASSENGER LISTS
Passenger records, which include
passenger lists and passenger cards,
provide a rich source of family history

information. For example, each vessel arriving at the Australian ports was required to lodge a list of incoming passengers. Arranged by date and port of arrival, the lists include each passenger's name and, in earlier lists, details such as age or marital status. There are no name indexes to these records which makes a search difficult unless date and port of arrival are known. Passenger lists survive for all Australian ports from 1924, with some gaps. Some ports have lists dating before 1924, for example Fremantle, where lists start in the 1880s.

• POLICY FILES AND LISTS OF CHILD MIGRANTS

Most of the records held by the National Archives of Australia are general policy files. Some series of child migrant case files are held by a number of Australian state archives.

The Commonwealth Department of Immigration was responsible for approving the entry of individuals and recording their arrival. Matters such as accommodation, welfare and reception arrangements generally lay with state governments or charitable bodies. Schemes and bodies included are the Dreadnought Scheme, Fairbridge Farm Schools, the Big Brother Movement, the Roman Catholic Church, the Church of England, the Salvation Army, the Presbyterian Church and the Children's Overseas Reception Board Scheme.

Records relating to child migrants — including migrant selection documents, passenger lists and immigration policy files — are held by the various state archives, details of which are available at the website for the National Archives of Australia, *www.naa.gov.uk*.

• THE PERSONAL HISTORY INDEX

The database of the Personal History Index (PHIND) has been developed by the Christian Brothers, the Sisters of Mercy and the Sisters of Nazareth in Western Australia. It records the location of records held by institutions in Western Australia concerning child migrants. Information recorded on the database includes name, date and place of birth, parent's names (if known) and age at departure from the UK. They also feature shipping details, the name and location of sending order in the UK, the destination order in Australia, initial residence and any transfers between homes and schools. A copy of this database is held by the National Archives in Perth. Access to PHIND is primarily for former child migrants and their families.

A database at *www.cbers.org* similarly details where to find records held in Australia for the 3,000 children resident in orphanages managed by the Christian Brothers, the Sisters of Mercy and the Poor Sisters of Nazareth between 1938 and 1965.

• BARNARDOS AUSTRALIA

Barnardo's Aftercare Services at *www.barnardos.org.au* provides a search facility for child migrants who were brought to Australia under Barnardo's schemes. The records consist primarily of a card index of all Barnardo migrants who came to Australia. Information on the card index includes name, date of birth, ship name and date of arrival, as well as details of any placement within New South Wales. The Aftercare Services can also retrieve the individual case records which are held in the Mitchell Library in Sydney. Access to these records is restricted to the surviving child migrant or their immediate next-of-kin only.

Useful addresses

The contacts below may hold private archives and documents relating to child migrants and migration schemes. Former child migrants have donated their stories to these institutions; many have been published or are available via the websites.

UNITED KINGDOM AND IRELAND

BARNARDO'S
  Tanners Lane
  Barkingside
  Ilford
  Essex IGI IQG
  Tel: +44 (0) 20 8550 8822
  www.barnardos.org.uk

BRITISH BOYS MOVEMENT
  (formerly Big Brother Movement)
  Canberra House
  10–16 Maltravers Street
  London WC2R 2EE

CATHOLIC CHILD WELFARE
  COUNCIL
  c/o Catholic Children's Society
  (Southwark)
  49 Russell Hill Road
  Purley, Surrey CR8 2XB
  Tel: +44 (0) 20 8668 2181

THE CATHOLIC CHILDREN'S
  RESCUE SOCIETY
  390 Parrs Wood Road
  Didsbury
  Manchester M20 5NA
  Tel: +44 (0) 161 445 7741
  Tel: +44 (0) 845 300 1128
  www.childrenssociety.org.uk

CATHOLIC CHILDREN'S SOCIETY
  73 St Charles Square
  London W10 6EJ
  +44 (0) 20 8969 5305
  www.cathchild.org

CHILDREN'S HOME AND MISSION
  Mill Grove
  10 Crescent Road
  South Woodford
  London E18 1JB

CHILDREN'S SOCIETY
  (formerly the Church of England
  Children's Society)
  Edward Rudolf House
  Margery Street
  London WC1X 0JL

CHURCH ARMY HEADQUARTERS
  Independents Road
  Blackheath
  London SE3 9LG

THE FAIRBRIDGE SOCIETY
  207 Waterloo Road
  London SE1 8XD
  Tel: +44 (0) 20 7928 1704
  www.fairbridge.org.uk

FAMILY TRACING SERVICES
  The Director
  Family Tracing Services
  105–109 Judd Street
  Kings Cross
  London WC1H 9TS

FATHER HUDSON'S HOMES
  The Director
  Father Hudson's Homes
  Coleshill
  Birmingham B46 3ED
  Tel: +44 (0) 1675 434000
  www.fatherhudsons.org.uk

INTERNATIONAL RED CROSS
  Welfare Section
  9 Grosvenor Crescent
  London SW1X 7EJ
  Tel: +44 (0) 870 170 7000
  www.redcross.org.uk

INTERNATIONAL SOCIAL SERVICES
  Cranmer House
  39 Brixton Road
  London SW9 6DD
  Tel: +44 (0) 20 7735 8941
  www.issuk.org.uk

INVALID CHILDREN'S AID SOCIETY
  The Director
  Invalid Children's Aid Society
  126 Buckingham Palace Road
  London SW1W OEJ

JEWISH WELFARE BOARD OF
  GUARDIANS
  The Director
  Jewish Welfare Board of Guardians
  315 Ballards Lane
  London N12 8LP

MIDDLEMORE HOMES
  The Director, Middlemore Homes
  55 Stevens Avenue
  Bartley Green
  Birmingham, B32 3SD
  Tel: +44 (0) 121 427 2429
  www.middlemore.org.uk

MR FEGAN'S HOMES, INC.
  The Director
  Mr Fegan's Homes, Incorporated
  160 St James Road
  Tunbridge Wells
  Kent TN1 2HE
  Tel: +44 (0) 1892 538288
  www.fegans.org.uk

THE NATIONAL ARCHIVES
  Kew, Richmond
  Surrey TW9 4DU
  Tel: +44 (0) 20 8876 3444
  www.nationalarchives.gov.uk

NATIONAL CHILDREN'S HOME
  85 Highbury Park
  London N5 1UD
  Tel: +44 (0) 20 7704 7000
  www.nch.org.uk

NUGENT CARE
  99 Edge Lane
  Liverpool L7 2PE
  Tel: +44 (0) 151 261 2000
  www.nugentcare.org

PACT
  15 Belgrave Road
  Rathmines
  Dublin 6
  Eire
  Tel: +353 (0) 1-4975155

POOR SISTERS OF NAZARETH
  Hammersmith Road
  Hammersmith
  London W6 8DB
  www.nazarethhouse.org

THE PRESBYTERIAN ORPHAN &
  CHILDREN'S SOCIETY
  Glengall Exchange
  3 Glengall Street
  Belfast BT12 5AB
  Northern Ireland
  Tel: +44 (0)28 9032 3737

QUARRIER HOMES
  Bridge of Weir
  Renfrewshire
  PA11 3SX
  Tel: +44 (0) 1505 612224
  www.quarriers.org.uk

SALVATION ARMY
  Salvation Army International
  Headquarters
  101 Queen Victoria Street
  London EC4P 4EP
  Tel: +44 (0) 20 7367 4924
  www.salvationarmy.org.uk

SHAFTESBURY YOUNG PEOPLE
  The Chapel
  Ropay Victoria Patriotic Building
  Trinity Road
  London SW18 3SX
  Tel: +44 (0) 20 8875 1555
  www.shaftesbury.org

THOMAS CORAM FOUNDATION
  49 Mecklenburgh Square
  London WC1N 2QA
  Tel: +44 (0) 20 7520 0300
  www.coram.org.uk

THE UNIVERSITY OF LIVERPOOL
  DEPT OF SPECIAL COLLECTIONS
  & ARCHIVES
  Sydney Jones Library
  The University of Liverpool
  PO Box 123
  Liverpool L69 3DA
  Tel: +44 (0) 151 794 2696
  http://ca.lib.liv.ac.uk/collections

AUSTRALIA

ANGLICAN CHURCH ARCHIVES
373 Ann Street
GPO Box 421
Brisbane QLD 4001

AUSTRALIAN CHILD MIGRANT
FOUNDATION
Level 2, 459 Hay Street
Subiaco WA 6008

THE BIG BROTHER MOVEMENT
NSW Office, Level 4/5
Hunter Street, Sydney NSW 2000
Tel: +61 (0)2 9233 4005
www.bbm.asn.au

CHRISTIAN BROTHERS EX-
RESIDENTS SERVICES
PO Box 1129
Bentley Delivery Centre
Bentley WA 6952
www.cbers.org

THE DREADNOUGHT SCHEME
Canon Harold Rawson
Custodian, Dreadnought Scheme
Claremont Lane
Windsor NSW 2756

THE FAIRBRIDGE FOUNDATION
The Secretary
The Fairbridge Foundation
Trust Building, 155 King Street
Sydney NSW 2000

INTERNATIONAL ASSOCIATION OF
FORMER CHILD MIGRANTS
Sybil McLaren-Carr
International Association of Former
Child Migrants
PO Box 124
Christies Beach SA 5165

NATIONAL ARCHIVES AUSTRALIA
Queen Victoria Terrace
Parkes
Canberra ACT 2600
Tel: + 61 (0)2 6212 3600
www.naa.gov.au
—120 Miller Road
  Chester Hill
  Sydney NSW 2162

Tel: +61 (0)2 9645 0110
www.naa.gov.au
—Victorian Archives Centre
  99 Shiel Street
  North Melbourne VIC 3051
Tel: +61 (0)3 9348 5600
www.naa.gov.au
—16 Corporate Drive
  Cannon Hill
  Brisbane QLD 4170
Tel: +61 (0)7 3249 4226
www.naa.gov.au
—384 Berwick Street
  East Victoria Park
  Perth WA 6101
Tel: +61 (0)8 9470 7500
www.naa.gov.au
—85 Macquarie Street
  Hobart
  TAS 7000
Tel: +61 (0)3 6230 6111
www.naa.gov.au
—Kelsey Crescent
  Millner
  Darwin NT 0810
Tel: +61 (0)8 8985 0300
www.naa.gov.au

SALVATION ARMY
Salvation Army Archives
69 Burke Street
Melbourne VIC 3000
Tel: +61 (0)3 9639 3618
www.aus.salvationarmy.org

WA INSTITUTIONS
RECONCILIATION TRUST
Level 6, 55 St George's Terrace
Perth WA 6000

CANADA

LIBRARY AND ARCHIVES CANADA
395 Wellington Street
Ottawa, ON KIA ONA
Tel: +1 613 996 5115
www.archives.ca

HERITAGE RENFREW HOME
 CHILDREN COMMITTEE
107 Erindale Avenue
Renfrew, ON K7V 4G3
CANADIAN CENTRE FOR HOME
 CHILDREN
Mr John Willoughby, Chairman
Canadian Centre for Home Children
PO Box 2601
Charlottetown
Prince Edward Island CIA 8C3

NEW ZEALAND

ARCHIVES NEW ZEALAND
Head Office
10 Mulgrave Street, Thorndon
Wellington 6011
• Correspondence address:
PO Box 12-050, Wellington
Tel: +64 (4) 499 5595
www.archives.govt.nz

SOUTH AFRICA

NATIONAL ARCHIVES OF
 SOUTH AFRICA
Head Office
24 Hamilton Street, Arcadia,
Pretoria, Transvaal
• Correspondence address:
Private Bag X236
Pretoria 0001
Tel: +27 (12) 323 5300
www.national.archives.gov.za/

ZIMBABWE

NATIONAL ARCHIVES OF
 ZIMBABWE
Head Office
Borrowdale Road
Gunhill, Harare
• Correspondence address:
Private Bag 7729
Causeway, Harare
Tel: +263 (4) 792 741
www.natarchives.gov.zw/

Selected websites

www.biographi.ca/EN/Results.asp
 Dictionary of Canadian Biography
www.bifhsgo.ca British Isles Family
 History Society of Greater Ottawa,
 for information on Home Children,
 particularly Middlemore Homes
http://clutch.open.ac.uk/schools/
 watlingway99 Fegan's Homes
www.isle-of-man.com/manxnotebook
 /famhist/genealgy/can2.htm
 Child emigrants to Canada from
 the Isle of Man
http://ist.uwaterloo.ca/~marj/
 genealogy/homeadd.html
 Organizations which sent young
 immigrants to Canada complied by
 Marjorie Kohli of the University of
 Waterloo, Canada
www.merchantnavyofficers.com/all
 .html The Allan Line
www.newadvent.org Catholic
 Encyclopedia
http://olivetreegenealogy.com Special-
 izes in free primary source records
www.publications.parliament.uk/pa/
 cm199798/cmselect/cmhealth/755/
 8061101.htm House of Commons
 publications on the internet
www.workhouses.org.uk Organizations involved in child emigration
*www3.telus.net/Home_Children_*
 Canada Home Children Canada
www.theshipslist.com Information
 about ships and passenger lists
www.umanitoba.ca/colleges/st_pauls/
 ccha/index2.html Canadian
 Catholic Historical Association
www.blaisdonbrotherhood.info
 Christian Brothers
www.fairbridge.asn.au Fairbridge
www.dh.gov.uk/en/Publicationsand
 statistics/Pressreleases/DH_4025086
 Department of Health
www.childmigrantstrust.com
 Child Migrants Trust

Bibliography

Anyone writing about child emigration is indebted to those who have researched and written so movingly about the practice. The voices of those directly involved have a unique resonance, and we would like particularly to thank Philip Bean and Joy Melville, Ann Howard and Eric Leonard, Marjorie Kohli, Joy Parr and Gillian Wagner. Their books vividly portray both the experience of migration and the context in which it took place, and we thoroughly recommend their work to anyone interested in learning more.

BOOKS

K. BAGNELL, *The Little Immigrants*, new edn (Dundurn Press, 2001)

S.L. BARNARDO and J. Marchant, *Memoirs of the Late Dr Barnardo* (Hodder & Stoughton, 1907)

T.J. BARNARDO, *Something Attempted, Something Done* (John F. Shaw, 1889)

P. BEAN and J. Melville, *Lost Children of the Empire* (Unwin Hyman, 1989)

CANON J.O. BENNETT, *Father Nugent of Liverpool* (Birkenhead Press, 1993)

THE BIG BROTHER MOVEMENT, *British Youth Migration 1925–1987*, (Strathfield, NSW, 1987)

L.M. BIRT, *The Children's Home-Finder* (James Nesbit, 1913)

N.R.P. BONSOR, *North Atlantic Seaway* (David & Charles, 1975)

B.M. COLDREY, *The Scheme: The Christian Brothers and Childcare in Western Australia* (Anglo-Pacific, 1993)

B.M. COLDREY, *Good British Stock: Child and Youth Migration to Australia, 1901–83*

(National Archives of Australia, 1998)

G.H. CORBETT, *Nation Builders: Barnardo Children in Canada*, new edn (Dundurn Press, 2002)

K. FAIRBRIDGE, *Veld Verse* (Oxford University Press, 1928)

M. FETHNEY, *The Absurd and the Brave: CORB — The True Account of the British Government's World War II Evacuation of Children Overseas* (The Book Guild, 1990)

J. HALLS, *Miracle of Fairbridge* (Hesperian, 1999)

P. HARRISON (ed.), *The Home Children* (J. Gordon Shillingford, 1979/2003)

A. HOWARD, *C'mon Over!* (TARKA Publishing, 2002)

A. HOWARD, and E. Leonard, *After Barnardo: Voluntary Child Migration from Tilbury to Sydney, 1921 to 1965* (TARKA Publishing, Australia, 1999)

L. HUMPHREYS, *A Chip Off What Block?* (Laurie Humphreys, Samson, Australia, 2007)

M. HUMPHREYS, *Empty Cradles* (Corgi, Transworld, 1994)

R. INGLIS, *The Children's War: Evacuation 1939–1945* (Collins, 1989)

M. KOHLI, *The Golden Bridge* (Natural Heritage Books, 2003)

J. LANE, *Fairbridge Kid* (Fremantle Arts Centre Press, 1990)

Lost Innocents: Righting the Record; Report of Child Migration (Senate Community Affairs References Committee, 2001)

A. MOORE, *Growing up with Barnardo's* (Hale and Iremonger, 1990)

T. NAGORSKI, *Miracle on the Water* (Robinson, 2006)

J. PARR, *Labouring Children: British Immigrant Apprentices to Canada, 1869–1924* (Croom Helm 1980)

J. Rose, *For the Sake of the Children: Inside Dr Barnardo's* (Hodder & Stoughton, 1987)

E. Rudolf, *The First Forty Years (1881–1920)* (SPCK, 1922)

M. de M. Rudolf, *Everybody's Children* (Oxford University Press, 1950)

P. Runaghan, *Father Nugent's Liverpool 1849–1905* (Countyvise, 2003)

J. Stroud, *Thirteen Penny Stamps* (Hodder & Stoughton, 1971)

Reverend J. Urquhart, *The Life Story of William Quarrier* (S.W. Partridge, 1904)

G. Wagner, *Barnardo* (Weidenfeld & Nicolson, 1979)

G. Wagner, *Children of the Empire* (Weidenfeld & Nicolson, 1982)

N. Wymer, *Father of Nobody's Children* (Hutchinson, 1954)

OTHER SOURCES

Barnardos: Annual Reports; magazines *Night and Day, Ups and Downs*

Catholic Society: Annual Reports; magazines *Across the Sea, Boys and Girls, St Peter's Net*

Church Army: Annual Reports

Church of England Waifs and Strays Society: Annual Reports; magazine *Our Waifs and Strays*

A. Morrison, *Thy Children Own Their Birth*, Ph.D thesis

Oxford Dictionary of National Biography

Report by Andrew Doyle to the President of the Local Government Board on Emigration of Pauper Children to Canada, 1875 (Parliamentary Papers LXIII)

Down Memory Lane 1902-84, Henry Dickenson, unpublished account

ARTICLES

Father A.F.M. Conlon, *The Flaminian Gate Revisited*, a talk given at the Faith of Our Fathers 2000 Conference in London, online at *www.latin-mass-society.org /flaminian.htm*

F.J. McEvoy, '"These Treasures of the Church of God": Catholic Child Immigration to Canada', Canadian Catholic Historical Association, *Historical Studies* 65 (January 1999), online at *www.umanitoba .ca/colleges/st_pauls/ccha/Back% 20Issues/CCHA1999/McEvoy.htm*

P. Roberts-Pichette, *John Throgmorton Middlemore and the Children's Emigration Homes*, online at *www.bifhsgo.ca/pdf/jtmiddle more.pdf*

'Lost Innocents: righting the record: report of child migration', Senate Community Affairs References Committee, 2001

Index

Numbers in *italic* refer to plate numbers.

Act to Regulate the Immigration into Ontario of Certain Classes of Children 1897 64–5, 116
adoption 38, 39, 49, 73
aftercare: Doyle Report 38–9; Fairbridge Farm Schools 155–6, 163
Allan, Alexander 78
Allan Line 78–87
Allen, Francis 14, 129–30
America 13; *see also* United States of America
American Committee for the Evacuation of Children 172–3
Anderson, Robert 91
Appleby, Mark 31
Approved Schools 197
Arandora Star 174
Arden, Cecil 135, 136
armed forces 185–6
Ashfield Barnardo's Home 200
Australia 10, 11, 13, 13–14, 17–18, 116, 141, 193–228, 229, 231–3; Barnardo's Homes 193–4, 197–205, 215–16, 217; Big Brother Movement 194, 205–9, 222–5, 228, 232; Christian Brothers 194, 209–15, 217–22, 232; CORB 174, 176, 177, 184, 185, 186, 190, 191; farm schools 144–52, 154, 157–69, 209–22; Garnett Report 160–63, 215–17, 218–21
Australian Assisted Passage Scheme 195, 214–15, 223, 228
Austrian 78
Baker, William 198, 199
Baldwin, Stanley 153
Balfour, Alexander 33
Ball, Alec 167

Bans, Emmanuel 134–6, 137
Barber, Emma 30
Barkingside Girls' Village Home 62, 95–6, 99, 117, 201
Barnardo, Dr Thomas 7, 8, 9, 10, 28, 75, 76, 77, 90–118, 143; Catholic children 126–9; court cases 96, 110, 126–8; early years 91–6; emigration as a solution 97–101; list of assurances 103; 'philanthropic abduction' 9, 110–11; visits to Canada 101–5 'Barnardo trunk' 100–101
Barnardo's Homes 14, 96, 228, 232; Australia 193–4, 197–205, 215–16, 217; Canada 105–18; Girls' Village Home 62, 95–6, 99, 117, 201; Picton Farm School 159–60, 203–5, 215, 217; Russell industrial farm 103–5, 108, 143; Stepney Home for Boys 94, 95, 201
Barrett, H.D. 53, 54–5, 85–6
Batory 180, 181
Bedford, Peter 15
Benyon Home 55
Big Brother Movement (later Big Brother Youth Migration Movement) 28, 29, 30, 10, 194, 205–9, 222–5, 228, 232
Bilborough, Ellen Agnes 29, 32, 48, 49, 63–4
Birmingham 70
Birt, Lillian 50
Birt, Louisa 32, 33–4, 44–5, 50
Blair Atholl farm, Galt 29–30, 32
Blantyre, Lord 76–7
boarding out 14, 107
Boards of Guardians 14
Bogue Smart, George 65, 74, 77, 117, 136
Bondfield, Margaret 118, 140

Booth, William 60
Bourne, Cardinal 140
Bowman Stephenson, Thomas 8, 65–9, 98
Bowman Tucker, William 86, 88
Bradshaw, William 63
Brassey, Lord 116, 198
Brenton, Edward Pelham 15–17
Bridger, John 52, 53
British Overseas Settlement Committee 139–40, 196
Buenos Ayrean 79–81
Bum, Dr Martin 188–9
Burges, Agnes 64, 65
Burges, James 64, 65
Burwood Barnardo's Home 204, 217
Caesar, Hugh 113–14
Cameron, Mabel 199
Canada 8–10, 11, 18, 88–9, 143–4, 172, 192–3, 230; Allan Line 78–87; ban on entry of unaccompanied children 193; Barnardo 97–118; Bowman Stephenson 66–9; Catholic emigration movement 122–41; Church Army 59–60; CORB 174, 175–6, 177, 184–5, 185–6, 190, 191; Doyle Report 35–43, 97, 142; farm schools 153–4, 168, 169, 186; Fegan 74–7; Laurie 34–5; Macpherson 28–33; Middlemore 70–74; Quarrier 62, 63–5; Report of the Proceedings of the Committee of the House of Commons on Immigration and Colonisation 39–43; Rye 21–6; Salvation Army 60; Waifs and Strays Society 52–9
Canadian Catholic Emigration Society 124, 134
Canadian Pacific 82
Carlile, Wilson 59

Catholic children:
  Barnardo and 126–9;
  Quarrier and 63
Catholic Emigrated Old
  Boys and Girls Society
  135–6
Catholic Emigration
  Association *15*, 8, 125,
  134–41
Catholic emigration
  organisations 10, 228;
  Australia 141, 209–15,
  217–22; Canada 119–41;
  early years 122–5; 'tug
  of faith' children 125–30
Catholic Emigration
  Society 140
Catholic Relief Act 1829
  120
CBERS Consultancy 232
Charity Organisation
  Society 96
Child Emigration Society
  143, 144, 145; *see also*
  Fairbridge Society
Child Migrant Trust 229,
  231
Children and Young
  Persons Act 1933 197
Children's Aid Society
  184
Children's Emigration
  Homes 70–71
Children's Friend Society
  15–17
Children's Home
  movement 14, 65–9, 157
children's homes 14
Children's Overseas
  Reception Board (CORB)
  24, 168, 170–91; *City
  of Benares* 179, 181,
  186–90, 191; early days
  171–3; operation of
  173–5; overseas organization of 175–8; return
  home 190–91; settling
  into new lives 182–6;
  voyage overseas 178–82
Chilton Thomas, Arthur
  134–6, 137
China Inland Mission 92
cholera epidemic 92
Christian Brothers 22, 23,
  10, 141, 194, 209–15,

217–22, 232
Church Army 59–60
Church of England 193,
  225
Church of England Waifs
  and Strays Society (later
  Children's Society) 14,
  22, 50, 51–9
Circassian 84, 86–7
City of Benares 179, 181,
  186–90, 191
City Brigades 94
Clontarf Boys' Home
  210, 212, 213, 220
Close, Elinor 143–4
clothing 100–101, 147,
  180–81, 184
Coles, Rhoda 129–30
Colonization Scheme
  104–6
communication 184
Conabree, William
  Francis 136–7
Conlon, Reverend
  Brother 211–12
Cox, George 98
crime 13, 14–18
Cross, Ronald 217–18
Crouch, R.W. 149–50
cruelty 36–7, 113–16,
  136–7
Cruikshank, George 22
Crusade of Rescue 125,
  141, 210, 212, 221
Custody of Children Act
  1891 (Barnardo Act)
  129
Day, Marjorie 181
Depression 58–9, 118,
  140, 193
Dew, Rosina 32
Dickens, Charles 15
Dickenson, Harry 84–5
Dixon, William 25–6
Dobson, Frank 229
Doyle, Andrew 25, 26, 45,
  46, 47–8, 79, 142–3
Doyle Report 35–43, 97,
  142
Dreadnought Scheme 194
Dufferin, Lord 66
Dundas, William 91
Dutton, Capt. Joseph 86
East End Juvenile
  Mission 93

economic depression
  58–9, 118, 140, 193
Edinburgh Castle (gin
  palace) 95
education 31, 121, 168–9;
  CORB children 184–5
Education Act 1870 18
Empire Settlement Acts
  11, 195, 197, 213, 216,
  227; 1922 Act 117, 140
escorts, CORB 178–9
evacuation 170, 171; *see
  also* Children's
  Overseas Reception
  Board (CORB)
Evangelical Revival,
  Dublin 91
fact-finding mission
  report 226–7
Fairbridge, Kingsley 10,
  96, 144–51, 193
Fairbridge, Ruby 145
Fairbridge farm schools
  18, 19, 62, 144–57,
  159–60, 161–3, 166–9,
  186, 193, 203, 215;
  growth of 151–7;
  Pinjarra 17, 10, 145–51,
  152, 159–60, 161, 166–7,
  168, 169, 218
Fairbridge Society 74, 143,
  151, 155, 156, 163, 168
Fairknowe 64
Fairview 73–4
family: Barnardo's
  children and 109–12;
  discovery of true
  circumstances 12;
  keeping in touch with
  31, 111–12, 183, 184
Farm School Management
  Committees 162–3, 215
farm schools 142–69;
  Australia 144–52, 154,
  157–69, 209–22; Canada
  153–4, 168, 169, 186;
  changing world 159–69;
  Christian Brothers 209–
  15, 217–22; Fairbridge
  see Fairbridge farm
  schools; Garnett Report
  160–63, 215–17, 218–21;
  Northcote 157–9, 159–
  60, 163–6, 169; Picton
  159–60, 203–5, 215, 217

Father Hudson's Homes
134, 232
Fegan, James 8, 74–7, 98
Female Middle Class
Emigration Society 20–
21
Fielder, Reverend 98
Findlay, Helen 115–16
Findlay, Pastor 65
First World War 9, 10, 58,
74, 117, 139, 145–6
Flint, Senator 41–2
food 147–8, 180
foster parents 107, 177–8,
183
Francis, Mother 139, 140
French-speaking families
137–9
Fry, Elizabeth 91
Gaisford, Basil 131
Garner Committee report
217
Garnett Report 160–63,
215–17, 218–21
Gibbs Home 52–3, 54, 56,
58, 59
Girls' Village Home 62,
95–6, 99, 117, 201
Glasgow Brigades 61
Gooderham, William 77
Gossage, Harry 126–7
Goudhurst 77
Gough, Helen 114
Grainger, Allendale 26
Green, George Everitt
115–16
Gunning Lodge 223–4
Guthrie House 72–3
Halls, Joan 202–3
Hamilton Children's
Home 66–9
hammocks 84
Hammond, Tom 75
Hancock, Mr 158
Hannigan, Michael 212–
13, 218, 220, 222
Hardy, Arthur 65
Harrison, Phyllis 88–9
Harvey, Ishbel 186
Hayward, Dr 24
Hayward, Elizabeth 13
Hazelbrae home 98–9,
101–2, 118
Heath, Colonel 158
Hibernian 78

Hills, Mr and Mrs Frank
67
Hinchcliffe, David 229
holidays 185; farm
schools 149, 168
Hope Place school 93
Horner, Francis 65, 66, 67
House of Commons
Health Committee 229
Hudson, George Vincent
134
Humphreys, Laurie 12,
214, 219, 222
Humphreys, Margaret
231
Hunter, W.J. 64
illness 85
ill-treatment 36–7, 113–16,
136–7
imperialism 9
'in care' children 197
Interdepartmental Com-
mittee on Migration
Policy (Syers Commit-
tee) 216–17
Irish Potato Famine 7,
32–3, 119–20
Jarvis, Jim 93–4
Karmsley Hills Farm 206
Kelso, John Joseph 50,
116
Kilby, Charles Herbert
180, 181, 182
King, William H. 181
Knowlton Home 30, 32,
44–5, 50, 62
Lacy, Margaret 125
Lane, John 148, 149, 152,
155, 168–9
Langham Place Group 20
Latham, C.G. 212
Laurie, James Wimburn
34–5
Liesching, Sir Percivale
166–7
Linton, Sir Richard 10,
194, 206
Little Brothers 30, 205–9,
222–5, 232
Liverpool 32–3, 53,
119–20
Liverpool Board of
Guardians 24
Liverpool Catholic
Children's Protection

Society 124–5
Liverpool Sheltering
Homes 33–5, 50, 118
Local Government Board
14, 26, 43, 76, 98, 132,
146
Logan, Harry 154
London Board of
Guardians 24–5
London Hospital 92, 94
Lowe, John 39–40
Macpherson, Annie 8,
19–20, 25, 26–33, 44,
47–8, 50, 51, 61, 79, 93,
97, 118; Doyle report
35–43
Mager, Alfred 65
Manning, Henry Edward
121
Marchmont Home 4, 29,
32, 63, 118
matchbox makers 27
Meiklejohn, Elizabeth 44
Methodist Church 225
Middlemore, John
Throgmorton 8, 69–74
Ministry of Health 14,
190
Molong Farm School 154,
159–60, 168
Montreal Steam Ship
Company (Allan Line)
78–87
Morrison, Andrew 230,
231
Moss report 217
Mowbray Park farm
school, Picton 159–60,
203–5, 215, 217
Murphy, William 128
musical tours 198
Napier, Sir George 16, 17
National Children's
Home 14, 65–9, 157
National Society for the
Prevention of Cruelty
to Children (NSPCC)
109
Nazareth House,
Melbourne 221
New Orpington Lodge
130–31, 135; *see also*
St George's Home
New Southwark farm
131–2

New Zealand 13, 21, 198;
CORB 174-5, 176, 177,
184, 185, 190, 191
Normanhurst Barnardo's
Home 215-16, 217
Northcote Farm School
157-9, 159-60, 163-6,
169
Norton, William 126
Nugent, James 8, 122-4
Okanagan Valley farm
school 153-4, 168
O'Keefe, Mother
Evangelist 136, 138, 139
Old Fairbridgians'
Association 155-6,
232-3
Orphan Homes of
Scotland 63
Osgood, Mrs 54
Our Western Home *1*, 22-
6, 48, 49, 50, 56, 57, 58
Overseas Settlement
Board 139-40, 196
Owen, Alfred de Brissac
84, 86-7, 107-8
Parisian 81
Patullo, T.D. 154
'philanthropic abduction'
9, 110-11
Philanthropic Society *10*,
14-15
philanthropists 7-9; *see
also under individual
philanthropists*
Picton Farm School 159-
60, 203-5, 215, 217
Pinjarra Farm School 17,
10, 145-51, 152, 159-60,
161, 166-7, 168, 169, 218
Piers, H. 16
Piper, Sarah 16
Point Puer 13-14
Poole, Dorothy 146
Poor Law Acts 121; 1834
Act 14
Poor Law Board 14
Poor Law Commissioners
14
Port Brisbane 179
Port Wellington 179
Potato Famine, Irish 7,
32-3, 119-20
poverty 7, 90, 92-3
Presbyterian Church 225

Prevention of Cruelty to
Children Act 1889 110
Prince of Wales appeal
18, 153
Prince of Wales
Fairbridge Farm School
74, 153-4, 168, 169, 186
Proctor, Miss 132-3
punishment 14-18
Quarrier, William, and
Quarriers 8, 14, 32, 60-
5, 80, 82
Ragged School Union
17-18
ragged schools 17-18, 93
Rangitane 179
Ray, William 74
Redhill Farm School *10*,
14-15
Reformatory School Act
1854 15
religious education 100
Rennie, Michael 25, 181,
188, 189
returning home 190-91
Revival Homes 27-8
Rhodesia Fairbridge
Memorial College 154-5
Rickard, Sir Arthur 199
Robbins, George 138
Roddy, John James 127-8
Romande, Gertrude 127
Rourke, Kathleen 200-201
Royal Commission on the
Poor Law 14
Royal Overseas League
176
Rudolf, Edward 51, 52,
53, 56-7, 81-2, 83, 88
Rudolf, Mildred 58-9
Rudolf, Robert 51
Russell industrial farm
103-5, 108, 143
Rye, Maria 2, 8, 18,
19-26, 45-50, 51, 52,
56; Doyle Report 35-43,
45-6; lack of sensitivity
to children 42, 46-7; Our
Western Home 22-6
Rye Home 58, 59
Salford Catholic Protec-
tion and Rescue Society
125
Salvation Army 60, 225-6
Sanderson, Milly 99

Sands, John 95
Sardinian 79
Sarmatian 79
Scaddon, Sir John 145
scattered farm system
143-4
Scone Barnardo's Farm
School 217
sea voyage 82-7, 178-82
Sears, George 138-9
Second World War
170-71, 194-5; *see also*
Children's Overseas
Reception Board (CORB)
Seddon, Richard 124, 134
settling in 182-6
Shaftesbury, Lord 17, 20,
93, 95
Shakespeare, Geoffrey
171, 188
Short, John 189-90
Sisters of Charity of St
Paul 121, 136
Sisters of Mercy 121
Sisters of Notre Dame
121
Smith, Samuel 33, 76, 94,
97-8
Smith, Capt. William
85-6
Society for Lessening the
Causes of Juvenile
Delinquency in London
15
Society for Promoting the
Employment of Women
20
Society for the
Suppression of Juvenile
Vagrancy 15
Somers, John 94
South Africa 15-17; CORB
174, 176-7, 184, 185,
186, 190, 191
Southwark Catholic
Emigration Society
130-31, 134
St Ann's Home, Montreal
88, 132-3
St George's Home 135,
136, 140
St John, Edward 130,
131-2
St John Bosco Boys'
Town 221

St Joseph's Farm School,
  Bindoon 213–14, 219
St Joseph's Home,
  Manchester 125
St Joseph's Home,
  Neerkol 221
St Vincent's Orphanage
  213, 218–19, 221
Stepney Home for Boys
  94, 95, 201
Stobo, Reverend 62
Swan Homes 225
Sydney Millions Club
  194, 198–9
Syers Committee 216–17
Tardun Farm School 141,
  210, 211–12, 213, 218,
  219–20, 221
Taylor, Colin 76
Taylor, Hudson 92
temperance movement
  95, 101
Tonkin, William 75–6
Toronto Barnardo's
  Home 101, 118
torpedoes 174, 179, 186–7
Trades and Labour
  Council 116
train journeys 87–8

transportation of
  criminals 13–14
'tug of faith' children
  125–30
Tupper, Sir Charles 103–4
Turrell, Arthur 199–200
Tye, Martha Ann 127
'undeserving poor' 109–
  10
United States of America
  172–3
Van Meter, W.C. 21, 22,
  28
Vaughan, Herbert 125,
  129
Victoria, Queen 56
Victorian 81–2
Virginia Company 13
Virginian 81–2
Volendam 179
voluntary organisations
  14, 196–7, 225–8; *see
  also under individual
  organisations*
voyage out 82–8, 178–82
Waifs and Strays Society
  (later Children's
  Society) 14, 22, 50, 51–9
Walden, Louis 25, 189

Walker, Doris 188
War Orphans Act 214
Weigall, Matron 199
West Indies 13
Westminster Archdiocese
  120–22, 124
Whitton, Charlotte 192
Wilberforce, William 91
Williamson, Stephen 33
Winnipeg Barnardo
  Home 107–8
Wiseman, Nicholas 120–
  21
Women's Volunteer
  Services (WVS) 181
workhouses 14
York, Duke of 152
Young, Robert 14
Youth's Labour House
  106

ACKNOWLEDGEMENTS

The Authors would like to thank the many people whose kindness and assistance have helped in the creation of this book including: *Adrian Allen*, Archivist, Sydney Jones Library University of Liverpool; *Pam Barr*, Quarrier's; *Joan Kerry*, National Children's Homes; *Martine King*, *Chris Reeve* and *Anne Newill*, from After Care Barnardo's; *Pat Lee*, The Church Army; *Pat McEvoy*, Nugent Care; *Carol Roper*, from the Catholic Children's Society (Westminster); *Ian Wakeling*, The Children's Society Archives; *Philippa White*, CBERS consultancy, and (from The National Archives) *Catherine Bradley*, publisher, *Ken Wilson*, designer, and *Gwen Campbell*, picture researcher. The author and publishers are particularly grateful to former child migrants *Michael Hannigan*, *Laurie Humphreys* and *Dennis M.* who have shared their experiences in the book.

PHOTOGRAPHIC CREDITS

The Publishers would like to thank the following for permission to reproduce the images featured in this book:

FRONT COVER: Hulton Deutsch Collection / Corbis.
BACK COVER: By courtesy of the University of Liverpool Library Special Collections and Archives.

PLATES 1, 2: NHS *Niagara*; PLATES 4, 6, 16, 21: By courtesy of the University of Liverpool Library Special Collections and Archives; PLATES 9, 10, 12, 13, 27: Library and Archives Canada; PLATES 11, 20, 26: Barnardo's; PLATE 15: Hulton Deutsch Collection / Corbis.

All other images are from The National Archives.